# THE WHOLE MUSIC OF PASSION

'Atalanta in Calydon' by Aubrey Beardsley

# The Whole Music of Passion

## New Essays on Swinburne

edited by
Rikky Rooksby and Nicholas Shrimpton

Scolar Press

Published by
SCOLAR PRESS
Gower House
Croft Road
Aldershot
Hants GU11 3HR
England

Ashgate Publishing Company
Old Post Road
Brookfield
Vermont 05036
USA

British Library Cataloguing-in-Publication Data.
A catalogue record for this book is available from the British Library.



ISBN 0 85967 925 X

Printed in Great Britain at the University Press, Cambridge

# Contents

# Introduction

Swinburne was a writer of exceptional versatility. Dramatist, novelist, critic, translator, parodist, pornographer, satirist, literary theorist, scholar and wit, he worked with distinction in almost every possible field of literary activity. But the central fact about him, as Cecil Lang reminded us in 1959, is that 'he was a poet and wrote great poems' (*Letters* 1.xviii). This volume of essays is concerned with that poetry, and with its status today.

It is a surprisingly uncertain status. Half a century of notoriety and half a century of neglect would be a good broad summary of Swinburne's reputation in the years since the first appearance of *Atalanta in Calydon* in 1865. Lang's edition of the *Letters* was the first phase of an important revaluation, which gathered pace in the 1960s. But even in the 1990s his standing remains uncertain. Too major a figure to be readily excluded from the canon of Victorian poetry, yet too distinctive and disturbing a writer to be fitted easily into established categories, his rediscovery has been delayed and unconfident.

In the 1860s no serious reader of poetry could be in any doubt about the importance of Swinburne. 'The poetical atmosphere,' in J. W. Mackail's vividly meteorological metaphor, 'was exhausted and heavy, like that of a sultry afternoon darkening to thunder. Out of that stagnation broke, all in a moment, the blaze and crash of *Atalanta in Calydon*. It was something quite new, quite unexampled. It revealed a new language in English, a new world as it seemed in poetry'.[1] George Saintsbury who, unlike Mackail, was old enough to bear direct witness, chose a similarly explosive image for the effect of Swinburne's next volume, in the Autumn of 1866. Unable to obtain a copy of *Poems and Ballads* before he went up to Oxford for the Michaelmas Term, Saintsbury used a trip to London to 'eat dinners' at the Inns of Court (a required qualification for a career as a lawyer) to get one. 'Three copies of the precious volume accompanied me back that night, together with divers maroons for the purpose of enlivening matters on the ensuing Fifth of November. The book was something of a maroon in itself. We sat next afternoon, I remember, from luncheon time till the chapel bell rang, reading aloud by turns in a select company "Dolores" and "The Triumph of Time," "Laus Veneris" and "Faustine," and all the other wonders of the volume.' [2] Earlier that year Thomas Hardy, as a young architectural assistant, had been walking the crowded London streets, between his lodgings in Paddington and Blomfield's office in Adelphi Terrace, compulsively reading the same poems. Forty-four years later he would remember the experience in his great elegy for Swinburne, 'A Singer Asleep', stressing once again the startling novelty of this poetic language:

O that far morning of a summer day
When, down a terraced street whose pavements lay
Glassing the sunshine into my bent eyes,
I walked and read with a quick glad surprise
  New words, in classic guise

Harold Nicolson, in 1926, tried to distinguish the components of this fierce early enthusiasm. 'A flaming symbol of emancipation, the very wine of freedom, the zest of heresy, the whole music of passion. . . the wide adventure and the wider hope; the excitement of discovery; the sharp throb of youth'[3]. Though we have borrowed one of Nicolson's more discerning phrases for the title of this collection of essays, we cannot hope, in the 1990s, to recreate quite this atmosphere of feverishly topical excitement. But excitement is still what Swinburne's verse offers, and this volume has been assembled as the latest contribution to the revival of intelligent interest in it.

As Rikky Rooksby suggests in his polemical survey of twentieth-century scholarship and criticism, 'A Century of Swinburne', the Modernist marginalization of the early and middle years of the century is giving way to a fresh and various appreciation of his achievement. Though still by no means a canonical author, Swinburne has begun to establish himself as an indispensable point of reference, at least in the academic discussion of Victorian poetry. Dorothy Mermin, for example, rescuing Elizabeth Barrett Browning from a similar period of neglect, commented in 1989 that, 'Her style tends to be expansive rather than lapidary, and like that of Swinburne (another major Victorian poet whom we have only recently learned how to read) has deterred critics from seeking the hard structure of meaning behind its dazzling impulsions of verbal energy'.[4] The work of critics such as William Empson, John Rosenberg and Jerome McGann who have thus taught us how to read Swinburne, and – more particularly – how to identify the hard structure of meaning behind his exhilarating verbal surface, is the foundation on which the present volume is built.

If there is a common theme to this consciously diverse collection of essays, in fact, it is a shared rejection of that subtle damnation with faint praise by which T.S. Eliot relegated Swinburne's verse to a peculiar realm of semantic nullity.

'The meaning,' Eliot wrote in 1920, 'is merely the hallucination of meaning, because language, uprooted, has adapted itself to an independent life of atmospheric nourishment'.[5] As early as 1930, William Empson, diagnosing the fifth type of ambiguity in 'Laus Veneris', was insisting that Swinburne is 'a very full and direct writer' and remarking how odd it was that 'people are. . . determined to regard Swinburne as an exponent of Pure Sound with no intellectual content'.[6] Edouard Roditi, in 1947, commented acidly on the way in which, 'since Eliot's essay on him', Swinburne is scorned, 'in quarters where Verlaine, who would deserve to be condemned on the same principles, is still admired'.[7] The scorn – and the misunderstanding on which it is based – persist, and this volume is an attempt to correct them. In Nicholson's terms, Swinburne's best poetry is a 'whole music of passion', not in the sense that it is somehow wholly (or merely) musical, but rather because its lyricism efficaciously embodies strong feelings and passionately held intellectual convictions.

In other respects the approaches taken here to Swinburne's poetry are very various. They range from David Riede's Bakhtinian discussion of Swinburne's struggle with the problematics of literary authority, or Thaïs E. Morgan's use of Riffaterre's theory of intertextual triangulation to elucidate the relationship between the poetics of Swinburne and Eliot, to Rikky Rooksby's humanist insistence on the possibility, in *Tristram of Lyonesse*, of metaphysical assertion, and on the poem's 'deep roots in Swinburne's life'. Like the critical methodologies adopted, the topics addressed are diverse. Both David Riede and Terry L. Meyers are concerned with Swinburne's use of literary precedent, Riede in the general sense of his need to construct a more than merely subjective basis for poetic utterance from a 'church of rebels' – an authorizing tradition whose principal hierophants are Blake and Shelley. With a deconstructor's eye for paradox, Riede explores the logical problems of a transgressive authority, and suggests that the formal and political conservatism of Swinburne's later work may have followed inevitably from this contradiction. Meyers discusses, in a more particular way, the precise nature of Swinburne's much-cited debt to Shelley. Even in the most explicitly Shelleyan of his volumes, *Songs before Sunrise*, he argues, the influence is a qualified one, muted by the hard-won political scepticism of the later nineteenth century and expressed only as part of a chorus of alternative views.

Nicholas Shrimpton's concerns, by contrast, are with a generic problem: the vexed question of to what extent Swinburne's poems are or are not 'dramatic'. If Swinburne himself, for reasons of self-protection, over-stated the dramatic impersonality of the 1866 *Poems and Ballads*, recent commentators have allowed too little to his capacity for the invention of voices which are not the self. As a consequence, they have under-valued his contribution to the great Victorian genre of the dramatic monologue. Recent work on the technical distinctions between dramatic and near-dramatic lyric modes permits a more precise account of Swinburne's (versatile) practice, and suggests new readings of the 'Hymn to Proserpine' and the neglected 'At Eleusis'. Rikky Rooksby's second essay is an attempt to do justice to the complexity of what Gosse saw as Swinburne's 'one epic' *Tristram of Lyonesse*. A late poem by date of publication (1882), though begun in the 1860s, Rooksby argues that it can be seen as a 'compendium' of the best features of the later poetry. It constitutes – to use what would once have been taken to be a contradiction in terms – a Putney masterpiece. This status Rooksby attributes both to its technical mastery and to the force with which it makes a quasi-religious assertion of the principle of unity.

The next group of essays is concerned with Swinburne's place on the map of late-nineteenth-century literature and culture – a map which has, we believe, been seriously distorted in recent decades by his absence. If Swinburne is omitted, the other landmarks do not assume their proper relationships, and the directions fail to make sense. Judith Stoddart attacks the stock contrast between Swinburne, the aesthetic immoralist and Ruskin, the moralist of art. As their friendship and frequent expressions of mutual esteem should imply, their work is less different than has been conventionally assumed. Swinburne, Stoddart argues, echoes in both prose and verse the humanist assumptions of Ruskin's later thought, and absorbs the Ruskinian notion of a morality embodied 'not in a set of doctrines, but in a way of seeing'. Ruskin, correspondingly, comes increasingly to insist that the artist's obligation to the truths of his own vision should take precedence over social or religious duty.

Dorothea Barrett addresses another stock contrast, that between Swinburne and George Eliot. In fact, these writers share an important sense of the connections between sexual and political issues, and their strongly erotic and subversive imaginations work to similar effect. In particular, Barrett points to the way in which Swinburne's sado-masochistic imagery can be compared with those passages in the novels of George Eliot where a discourse of the body runs counter to the more conventional language of intellect, in ways which undermine Victorian domestic convention. Murray Pittock's essay gives substance, for the first time, to the frequent vague claims for a Swinburneian influence on the writing of the 1890s. The relationship, Pittock suggests, is not one merely of occasional allusions and verbal echoes. Rather, Swinburne's commitment to artifice, and his counter-natural interiority of landscape, anticipate Symbolist practice, while his Jacobite 'ethic of the past' and marine imagery have important effects on the work of Symons, Dowson, Wilde, Johnson and Yeats. Thaïs E. Morgan extends this charting of literary relationships into the twentieth century, using the theoretical formulations of Bloom and Riffaterre to explore T. S. Eliot's troubled response to Swinburne. Eliot, she argues, uses 'intertextual triangulation in order to marginalize Swinburne's poetry'. But at the same time his essays on Swinburne represent an intertextual site on which he builds his conception of the new poet.

T. S. Eliot's subtle suggestion of semantic emptiness is not the immediate topic of Timothy Burnett's article, which is actually a response to Robert Browning's cruder accusation of 'florid impotence' and 'the *minimum* of thought and idea in the *maximum* of words' (*Hyder* 115). But Burnett's essay is, none the less, in many ways the most concrete and specific of all the essays collected here in the reply which it suggests to Eliot's claims. Burnett gives a textual editor's account of the manuscript revisions to the first page of 'Anactoria'. He does so in order to demonstrate, in detail, how closely Swinburne was concerned with the sense (as well as sound) of his poetry. Edmund Gosse discussed this manuscript in his article 'The First Draft of Swinburne's "Anactoria" ' (collected in his *Aspects and Impressions*, 1922), commenting that 'It would baffle the most meticulous investigation to restore the innumerable false starts, broken lines, and rejected readings which underlie the text of the Draft'. Burnett's meticulous investigation, concentrating solely on the first page of the manuscript, achieves precisely that restoration of the process of composition. His conclusions confirm Gosse's judgement that 'nothing could be more opposed to the popular notion of Swinburne as the inspired improvisatore than all this evidence of intense laborious application to his creative task',[8] and his detailed evidence shows just how wrong it is to suppose that Swinburne was 'for ever paring away at precision in order to achieve a vague and dreamy music'. We are grateful to the Harry Ransom Research Center, the University of Texas at Austin, for permission to print the reproduction of the manuscript which Timothy Burnett is analysing.

The final section of this book consists of three previously unpublished poems. Though they would be conventionally regarded as juvenilia, that term has a rather peculiar meaning when applied to the early work of Swinburne. Between the appearance of the first canto of 'Queen Yseult' in *Undergraduate Papers* in December 1857 (when he was twenty) and the publication of *Atalanta in Calydon* in March 1865, Swinburne published no verse except for the plays *The Queen Mother* and *Rosamond* (1860) and eight poems in the *Spectator* and *Once a Week* in 1862. Yet during those eight years he was very far from being a casual, amateur, or naive poet. On the contrary, he was subjecting himself to a conscious, and unusually rigorous, poetic apprenticeship. Gosse's account of the period between 1857 and 1862 is, if a touch rhetorical, none the less broadly correct: 'His verses at this time were corrected, torn up, rewritten from memory with divers modifications, revised again and put away' (*Works* 19.77). Even the medievalist poems written in imitation of William Morris between 1857 and 1859, though derivative, were derived from distinctly avant-garde models, and Morris, famously, commented that 'Queen Yseult' was actually 'much better' than the poems on which it was based (*Letters* 1.13).

By 1876 Swinburne was expressing a wish to publish a volume of 'Early Poems', in which he could collect the work which he had, in Gosse's phrase, 'put away' in the severely self-critical spirit of the late 1850s and early 1860s (*Letters* 3.199–207). Andrew Chatto declined to oblige, and those early texts which had not been included in the first series of *Poems and Ballads* were left to trickle, gradually, into print in such places as Gosse and Wise's *Posthumous Poems* (1917), the first volume of the Bonchurch Edition (1925), T. J. Wise's *A Swinburne Library* (1925), Lafourcade's *La Jeunesse de Swinburne* (1928), and Cecil Lang's *New Writings by Swinburne* (1964). We print three further poems, partly on grounds of their intrinsic merit, and partly because of the way in which they help to complete our picture of Swinburne's writing in this important early period.

'King Ban' is an Arthurian narrative poem, possibly written as early as 1857. A fragment of 120 lines of the poem (Folios 1–4) was published by Gosse and Wise in their *Posthumous Poems* (1917). Timothy Burnett has here, for the first time, assembled and reconstructed the entire text. The poem is printed by kind permission of the British Library (where Folios 1–4 are Ashley MS 5097) and The John S. Mayfield Collection, USA (Folio 6,) Folio 5, formerly in a private collection in New York, is now unlocated, and is printed here from a photocopy in the possession of Timothy Burnett,

'The White Hind', probably written in 1858, is an early draft of the poem printed in *Poems and Ballads* (1866) as 'The Two Dreams', and is based on a story in Boccaccio's *Decameron*. It is printed here by kind permission of the British Library, where it is Ashley MS 1840.

'By the sea-side' is an early landscape poem, incorporating the recurrent Swinburneian topic of romantic estrangement and the (equally characteristic) motif of the *femme fatale*. Georges Lafourcade, who printed the first twelve lines of the poem, suggested that it was probably written in 1859 or 1860 (*Lafourcade* 2.67–8, 590). It is printed here by kind permission of the Brotherton Collection, Leeds University Library. We are grateful to William Heinemann, Ltd and the Octopus Publishing Group (part of Reed International Books), the owners of the copyright, for permission to publish all three of these poems, and to the Trustees of the British Museum for permission to reproduce Aubrey Beardsley's ink and wash drawing 'Atalanta in Calydon'.

In the 'Dedication' of the first series of *Poems and Ballads* to Edward Burne Jones, Swinburne asked modestly whether there might be 'room' for his poems in the painter's 'world of delight', and wondered more generally whether there is 'hearing for songs that recede'. The task of literary criticism is, at root, to rescue the best texts from the temporal processes which cause them to recede from our attention and understanding. With the rapid growth of interest in the art and literature of the Aesthetic Movement, Pre-Raphaelitism, and (in our own *fin-de-siècle*) the Decadence, the recovery of a hearing for Swinburne is indispensable. Our hope for this volume is that it might, in some small way, accelerate that process.

Rikky Rooksby
Nicholas Shrimpton

## Notes

1. J. W. Mackail, *Swinburne*, Oxford, 1909, 8–9.
2. G. Saintsbury, 'Mr Swinburne', in *Corrected Impressions*, 1895, 61-2.
3. H. Nicolson, *Swinburne*, 1926 (reprinted 1969), 145.
4. D. Mermin, *Elizabeth Barrett Browning, The Origins of a New Poetry*, 1989, 9.
5. T. S. Eliot, 'Swinburne as Poet' in *The Sacred Wood*, 1920 (4th ed, 1943), 149.
6. W. Empson, *Seven Types of Ambiguity*, 1930 (reprinted 1973), 194–5.
7. E. Roditi, *Oscar Wilde*, New York, 1947, 2.
8. E. Gosse, 'The First Draft of Swinburne's "Anactoria" ' in *Aspects and Impressions*, 1922 (reprinted 1928), 110.

# Notes on contributors

**Dorothea Barrett** (*The Politics of Sado-Masochism: Swinburne and George Eliot*) has taught English at Cambridge and Glasgow Universities, and now works in Italy. She is the author of *Vocation and Desire: George Eliot's Heroines* (1989).

**Timothy Burnett** (*Swinburne at Work: the First Page of 'Anactoria'*) is Manuscript Librarian in the Department of Western Manuscripts at the British Library. He is the author of *The Rise and Fall of a Regency Dandy: The Life and Times of Scrope Berdmore Davies* (1981), and is currently at work on critical editions of Browning's *The Ring and the Book*, and of Swinburne's complete poems.

**Thaïs E. Morgan** (*Influence, Intertextuality and Tradition in Swinburne and Eliot*) is an Associate Professor of English at Arizona State University, and has published articles on Victorian poetry and on critical theory in *Victorian Newsletter*, *Semiotica*, *The American Journal of Semiotics*, and *Victorian Poetry*. She has translated Gérard Genette's *Mimologics: A Voyage into Cratylusland* (forthcoming, University of Nebraska Press), and is the editor of *Victorian Sages and Cultural Discourse: Renegotiating Gender and Power* (1990), and co-editor of *Reorientations: Literary Theories and Pedagogies* (1990). Her current project is a book on the construction of masculinities and the literary canon.

**Terry L. Meyers** (*Swinburne, Shelley and 'Songs Before Sunrise'*) teaches in the English Department of the College of William and Mary, Williamsburg, Virginia. He has published a number of articles on Swinburne, and is completing work on an edition of Swinburne's correspondence to include over 400 previously uncollected letters by Swinburne. He published an edition of Swinburne's short poem *Milton* in 1987.

**Murray G. H. Pittock** (*Swinburne and the 'Nineties*) is a Lecturer in English Literature at the University of Edinburgh. He is an associate editor of *The Eighteen Nineties: An Encyclopedia of British Culture* (forthcoming, Garland), and is the author of *The Invention of Scotland: the Stuart Myth and the Scottish Identity* (1991), and editor of *Lionel Johnson: Selected Letters* (1988). He is currently working on a biography of Lionel Johnson.

**David G. Riede** (*Swinburne and Romantic Authority*) is a Professor in the Department of English at Ohio State University, Columbus. His books include *Swinburne: A Study in Romantic Mythmaking* (1978), *Dante Gabriel Rossetti and the Limits of Victorian Vision* (1983), and *Matthew Arnold and the Betrayal of Language* (1988). He has since completed *Oracles and Hierophants: Constructions of Romantic Authority* (forthcoming, Cornell University Press), and *Dante Gabriel Rossetti Revisited* (forthcoming, G. K. Hall). He was a Guggenheim Fellow in 1984–85, and is a member of the editorial boards of *Victorian Poetry* and *Victorians Institute Journal.*

**Rikky Rooksby** (*A Century of Swinburne; The Algernonicon, or Thirteen Ways of Looking at 'Tristram of Lyonesse'*) is a Tutor in English at St Michael's Hall, Oxford. He has published a number of articles on Swinburne in *Victorian Poetry*, *Victorians Institute Journal*, *Review of English Studies*, and *Notes and Queries*. As well as a critical study of the later poetry, he is at work on a full scholarly biography of Swinburne.

**Nicholas Shrimpton** (*Swinburne and the Dramatic Monologue*) is Fellow and Tutor in English at Lady Margaret Hall, Oxford. He has published articles on Blake, Arnold, Ruskin, and Rossetti, and is, with Miriam Allott, currently completing a critical edition of the complete poems of Matthew Arnold.

**Judith Stoddart** (*The Morality of 'Poems and Ballads': Swinburne and Ruskin*) is an Assistant Professor at Michigan State University, and has published articles on Ruskin in P. Scott & P. Fletcher, eds., *Culture and Education in Victorian England* (1990), and *Victorians Institute Journal.*

# Short titles

References to Swinburne's published works and correspondence have been standardized and are given in the text in the following forms:

| | |
|---|---|
| *Works* | *The Bonchurch Edition of the Complete Works of Algernon Charles Swinburne*, eds Sir Edmund Gosse and Thomas James Wise, 20 vols., London and New York, William Heinemann and Gabriel Wells, 1925–27, cited by volume and page number. |
| *Poems* | *The Poems of Algernon Charles Swinburne*, 6 vols., London, Chatto and Windus, 1905, cited by volume and page number. |
| *Tragedies* | *The Tragedies of Algernon Charles Swinburne*, 5 vols., London, Chatto and Windus, 1904, cited by volume and page number. |
| *Hughes* | *Lesbia Brandon*, by Algernon Charles Swinburne, ed. Randolph Hughes, London, Falcon Press, 1952. |
| *Letters* | *The Swinburne Letters*, ed. Cecil Y. Lang, 6 vols., New Haven and London, Yale University Press and OUP, 1959–62. |

In like manner:

| | |
|---|---|
| *Hyder* | *Swinburne: The Critical Heritage*, ed. Clyde K. Hyder, London, Routledge and Kegan Paul, 1970. |
| *Gosse* | Edmund Gosse, *The Life of Algernon Charles Swinburne*, London Macmillan, 1917. |
| *Lafourcade* | Georges Lafourcade, *La Jeunesse de Swinburne (1837–1867)*, 2 vols., Paris and Oxford, Société d'Edition: Les Belles Lettres and OUP, 1928. |
| *Henderson* | Philip Henderson, *Swinburne: The Portrait of a Poet*, London, Routledge and Kegan Paul, 1974. |
| *McGann* | Jerome J. McGann, *Swinburne, An Experiment in Criticism*, Chicago and London, University of Chicago Press, 1972. |

# 1 A century of Swinburne

Rikky Rooksby

Algernon Charles Swinburne died in 1909. With nearly a century, now, of posthumous commentary on his life and work, there remains a striking discrepancy between the conventional estimation of his achievement and the view formed by those few critics who have taken the trouble to read him closely and patiently.

For the general reader, consulting the standard reference books and potted literary histories, entries dealing with Swinburne often (and with no excuse) appear to be a Land That Time Forgot. Writing in 1936, Miriam Allen de Ford observed 'it is the fashion nowadays to depreciate Swinburne as a poet, to speak, in our later sophistication, of his dull wordiness, his meretricious hypnosis of music.'[1] In many quarters it remains the fashion. A consultation of two reputable dictionaries of English literature published quite recently uncovers statements such as his verse 'is extremely melodious and very varied in the handling of metre, but as vague and shallow in content as it is emotionally intense',[2] and that it is 'chiefly notable for its verbal cascades, luxurious imagery and metrical pyrotechnics, for it would be difficult to make a case for its spiritual, philosophical or political profundity.'[3] In the first instance, why is intense emotion not qualified to be 'content'? In the second, there are at least three dozen recent essays that amply demonstrate the 'profundity' of Swinburne's best writing. But outside a small circle of Swinburneians and Victorian specialists these essays have gone unread, and so, to use a phrase of Swinburne's, the deep division between the two persists, with the result that the authors of such dictionary entries, histories, and reviews go on mouthing clichés.

Nor has the revised view of his status as a major Victorian poet who wrote a number of fine lyrics after 1879 yet been reflected in anthologies of Victorian poetry. W. H. Auden omitted Swinburne from his *Nineteenth Century Minor Poets* (1966), in the company of Tennyson, Browning, Arnold and Hopkins, on the good grounds that he is a major poet. In other anthologies he continues to be under-represented with little excuse, and appears all too frequently as the author of two choruses from *Atalanta in Calydon* (1865) and a few pieces from *Poems and Ballads* (1866). The *New Oxford Book of Victorian Verse* (1987), edited by Christopher Ricks, had room for only nine poems, seven from the 1866 volume, an untitled eight lines from the pamphlet *Notes on Poems and Reviews* (1866), and 'A Forsaken Garden' from *Poems and Ballads* (1878), yet found a place for ten poems by Charles Turner, sixteen by Robert Louis Stevenson, seventeen by A.E. Housman, and twenty-four by Christina Rossetti. Even on the basis that 'his pagan sensuality and life-affirming energy are a landmark, as significant a turning point in poetry as the Second Reform Bill of 1867 was in politics',[4] his early work merits a bigger selection. But what of 'The Triumph of Time', 'Ave Atque Vale', 'A Vison of Spring in Winter', the translations from Villon, 'By the North-Sea', 'Evening on the Broads', 'A Nympholept', 'The Lake of Gaube' or *Tristram of Lyonesse*? The Swinburne who wrote these things goes beyond the disciple of de Sade who thrust 'Dolores' or 'Faustine' or 'The Garden of Proserpine' at the soft underbelly of Victorian sensibility.

Without attempting to be exhaustive, my purpose here is to discuss the main phases of Swinburne criticism, and to analyse how Swinburne has been (and still is) marginalized and thus denied the recognition due to him as a poet, a pioneering critic, an important figure in the history of Aestheticism, and a timely rebel against oppressive cultural restraints.

Two essential works for delving into the world of Swinburne scholarship are Clyde K. Hyder's section on Swinburne in *The Victorian Poets: A Guide to Research*, edited by F.E. Faverty (second edition, 1968), and Kirk H. Beetz's A. C. Swinburne, *A Bibliography of Secondary Works, 1861–1980* (1982). Beetz includes references taken from Ehrsam, Deily and Smith's *Bibliographies of Twelve Victorian Authors* (1936, reprinted 1968) and the reader may wish to consult this. The journal *Victorian Poetry* publishes an annual guide to the year's work in Victorian poetry in which Swinburne irregularly features. For a substantial introduction to Swinburne readers should consult the encyclopaedic *Twentieth Century Literary Criticism* (volume 36, 1990).

The first phase of serious Swinburne criticism was initiated by the poet's death in 1909 and culminated in that green elephant of Swinburne editions, the Bonchurch *Complete Works* (1925–27, reprinted 1965), of which it must be said that it is not complete and hardly works.[5] Inaccurate and misleading, the Bonchurch unfortunately remains the only edition of Swinburne's poetry and prose. One critic described it as 'more like a tomb than a living memorial',[6] a tomb at which many scholarly curses have been uttered. Its editors (or perpetrators), Sir Edmund Gosse and Thomas J. Wise, exerted considerable influence over Swinburne's literary fortunes in the period 1909–27, and a firm grip on the fate of his published and unpublished manuscripts. Putting aside their cottage industry of limited edition pamphlets (numbering more than seventy), Gosse and Wise were responsible for *Posthumous Poems* (1917), a two-volume *Letters* (1918), *Contemporaries of Shakespeare* (1919) and a *Selected Poems* (1919) intended to replace the much reprinted *Selections* of 1887. Hampered by the obstructive attitude of Watts-Dunton, Isabel Swinburne (the poet's sole surviving sister), and Mrs Disney-Leith (his cousin), and by his own mixed feelings, Gosse published the first *Life* in 1917 (revised as volume nineteen of the *Works*). It is a flawed, if readable, biography and contains interesting accounts by Swinburne's contemporaries, but Timothy A. J. Burnett has provided a salutary warning:

> Gosse never got over his jealousy of Swinburne's eminence, and there is an element of carping and of making fun of Swinburne in all that he wrote. I do not believe that any statement by Gosse should be used as evidence unless corroborated, and if this is impossible then it should be signposted for what it is.[7]

For his part, Wise wrote a two-volume *Bibliography* (1920, reprinted 1966). This together with his later *A Swinburne Library* (1925) and volume twenty of the *Works*, remains the standard reference. These books retain this status despite their incompleteness and the fact that they are peppered with Wise's own forgeries and piracies.[8]

No studies of any consequence were published during Swinburne's life, and the ruby boards of Theodore Wratislaw's 1900 book on Swinburne in the 'English Writers of To-day' series will interest only the ardent collector. After his death there were a number of books of reminiscence, of which the most important are Mrs Disney-Leith's *The Boyhood of Algernon Charles Swinburne* (1917), the only source for a number of family letters she had destroyed, and Clara Watts-Dunton's endearing account of life in Putney, *The Home Life of Swinburne* (1922).[9] Of the briefer tales of visits to the elder Swinburne pride of place must go to Max Beerbohm's 'No. 2 The Pines' in *And Even Now* (1921).[10] Gosse and Wise were not the only ones to print corrupt versions of Swinburne's texts during these years, as T. Hake and A. Compton-Rickett's volume of *Letters* (1918) and W. A. MacInnes's *Ballads of the English Border* (1925) both show.

There was a handful of more literary judgements, including good essays by Oliver Elton in *A Survey of English Literature*, 1830–1880 (1920) and Lafacadio Hearn's 'Studies in Swinburne' in *Pre-Raphaelite and Other Poets* (1911, reprinted 1968). Harold Nicolson tried to distinguish various facets of Swinburne's output in his interesting *Swinburne* (1926), and argued for the presence of a persistent tension between the impulses of rebellion and submission in his writing. In the same year Nicolson also published the comparative 'Swinburne and Baudelaire' in *Essays by Divers Hands*. W. B. Drayton Henderson wrote *Swinburne and Landor* (1918), and two poets associated with the Georgian movement, Edward Thomas and John Drinkwater, published intermittently engaging books on Swinburne in 1912 and 1913 respectively. Their studies remind us that the change of taste signified by the inception and popular success of Edward Marsh's *Georgian Poetry* anthology was a factor in the decline of Swinburne's reputation just as much as the Modernist reaction against him, not to mention the cultural upheaval of the Great War.[11]

By the 1920s, critics sympathetic to Swinburne often seem to be on the defensive. T. Earle Welby, who wrote on Swinburne in *The Victorian Romantics 1850–70* (1929), and at full-length in the sensitive *A Study of Swinburne* (1926), commented:

> To write another book on Swinburne, I am assured, is either superfluously to restate [the general verdict] or to argue against it in sheer perversity. There is no Swinburne problem; there is nothing to elucidate. He is the simplest, the most readily and completely understood of our great poets. (1–2)

If the word 'great' were omitted, this could easily be a contemporary view.

As for the Modernist reading of Swinburne, Ezra Pound, in his review 'Swinburne Versus His Biographers', found faults 'by the bushelful' in the Victorian poet, but quickly conceded Swinburne's genius and praised the uniqueness of his music.[12] T. S. Eliot's 'Swinburne as Poet' (originally published as 'Swinburne' in *The Athenaeum* 4681, 16 Jan. 1920; revised in *The Sacred Wood*, 1920), however, has proved to be an effective and enduring depreciation. Often quoted on the dust-jackets of selections from the poetry under the mistaken belief that what Eliot had to say was complimentary, 'Swinburne as Poet' came to be regarded as a definitive pronouncement. In the words of Geoffrey Tillotson, 'forty years ago Mr Eliot said some damning things about that poetry, and he spoke for most people then and since that date.'[13] The persistent authority of this essay is evident in a recent remark that Swinburne 'seems precious and limited; and we are prone to accept the reservations of Hopkins . . . and T. S. Eliot ('Swinburne as Poet') as the last word not only on the poems but the whole career.'[14]

Close inspection easily demonstrates the inadequacy of the essay. It has the corrosive understatement of Eliot's comment that we respect Blake's philosophy as we would 'an ingenious piece of home-made furniture: we admire the man who has put it together out of the odds and ends about the house.'[15] It is not an attempt to cloak a poetic debt to Swinburne, but should rather be read in the light of Eliot's own defence of Pound's critical writings, for 'any pioneer of a revolution in poetry . . . is sure to attack some venerated names' because 'a great writer can have, at a particular time, a pernicious or merely deadening influence'.[16] Eliot marginalized Swinburne by damning with faint praise, advancing the proposition that,

> the words which we use to state our grounds of dislike or indifference cannot be applied to Swinburne as they can to bad poetry. The words of condemnation are words which express his qualities.[17]

This was to place Swinburne in a class of one, quite apart from English poetry as a whole. Referring to one of Swinburne's greatest poems, Eliot wrote:

> That so little material as appears to be employed in 'The Triumph of Time' should release such an amazing number of words requires what there is no reason to call anything but genius.

The phrase 'so little material' begs a serious question. 'The Triumph of Time' has always been read as autobiographical, inspired by a great disappointment in love. The power of experience to inspire great art does not depend on its quantity, but rather its quality and depth, and Eliot's 'so little material' is quite specious. Could his own use of a mystical experience in 'Burnt Norton' be described as 'so little material'? Furthermore, by using the word 'genius' in a context that gives it the connotation of 'conjuror', Eliot ensured that 'The Triumph of Time' was denied its human dimension and turned into an empty display of virtuosity. Throughout the essay, Eliot presented a Swinburne bound to alienate the general reader of poetry, as when he seemed to defend Swinburne from the charges brought against him by Victorian reviewers:

> None of the obvious complaints that were or might have been brought to bear upon the first *Poems and Ballads* holds good. The poetry is not morbid, it is not erotic, it is not destructive. These are adjectives which can be applied to the material, the human feelings, which in Swinburne's case do not exist.

Surely to say that a lyric poet's work has no human feelings is a devastating judgement, and a more damaging one than that of immorality. And what of Eliot's observation that the word 'beauty' 'is hardly to be used in connection with Swinburne's verse at all'? How could this be seriously maintained by anyone who takes the trouble to read attentively 'The Triumph of Time' or the 1878 *Poems and Ballads*? For Eliot, Swinburne was a poet of false impersonality; in his poetry word and object are united, as they are in 'healthy' language, only because,

> the object has ceased to exist, because the meaning is merely the hallucination of meaning, because language, uprooted, has adapted itself to an independent life of atmospheric nourishment.

Swinburne is thus consigned to a world of words, like Alice trapped behind the looking-glass in a dimension that reverses all the normal assumptions about good poetic craft. Set aside from the rest of English poetry, denied music, beauty, eroticism, human feeling, precision, structure, even the frisson of the immoral, and offering only the 'hallucination' of meaning. Swinburne's poetry was banished in a way which ensured that no sensible reader would want anything to do with it.

Eliot's *The Sacred Wood* also included an essay on Swinburne as an 'imperfect critic' that was rather more complimentary. But it was 'Swinburne as Poet' that had the influence. The book was reprinted in 1928 and 1932. Its impact is quickly apparent from J. H. Blackie's school edition of *Atalanta in Calydon* (1930), where it is one of only two critical works on Swinburne in the brief bibliography, and where one of the questions for essay practice is the quotation 'only a man of genius could dwell so exclusively among words as Swinburne'. In his preface, Blackie revealed another prejudice of the time, when he rounded off with this schoolmasterly injunction:

> It is sometimes asserted that the love of Swinburne is characteristic of youth, and that as we grow to manhood the music and the motion of his lines cease to move us as formerly. If this be so, and it is a condemnation not of his poetry but of ourselves, we must make the most of it while we may. (xi)

Eliot's picture of Swinburne inhabiting a linguistic universe of his own was echoed by a number of critics and editors through the second phase of Swinburne criticism that stretched (rather thinly at times) from about 1927 to 1959. Even if not intended, the marginalization of Swinburne was carried on in such comments as 'within his own territory, he stands as perfect as a poet could',[18] or 'in his own special sphere he is supreme',[19] or in a reference to the poetry's 'self-rapt generation in a cosmos of words.'[20] But the decline in Swinburne's reputation was due to a number of factors, including, as Cecil Lang pointed out, the advent of New Criticism, the decline of classical education, and the increased interest in Metaphysical poetry at the expense of the Victorians and the Romantics. When the first Swinburne centenary was reached in 1937, Laurence Binyon observed that it found him 'not so much depreciated as ignored',[21] and E. K. Brown that the centenary 'falls at a time when the excellences of Swinburne's poetry are unlikely to receive their due'.[22] Brown even felt Swinburne was 'in danger of becoming a forgotten poet'. Fortunately, this prophesy was false.

During the 1920s, 30s, 40s and 50s Swinburne continued to crop up in books and essays not written by confirmed supporters. Quite against the times William Empson discussed 'Laus Veneris' in *Seven Types of Ambiguity* (1930), concluding that 'when Swinburne comes off he is a very full and direct writer; it is no use saying these verses show interest in mere sounds or pattern of verbal cadence' (164). C. M. Bowra wrote on *Atalanta* in *The Romantic Imagination* (1949), and E. M. W. Tillyard printed a reading of 'Hertha' in *Five Poems* (1948). Swinburne also featured in books like Douglas Bush's *Mythology and the Romantic Tradition in English Poetry* (1937), J.W. Beach's *The Concept of Nature in Nineteenth-Century English Poetry* (1936), Leon Vivante's *English Poetry and its Contribution to the Knowledge of a Creative Principle* (1950), Jerome Buckley's *Victorian Temper: a study in Literary Culture* (1951), Ruth

Z. Temple's *The Critic's Alchemy* (1953), and Mario Praz's famous *The Romantic Agony* (translated into English, 1933). His poetry appeared in selections edited by Blakeney (1927), Burton (1927), Wolfe (with illustrations by Harry Clarke, 1928), Hyder and Chase (1937), Binyon (World's Classics, 1939), Church (with some prose, Everyman, 1940), Treece (1948), Hare (1949), Shanks (1950), and Foss (with prose, 1955).

More significant were the writings of Swinburne specialists, especially Georges Lafourcade, who edited *Swinburne's Hyperion* (1927), with an essay on the influence of Keats on Swinburne, wrote the huge *La Jeunesse de Swinburne* in two volumes (1928), an illuminating study of the life and works up to 1867 which still awaits translation into English, *Swinburne: a Literary Biography* (1932), a very readable life, and the foreword to the facsimile *Atalanta in Calydon* (OUP, 1930). Lafourcade was one of the ablest of the early critics and made a considerable contribution to the inception of a serious modern reappraisal of Swinburne.

Special mention must also be made of Clyde K. Hyder who, in addition to six articles on various aspects of Swinburne's oeuvre (1929–45, 1977), wrote *Swinburne's Literary Career and Fame* (1932, reprinted 1963) and edited several other texts that will be considered later. Two other significant books were William Rutland's *Swinburne: A Nineteenth Century Hellene*, which discussed in detail *Atalanta*, *Erechtheus* and the Hellenic poems (albeit in a splenetically anti-Modernist spirit), and Samuel Chew's more general *Swinburne* (both 1931). Other books like Humphry Hare's 1949 biography were a mixed blessing. Hare combined a heavy reliance on earlier sources with crude psycho-analysing, and exhibited a fatal (and not unique) impatience with Swinburne's life and writing at Putney – what Welby called 'that opening for cheap irony'.[23] Short, tetchy chapters on the last thirty years of Swinburne's life are usually indicative of a failure of response, with the consequence that major later poems like *Tristram of Lyonesse*, 'By the North-Sea', 'The Lake of Gaube' and 'A Nympholept' are ignored.

There was also the strange case of Randolph Hughes, who seemed determined to take possession of Swinburne studies lock, stock and barrel from the early 1940s until his death in 1955. His chief labour was the assembling of Swinburne's unfinished novel *Lesbia Brandon* (1952), which presages the revival of interest in Swinburne in the 1960s much as one of those unnatural births alluded to in whispers foreshadows great events in Shakespeare's history plays. It is a singular entity in every sense, and the invective of its footnotes legendary. Hughes clearly had a fervent desire to shatter the window of indifference where Swinburne was concerned, as his ferocious and expansive commentary (not to mention his book's brick-like shape) demonstrates. Hughes's writing on Swinburne was cranky and ill-mannered, but certainly committed. He edited two Swinburne texts for the Golden Cockerell Press, *Pasiphae* (1950) and *Lucretia Borgia: The Chronicle of Tebaldeo Tebaldei*

(1942). His projected 'veridic' biography and the intriguingly titled *Swinburne: The Arcane Side* were never published.

New light on at least one of Swinburne's relationships, with Charles Augustus Howell, came in Helen Angeli Rossetti's *Pre-Raphaelite Twilight* (1954), but otherwise no great advances were made in our knowledge of Swinburne's life during this period. He featured in William Gaunt's popular *The Pre-Raphaelite Tragedy* (1942) and *The Aesthetic Adventure* (1949), and in books like Frances Winwar's *The Rossettis and Their Circle* (1934). In these and similar books we find another way in which Swinburne has been marginalized over the years, with a distinctive note of fantastic caricature sounded in such descriptions as, 'there was the smell of sulphur about the demon who tore from his grandfather's to the Trevelyan estate two miles away, his mane and his mare's sweeping in the speed of his going, the air shivering to the shrill of his eldritch voice' (142). Compare Peter Quennell's account of Swinburne's impact on the 1860s:

> With his aureole of flaming red hair, his feverishly dancing limbs and perpetually fluttering hands, that prodigious youth had burst through the enchanted forest, the Tennysonian Broceliande of late-Romantic poetry, to the shrilling of bacchic flutes and the crash of corybantic cymbals.[24]

Given Swinburne's colourful appearance and mannerisms, his energy, his enthusiasm and his unusual psychology, it is hardly surprising that few travellers through this domain – whether they were tracking another subject (like Quennell), or day-visitors writing a brief review or entry in a historical survey – could resist this kind of writing. As they copied each other, the language became more and more exaggerated. Among English poets Swinburne is the most static of all sitting ducks for caricature. In the same vein, here is F. L. Lucas writing of how,

> the 'demoniac youth', as Ruskin called him, who had so fluttered the dove-cotes of the Victorians, turned at last into a healthy, methodical little old man of clockwork habits, his only dissipation a morning walk over Wimbledon Common and his only excitement (apart from literary quarrels of a quite frenzied ferocity) the dances of ecstasy he used to perform round every perambulator encountered on the way. . . The tiger-cat was tamed, the rebel subdued; once more Victorianism had won.[25]

This is moderate compared to Church's 'tadpole scholar' leaping on and off chairs 'like a wild creature', ' a syllable-addict, a word-drunkard'[26] or Treece's 'Eternal Boy, the rather roguish Peter Pan'.[27] One reviewer calls him a 'besotted logophile' and a 'versifying Roget'.[28] A recent critic introduces him as 'a small red-headed, bird-voiced eccentric of aristocratic lineage'.[29] This type of writing is a temptation to which anthologists and reviewers often succumb, and the result is Disneyesque. Caricature makes any serious engagement with

Swinburne seem pointless. The implication is that no one who could be so described would write anything of any depth. A similar argument says that Swinburne's creativity was dependent on his excesses, that as Rupert Croft-Cooke put it, 'he wrote no more of any great consequence after he had sobered up and ceased to undergo flagellation in St John's Wood'.[30] A context is thus established in which commentators ignorant of the past thirty years of Swinburne scholarship can credibly ask if it is possible to read him with a straight face. There was a time when stories of how 'the strident red-headed imp invaded the prim Victorian drawing room gleefully shouting indecencies and blasphemies in new and compelling poetic rhythms'[31] served to highlight an episode in literary history that was in danger of being obscured. That time has passed.

Caricature whether well-intentioned or not, conceals the historical significance and human content of Swinburne's work. It has also been common to find sympathetic and hostile critics alike conceding that he had a certain facility of expression. Graham Hough, for one, called Swinburne 'a virtuoso on the English metrical keyboard, much of whose significance lies in his versification for its own sake'.[32] It was recently stated that 'his basic greatness lies in his technical innovation and skill'.[33] Over the years Swinburne has been hailed as a 'prosodist magician',[34] a 'supreme technician',[35] 'the most consummate wizard in prosody',[36] whose,

> poetic gifts were astonishing, his facility extraordinary . . . In the technical way there was nothing he could not manage easily . . . not so much a master of language as immersed in it, swimming in a sea of words.[37]

Such praise may be justified. But Swinburne's relevance to us as a poet singing of the human condition, of the joys and sorrows of living, is easily obscured by it. We are left with a limelit figure pulling endless stanzas out of the top-hat of his poetic ingenuity like so many rabbits. What has this to do with the power of lines like 'Is it worth a tear, is it worth an hour,/ To think of things that are well outworn?', or 'But the world shall end when I forget' or 'who shall change with prayers or thanksgivings / The mystery of the cruelty of things?' or the exquisite balance of regret and consolation in the final stanza of 'A Vision of Spring in Winter'?

> The morning song beneath the stars that fled
>    With twilight through the moonless mountain air,
>    While youth with burning lips and wreathless hair
> Sang toward the sun that was to crown his head,
> Rising; the hopes that triumphed and fell dead,
>    The sweet swift eyes and songs of hours that were;
> These may'st thou not give back for ever; these,
>    As at the sea's heart all her wrecks lie waste,
>       Lie deeper than the sea;

But flowers thou may'st and winds, and hours of ease,
And all its April to the world thou may'st
Give back, and half my April back to me.

(*Poems* 3.97)

Defending Swinburne, Henry Treece once wrote that 'though one may allow oneself to be flippant about Swinburne's emotional development, one does not dare call into question his technical achievement'.[38] This is a damaging discrimination, and has been unconsciously restated by recent acknowledgements of Swinburne's technique that push caricature still further. Some readers of poetry might perhaps be attracted by the idea of a 'prosodist magician'. But who will respond to the statement that Swinburne was 'gifted' – as crack tennis stars are gifted – with a dazzling facility for delivering words at speed'?[39] And who would warm to the claim that, 'mention the sea or a garden or a lost love and Swinburne can talk forever. He is inexhaustible' ?[40]

Swinburne's detractors have often saved themselves the trouble of doing justice to his poetry by recounting the story of Swinburne's lost love, as given by Gosse in 1917. One major development in our thinking about his romantic disappointment came in the 1950s with the publication of two key articles. In 1953, John S. Mayfield published 'Swinburne's "Boo" ', in which he demonstrated that at the time Swinburne's proposal to Jane Faulkner was alleged (by Gosse) to have taken place, Jane would have been ten years old, and that there was no connection between her and the verses which Wise claimed had been written for her by Swinburne. By the end of the decade, Mayfield, Paul F. Baum (who published a fine reading of 'A Nympholept'), and Cecil Lang had all independently reached the conclusion that a much more likely candidate for this romance was Swinburne's cousin Mary Gordon (from 1865, Mrs Disney-Leith), and it was Lang who presented the case in 'Swinburne's Lost Love' (*PMLA* 1959). As he pointed out, if 'The Triumph of Time' was supposed to be a faithful record of this rejection in love (as Swinburne had told Gosse that it was), one line – 'Flesh of his flesh, but heart of my heart' – clearly indicated that the speaker had lost the woman to another man, probably in marriage. Mary Gordon had married in June 1865. Was it likely that Jane Faulkner at ten had had another suitor? There are many more writings by Swinburne and Mary Gordon which support this thesis.

The third phase of Swinburne studies was ushered in by the publication of Lang's indispensable *The Swinburne Letters* (1959–62), the book that launched a thousand footnote citations. It presented a massive amount of new information about all aspects of the poet's life and art, some 2,000 mostly unpublished letters, and came immaculately annotated and indexed, with a strong polemical introduction and, as an appendix, the first printing of the confidential note that Gosse had written on Swinburne's 'irregularities' and deposited in the British Museum. The idea of doing any serious work on Swinburne without it is unthinkable. As well as his edition of the letters, Lang has published ten articles (1948–62), a valuable commentary on the twenty-five Swinburne poems in his anthology, *The Pre-Raphaelites and their Circle* (1968), and a very useful miscellany of unpublished materials called *New Writings by Swinburne* (1964).

If a large part of the credit for a revival of interest in Swinburne during the 1960s must go to *The Swinburne Letters*, other reasons are not hard to find. With a waning preoccupation with Modernism and its values, there came a renewed interest in Romantic and Victorian poetry, and in the less stuffy aspects of Victorian culture generally. The market value of Pre-Raphaelite paintings began to climb. That side of the 1960s which delighted in the hedonistic, the exotic and the iconoclastic, was bound to find something attractive in Swinburne, as it did in Blake. This third phase could be said to have culminated in 1971. Between 1959 and 1971 the study of Swinburne was given a firm scholarly foundation. On the textual front, Clyde K. Hyder edited *Notes on Poems and Reviews* (1866), *Under the Microscope* (1872) and the 1904 'Dedicatory Epistle' as *Swinburne Replies* (1966), and a volume of early reviews of Swinburne in the Critical Heritage series (1970). Edmund Wilson's introduction to his edition of *The Novels of A. C. Swinburne* (1962) remains worth reading; Wilson argued that Swinburne deserved to be remembered more for his fiction than his poetry. Howard B. Norland edited *A Study of Ben Jonson* (1969), and Hugh J. Luke *William Blake. A Critical Essay* (1970). There were a number of selections made from the poetry by Edith Sitwell (1960), Bonamy Dobree (1961), and Morse Peckham, whose edition of *Poems and Ballads* and *Atalanta in Calydon* (1970) carried out Swinburne's proposed re-arrangement of the former text, sketched out in a letter of 1876. One of the best essays ever written on Swinburne, John D. Rosenberg's article in *Victorian Studies* (1967) became the introduction to his *Swinburne: Selected Poems and Prose* (1968). Rosenberg made the important claim that he found 'moments of astonishing strength'[41] in the later verse and that Swinburne had not died as a poet when he moved to Putney in 1879. Critics like Chew, William Sharp, and Lucas had felt, in the latter's words, that 'even in the later volumes, when the flame of his eloquence can find something real to feed it, the old splendour suddenly flames heaven-high again'.[42] Leon Vivante went so far as to call *Tristram of Lyonesse* 'by far the best of his poems'.[43] But the majority verdict had indeed been that the Putney poems were a 'strait waste place' at the end of 'the dense hard passage . . . that crawls by a track none turn to climb'. So the discovery that Swinburne's later poems were not the forsaken garden they were widely believed to be was exciting. Earlier critics were also aware of the observation Rosenberg made that Swinburne is not always lush but rather a master of the monosyllable. This employment of 'the bleak beauty of little words'[44] was noted by Drinkwater and G. K. Chesterton, who had observed that Swinburne's style was 'made of short English words like the short Roman swords'.[45]

New ground in the understanding of Swinburne's criticism was broken by Robert L. Peters' *The Crowns of Apollo: Swinburne's Principles of Literature and Art* (1965) and Thomas E. Connolly's *Swinburne's Theory of Poetry* (1964), both of which remain important for readers interested in this aspect of Swinburne's work. On the biographical front, John A. Cassidy published the contentious *Algernon C. Swinburne* (Twayne's English Authors, 1964) and Jean Overton Fuller pursued the Mary Gordon theme in her *Swinburne* (1968), sometimes to silly lengths. An increasing preparedness to see Swinburne not as an isolated phenomenon but in the wider context of nineteenth-century culture was evident from books like Rupert Croft-Cooke's *Feasting With Panthers* (1967), John Dixon Hunt's *The Pre-Raphaelite Imagination* (1968), Barbara Charlesworth's *Dark Passages: The Decadent Consciousness in Victorian Literature* (1965), which looks at Pater's debt to Swinburne, and E. W. Schneider's study of G. M. Hopkins *The Dragon in the Gate* (1968) in which she called Swinburne's influence 'one of the mainsprings of Hopkins's new rhythm' which 'may well have provided the first incitement to experiment' (57).

It becomes impossible after 1960 to mention the many essays about Swinburne in literary journals such as the *Journal of Pre-Raphaelite Studies* and *Victorian Poetry*. But the latter's specal issue of 1971 dedicated to Swinburne, and fittingly edited by Cecil Lang, signals that the rebirth of Swinburne studies was now complete. In his introduction, Lang remarked with justifiable satisfaction that 'the "sad, shapeless horror increate" that was Swinburne criticism . . . has ceased' and 'a new era has begun'. The essays he collected showed a sophistication and breadth of interest which hardly existed twelve years previously. The contributors discussed *Atalanta, Poems and Ballads* (1866), 'Ave Atque Vale', as well as late poems like 'The Lake of Gaube' and 'A Nympholept'. F. A. C. Wilson investigated the prose fiction of Mary Gordon.

The fourth phase of Swinburne studies, from 1971 to the present, has been a consolidation of what was achieved in the 1960s and a filling-in of detail. Benefiting from the immediate past, Swinburne's new readers were able to lift the quality of their discussions to new heights. Nowhere is this more apparent than in Anthony Harrison's *Swinburne's Medievalism* (1988), Margot K. Louis's *Swinburne and His Gods* (1990), and Jerome McGann's endlessly engaging *Swinburne: An Experiment in Criticism* (1972) which, in imaginary-dialogue form, examines many ways of reading Swinburne, and traces his preoccupations through poetry and prose, both published and unpublished. If there is a single indispensable critical study of Swinburne, this is it. David G. Riede's *Swinburne: A Study of Romantic Mythmaking* (1978) was important not least for championing the later poetry more than anyone else has done, before or since. Other important books on Swinburne include Meredith B. Raymond's *Swinburne's Poetics: Theory and Practice* (1971), Ross C. Murfin's

*Swinburne, Hardy, Lawrence and the Burden of Belief* (1978), and Kerry McSweeney's *Tennyson and Swinburne as Romantic Naturalists* (1981). Anne Walder published a monograph on Baudelaire's influence on *Poems and Ballads* (1976), and Ian Fletcher wrote a pamphlet on Swinburne in the 'Writers and Their Works' series (1973) in addition to editing *Decadence and the 1890s* (1979) which contained Chris Snodgrass's essay 'Swinburne's Circle of Desire'. Other recent essays worth consulting are Lionel Stevenson's chapter on Swinburne in *The Pre-Raphaelite Poets* (1972), William Buckler's 'The Poetry of Swinburne: An Essay in Critical Reinforcement' in *The Victorian Temper* (1980), Richard McGhee's 'Swinburne and Hopkins' in *Marriage, Duty and Desire in Victorian Poetry and Drama*(1980), Robert L. Peters's 'Swinburne: A Personal Essay and a Polemic' in *The Victorian Experience: The Poets* (edited by Richard A. Levine, 1982), 'Swinburne: The Sublime Recovered' in Pauline Fletcher's *Gardens and Grim Ravines* (1983), James Richardson's 'Swinburne: Purity and Pain' in *Vanishing Lives* (1988), Ekbert Faas's 'Swinburne, or the Psycho-pathology of Poetic Creation' in *Retreat Into The Mind* (1988), and Thaïs E. Morgan's 'Swinburne's Myth of Apollo' in *The Sun is God: Painting, Literature and Mythology in the Nineteenth Century* (edited by J. B. Bullen. 1989). Anthony H. Harrison published an essay on 'Swinburne, Wordsworth, and the Politics of Mortality' in his *Victorian Poets and Romantic Poems* (1990), and Richard Dellamora included a chapter on Swinburne in *Masculine Desire: The Sexual Politics of Victorian Aestheticism* (1990).

Most of these discussions show the much enhanced awareness that now exists of Swinburne's importance in the literary milieu of his day. His name is now routinely cited in studies of the Aesthetic movement and the 1890s.[46] As Ian Fletcher said, 'it was Swinburne who took the aesthetic standard from Ruskin and Baudelaire and passed it on to the generation that was to follow.'[47] William Buckler was surely right when he wrote:

> Swinburne's part in moving literary matters forward when they threatened to stagnate in the acknowledged successes of Tennyson and Browning will gain firmer and crisper, if not universal recognition and acknowledgement.[48]

Many new perspectives on Swinburne's poetry were opened up, like the use of Biblical typology to which George P. Landow drew attention in poems like 'Before a Crucifix', in his study *Victorian Types, Victorian Shadows* (1980). Another indication of change, and one that may have raised eyebrows in certain quarters, was the inclusion of 'Ave Atque Vale' alongside 'Lycidas', 'Adonais', *In Memoriam*, 'A Singer Asleep' and 'In Memory of Major Robert Gregory', in Peter M. Sacks's *The English Elegy* (1985); Sacks regarded Swinburne's elegy as 'one of the finest and least understood in the language' (204).[49]

A small number of Swinburne texts were reprinted or published for the first time. Clyde K. Hyder presented a very useful selection from the criticism in *Swinburne as Critic* (1972). Francis J. Sypher edited both *Undergraduate Papers* (1974), the extremely scarce journal to which Swinburne contributed five pieces in 1857–58, and his novel *A Year's Letters* (1974), at last establishing a reliable text for the latter.[50] Robert E. Lougy edited Swinburne's collaboration with Mary Gordon, *The Children of the Chapel* (1987), which further illuminated their relationship. Leonard M. Findlay was responsible for the latest volume of *Selected Poems* (1982), and Swinburne's Arthurian poems have made a welcome re-appearance in the 'Arthurian Poets' series (1990), introduced by James Carley.

When it comes to publications, an air of regret for what might have been clings to the otherwise eminent name of John S. Mayfield (who died in 1983), one of the staunchest supporters Swinburne ever had. His vital research into the life of Jane Faulkner ('Swinburne's "Boo" ') has already been cited, and he was responsible for a number of pamphlets printed in very small numbers. Nor are his two books easy to come by. *Swinburneiana* (1974), an entertaining if light-weight miscellany of notes, was limited to 500 copies, and a first printing of the early poem *Hide and Seek* (1975) to 250. His rumoured bibliography never materialized. The huge Swinburne collection he acquired, including more than one hundred first editions of *Atalanta*, bought to prove more than that number had been printed, will no doubt prove a treasure trove once it has been catalogued.

The 1970s and 1980s saw the publication of a number of books that have added to or refined the picture of Swinburne's life. Donald Thomas' *Swinburne: The Poet in his World* (1979) was good on the cultural background but not especially sympathetic, and it gave short shrift to the Putney period. His comment that the 1878 *Poems and Ballads* 'had an easy appeal' (194) seemed a tepid response to Swinburne's most poignant collection. A better book was Philip Henderson's *Swinburne: The Portrait of a Poet* (1974), a compact and elegant synthesis of material that may well continue for some time to win new readers for Swinburne, even if it was not based on very much original research. Mollie Panter-Downes' *At the Pines* (1971) was a sensitive treatment of the Putney years, and Swinburne's connection with the Isle of Wight was explored in detail in the pamphlet *Young Algernon Swinburne* (1978) by Richard J. Hutchings and Raymond V. Turley. Wolf Mankowitz's *Mazeppa* (1982) had a chapter on Swinburne's affair with Adah Isaacs Menken, and Raleigh Trevelyan's *A Pre-Raphaelite Circle* (1978) and Simon Reynold's *The Vision of Simeon Solomon* (1984) discussed other relationships.[51] Ian Gibson's *The English Vice* (1978) had a very interesting chapter on Swinburne's experience of and predeliction for the birch, and as an appendix printed two flagellant poems by Swinburne from 'The Pearl'. Gibson's account was welcome in its directness after so many damaging hints and whispers, and made Swinburne's sexual abnormalities seem a little less abnormal:

> Whoever Swinburne's flagellant ladies were, it is legitimate to assume that, having helped the poet to erection by acting out his fantasies for him, they proceeded to assuage his desires in a more conventional manner . . . We might note that the poet refers to the St. John's Wood establishment as a 'Sadice-Paphian' spring and not merely as a sadique one, suggesting that after the birch came the bed. (256–57)

This is a welcome corrective to so many biographical accounts or reviews that have made it seem that Swinburne's sexual life meant birching and nothing else. Gibson also quotes some striking passages from the commonplace books of Richard Monckton Milnes, including this one:

> Algernon Swinburne with a tutor who flogged him over the fallen branch of a tree, till the grass was stained with his blood and another time when wet out of the water after bathing.

If Swinburne was telling the truth, then here is light indeed shed on some of his fiction, for as Gibson commented 'it would seem from this account that Bertie Seyton's birching when wet from bathing in *Lesbia Brandon* derived from the author's own experience' (125). However, we are not yet in a position to be able confidently to distinguish between fact and fantasy in matters where Swinburne's emotions were so involved, and caution is needed.[52]

Our knowledge of Swinburne's life will be greatly enhanced when all the letters which have come to light since 1962 are gathered together. Terry L. Meyers, who has written several articles on the influence of Shelley on Swinburne and salvaged the text of Swinburne's speech to the Royal Literary Fund in 1866 (see *Modern Philology* 86, 1989), is nearing the completion of what will be the seventh volume of Swinburne's letters.

We now have a partial answer to one of the mysteries of Swinburne's life, his departure from Balliol in November 1859. Research into the College's archives has shown that Swinburne was reprimanded on three occasions, twice in 1858, and then officially sent away from Balliol ('rusticated') to fix his attention on his work. It had been thought that he withdrew on the advice of Jowett to his father. To some extent therefore, Swinburne was being true to life in *A Year's Letters*, not only throughout most of Captain Harewood's letter to his son Reginald, but also in a manuscript variant given by Sypher, 'as I looked back over my son's school and college days, on three memorable features in them . . . that he had got himself constantly flogged, twice plucked, and once rusticated.'[53]

The peculiarities of Swinburne's constitution and sensibility have also been examined in recent years by the qualified eyes of an American doctor. In his essay 'Swinburne's Masochism: Neuropathology and Psychopathology', in *Boswell's Clap* (1979, reprinted 1988), William B. Ober stated his intent was, 'to demonstrate that Swinburne's psychopathology had its root in neuropathology, that the specific primary event was anoxic brain damage incurred at birth, and that his masochism and other abnormal behaviour developed as a psychological overlay.'(44) Ober believed that Swinburne might have been born prematurely.

One other biographical issue that has swum from the deep concerns Jane Faulkner. A source for Gosse's story has at last turned up, in the guise of a letter written by the novelist Lucy Clifford (died 1929), informing Gosse (in case he did not know) that Jane Faulkner had been proposed to by Swinburne. Clifford did not state a year for this event and seemed unaware of the age problem, but claimed to have got the story from one of Jane's sisters, who presumably would have known Jane's age. The letter does not solve anything, and Gosse's reply has not yet come to light. Was the story concocted out of spite by Jane's sister? Nothing can now dislodge Mary Gordon from her place in the biography of Swinburne and she remains, quite rightly, the most likely candidate for the role of his lost love, and the Muse who inspired 'The Triumph of Time'. But perhaps there is some grain of truth yet to be filtered from the legend of Jane Faulkner.[54]

The growing diversity and intelligence of Swinburne criticism in the 1970s and 1980s was a pleasure to behold. Admittedly, the problem of caricature did not go away, and no doubt there will always be those who are convinced, like Yvor Winters, that Swinburne 'wrote no poems that will endure serious reading' and that 'the first chorus of *Atalanta* is probably the best poem. After that there is little to choose'.[55] But the best of the recent work has combined a firm grasp of the advances in textual and contextual scholarship with a high degree of theoretical sophistication. On occasion, however, the *nouvelle critique* has led to readings of Swinburne that are little more than a repetition of old sins in new guises, where the lilies and languors of Eliot are exchanged for the raptures and roses of Barthes or Derrida. Eliot's picture of Swinburne dwelling in a world of words was no problem for post-structuralists, since for them so was everyone else.

One such example of how not to read Swinburne was provided by Laurence Lerner in 1985, during an argument about the utility of the concept of self-reflexive poetry. The ghost of Eliot loomed large throughout Lerner's mishandling of 'The Triumph of Time', which was a catalogue of the sort of perverse critical practice that would be rejected out of hand if anyone had the temerity to apply it to a major poem by Yeats, Pound or Hopkins. To analyse the 'incantatory lilt' of its tenth stanza without acknowledging the context created by the previous nine was absurd. A barrage of literal-minded questions which few poems (particularly contemporary ones) could satisfy quickly led to the conclusion that 'it is impossible to translate this point into any aspect of the human situation'. 'The Triumph of Time' could not really be about love or swimming (the other possible topic!). It was not a 'psychological exploration but a game.'[56] So much for Swinburne's *cri de coeur*.

Perversely, similar readings were offered by critics attracted by the idea of Swinburne's supposed world of words. Here was a discourse seemingly made in the image of their own belief in the world as text. Often the old charge of mellifluous confusion was simply re-stated as grounds for a dubious praise. Thus Nicholas Tredell wrote:

> While it has long been recognized that *Tristram* undermines narrative, it has not been perceived that the poem also undermines quasi-theological hypostatizations, set symbolic patterns, and, indeed, language itself; that it is, in fact, radically subversive.[57]

Giving only passing mention of the poem's 'rhapsodic celebration of passional experience', Tredell's essay claimed that *Tristram*'s real innovation emanates from the use of language to break up the structures – of which language itself is perhaps the most basic – that order our perceptions and our lives. Why this should be a desirable aim or laudable achievement for a poet was left unexplained. Behind such a statement can be seen a lazy association of order with bourgeois restrictions and an adolescent notion of the value of anarchy. Any attempt, Tredell argued, to make of the poem a 'seamless unity, is dissolved by the text even as the materials for constructing it are presented'.[58] This left no alternative between viewing *Tristram* either as a self-deconstructing mess, or as a flawlessly signifying perfection; the former useless to humanity, the second unknown in the annals of literature. Aspects of Swinburne's technique, for example his similes, were to be read as a means of sharpening 'our awareness of the images as acts of language rather than as presentations of extra-linguistic reality'.[59]

Tredell's reading marginalized *Tristram of Lyonesse* as effectively as the most hidebound traditional criticism. In effect, the essay presented Swinburne as being, in the words of Eric Partridge, 'magnificent, purple, highfalutin' ', in order to demonstrate the unimportance of being those things. Why it should be desirable to undermine language, why this should occupy Swinburne on and off for something like thirteen years, and why he should take nine cantos to do it, are questions Tredell did not ask. Only in referential universes can poetry make anything resembling the 'dangerous voyage' of his title, where its essential function to signify to worlds of human concern is central. As Bonamy Dobrée wrote in 1961:

> His verse . . . is still superb, still magnificently exciting to anyone who has an ear for poetry, who can be stirred by the sheer complex music that Swinburne created, who does not approach poetry in that solely mental state which makes all poetry sterile.[60]

The same problems of interpretative practice showed up in some of the essays written about Swinburne's response to the natural world, especially in his later landscape and seascape poems. Susan E. Lorsch's reading of 'Evening on the Broads' tried to argue that the true theme of the poem was an interrogation of how language is applied to nature, rather than a response to nature itself; that the poem was an attempt to illustrate,

> the process by which humanity attempts to commune and communicate with a post-Romantic nature emptied of meaning; and it demonstrates the ultimate impossibility of relating to this natural setting without falsifying it by infusing it with meaning.[61]

Such a view immediately fails to account for the intensity of Swinburne's later poems. It also rests on the assumption that nature is without meaning, a belief that has only been held for an infinitesimal time in human history, and that is insistently challenged in ecological circles. The notion of humanity utterly divided from nature, upon which Lorsch's argument rested, might be just as validly read as a statement not of things as they are, but of a delusion under which we presently labour and that we exploit for selfish reasons. Swinburne's refrain 'Are we not as waves of the water, as notes of the song?' (*Poems* 5, 189) suggests he intuitively knew this too. As Rosenberg observed:

> The decadent, verbally sophisticated Swinburne was in another part of his being pre-civilized, a wind-worshipper and a sea-worshipper whose poetry springs from sources more antique than words.[62]

For Lorsch, the poem's use of indirect verbs, its strange grammar and syntax, the tactic of delaying the subject, and the plethora of negative suffixes like 'shadowless', 'breathless', and 'deathless', all constituted a 'language of negation' that insists the landscape has no inherent meaning. It could just as plausibly be argued that they are a language of wonder. To argue that 'the negating suffix tells us that the subject of the adjective lacks something, that it is without' is to approach poetry with the narrow view of a textbook of grammar. And only a modern scepticism would make the unwarranted assumption that right from the beginning of the poem 'the narrator begins with the implicit assumption or recognition that nature is without meaning'. It is hard to deny that Swinburne approached nature with wonder, when he writes:

> As a bird unfledged is the broad-winged night, whose
> winglets are callow
> Yet, but soon with their plumes will she cover her
> brood from afar,
> Cover the brood of her worlds that cumber the skies
> with their blossom
> Thick as the darkness of leaf-shadowed spring is
> encumbered with flowers.

World upon world is enwound in the bountiful girth
of her bosom,
Warm and lustrous with life lovely to look on as
ours.

(*Poems* 5. 59–60)

Lorsch's account dismissed this as the speaker 'caught up in his own rhetoric'. But where in the poem is the signal to tell the reader this? Why are we to assume that night 'does not merit such language'? Perhaps Swinburne felt it did, and that was why he wrote these lines. The majesty of 'Evening on the Broads' is not served by binding it in a strait-jacket of imposed irony alien to the imaginative freedom of the poem, thus turning it from being a real encounter with a living cosmos into a lengthy mutter about inarticulacy.

For all their vaunted modernity, interpretations like those of Lorsch, Tredell, and Lerner emasculated Swinburne's poetry; the poems turned dull under a layer of dust not so much of the library as the seminar room. Pauline Fletcher has described Swinburne's impact in the 1860s as being that of one 'throwing open the Victorian drawing room and exposing its inmates to the elemental clash of wind and waves'.[63] Perhaps there are other doors that need throwing open. As Arthur Symons once wrote, in a very different vein from the zinc-bright diction of modern criticism:

> Reading the earlier and the later Swinburne on a high rock around which the sea is washing, one is struck by the way in which these cadences, in their unending, ever-varying flow, seem to harmonize with the rhythm of the sea. Here one finds, at least, and it is a great thing to find, a rhythm inherent in nature. A mean, or merely bookish, rhythm is rebuked by the sea, as a trivial or insincere thought is rebuked by the stars.[64]

If the speaker in 'Evening on the Broads' fails to achieve the rapturous communion with nature that others among Swinburne's singers experience, then, Fletcher suggests, it may be because of a failure to transcend the limits of the ego. Like Anthony Harrison, Fletcher sees a place for recognizing the religious dimension in the later poetry's encounter with nature and the sea. Harrison has brought the notion of pantheism (even if that is not the exact term we may require) back into the debate about Swinburne's later work. This must be healthy.

Swinburne's oeuvre is rich enough to offer us many delights, some strange, some familiar, and in this sense the author of *Atalanta*, *Poems and Ballads* (1866 and 1878), *William Blake*, some of the *Songs Before Sunrise*, and *Tristram of Lyonesse*, is for all times. Yet his distinctive celebration of the organic unity of the world, and of our life in that unity, give him a particular relevance in the last years of the century which could hardly have been anticipated. It would be deeply unfortunate if a persistent preoccupation with his supposed status as a poet of disembodied words deafened us to his distinctive intimations of natural harmony.

## Notes

1. S.J. Kunitz (ed.), *British Authors of the Nineteenth Century* (New York, 1936), 600.
2. C. Gillie (ed.), *Longman Companion to English Literature* (1972), 814.
3. Ian Ousby (ed.), *Cambridge Guide to English Literature* (Cambridge, 1988), 965.
4. J.R. Watson (ed.), *Everyman's Book of Victorian Verse* (1982), xxi.
5. For valedictory notes after Swinburne's death see *The Bookman*, June 1909, and J. W. Mackail's lecture 'Swinburne' given on 30 April 1909 in Oxford, reprinted in *Studies in English Poets* (1926).
6. B. Ifor Evans, *English Poetry in the Later Nineteenth Century* (1933, rev. ed. 1966), 47.
7. T. A. J. Burnett, review of *Henderson, Victorian Poetry*, 14 (1975), 1, 85.
8. Gosse's 1912 essay on Swinburne is reprinted in *Portraits From Life*, ed. Ann Thwaite (1991). For an account of Gosse's relationship with Swinburne see her *Edmund Gosse: A Literary Landscape* (1984). For Wise see W. Partington's *Forging Ahead* (New York. 1939. repr. 1974), N. J. Barker and J. Collins's *Sequel to An Enquiry into the Nature of Certain Nineteenth Century Pamphlets* (1983) and their book on Wise and Harry Buxton Foreman, *Two Forgers* (1992).
9. See also James Douglas, *Theodore Watts-Dunton: Poet, Novelist, Critic* (1904).
10. N. John Hall (ed.) *Max Beerbohm's Rossetti and His Circle* (1987) includes many of Beerbohm's caricatures of Swinburne. For a brief but vivid account of a visit to 'The Pines' see Karl Beckson and John M. Munro (eds.), *Arthur Symons: Selected Letters 1880-1935* (1989), 149–151.
11. See also A. E. Housman, 'Swinburne', *American Scholar*, 39 (1969), 59–79.
12. T. S. Eliot (ed.) *Literary Essays of Ezra Pound* (1960), 294.
13. G. Tillotson, *Mid-Victorian Studies* (1965), 211.
14. B. Richards (ed.), *English Verse 1830-1880* (1980), 462.
15. T. S. Eliot, *Selected Essays* (3rd ed. 1951), 321.
16. *Literary Essays of Ezra Pound*, xi.
17. Eliot, *Selected Essays*, 323–327.
18. Henry Treece (ed.), *Selected Poems by Algernon Charles Swinburne* (1948), 17.
19. L. Binyon (ed.) *Selected Poems by Algernon Charles Swinburne* (1939), xviii.
20. Richard Church (ed.), *Swinburne: Poems and Prose* (1940), xv.
21. Binyon, vii.
22. E. K. Brown, 'Swinburne: A Centenary Estimate' in *Victorian Literature: Modern Essays in Criticism*, ed. Austin Wright (1961), 295.
23. Welby, 9.
24. Peter Quennell, *John Ruskin: The Portrait of a Poet* (1949), 204–05.
25. F. L. Lucas, *Ten Victorian Poets* (1940), 170.
26. Church, xi, xiii.
27. Treece, 12.
28. Jonathan Raban, 'The besotted logophile', *Sunday Times*, 9 May 1982.
29. Carl Woodring, *Nature Into Art* (Cambridge, Mass, 1989), 147.
30. R. Croft-Cooke, *Feasting with Panthers* (1967), 10.
31. Curtis Dahl in *The Victorian Period Excluding the Novel* (1983) ed. Arthur Pollard, 189.
32. Graham Hough, *The Last Romantics* (1949), 192.
33. Dahl, 190.
34. Brown, 301.

35. Edith Sitwell (ed.), *Swinburne: A Selection* (1960), 5.
36. E. Batho and B. Dobree. *The Victorians and After, 1830–1914* (1938), 64.
37. Julian Symons, 'The Stumbling Block', *Sunday Times*, 24 March 1974.
38. Treece, 12.
39. Raban, 'The besotted logophile'.
40. W. David Shaw, *The Lucid Veil: Poetic Truth in the Victorian Age* (1987), 171.
41. J. D. Rosenberg, 'Swinburne', *Victorian Studies*, 11 (1967), 152.
42. Lucas, 177.
43. Vivante, 265.
44. Rosenberg, 132.
45. G. K. Chesterton, *The Victorian Age in Literature* (1913), 185.
46. See Linda Dowling, *Language and Decadence in the Victorian Fin de Siècle* (Princeton, 1986.).
47. E. Warner and G. Hough (eds). *Strangeness and Beauty: An Anthology of Aesthetic Criticism* (1983), 224–5.
48. Buckler, 228.
49. See also Melissa Zeiger, 'A Muse Funereal: The Critique of Elegy in Swinburne's "Ave Atque Vale" ', *Victorian Poetry*, 24 (1986), 2, 173–88.
50. See also Gerald C. Monsman, 'Old Mortality at Oxford', *Studies in Philology*, 67 (1970), 359–89. Edward P. Schuldt, 'Three Unpublished Balliol Essays of A. C. Swinburne', *Review of English Studies*, 27 (1976), 108, 422–30; Rikky Rooksby, 'A Short Note on the Swinburne Manuscripts at Worcester College Oxford', *Victorians Institute Journal* 18 (1990), 175–83; and the appendix to Anthony Harrison's *Swinburne's Medievalism* (1988). For *A Year's Letters* see David G. Riede's 'Bard and Lady Novelist: Swinburne and the Novel of (Mrs) Manners', *Victorian Newsletter* 69 (1986), 4–7.
51. See also Derek Hudson's *Munby: Man of Two Worlds* (1972) and the many letters to Swinburne in Roger W. Peattie (ed.), *Selected Letters of William Michael Rossetti* (1990).
52. For a contrary view see T. A. J. Burnett, 'Swinburne's Life and Works', *Review*, 4 (Virginia, 1982), 54–5.
53. Sypher, 176. See Rikky Rooksby, 'The Case of Commoner Swinburne', *Review of English Studies*, 164 (1990) 510–20.
54. See Rikky Rooksby, 'Swinburne's "Boo" Rides Again', *Review of English Studies* (Feb. 1993). For the possible influence of an early death in the Swinburne family hitherto unrecorded, see 'A Swinburne Tragedy', *Notes and Queries* (June, 1992).
55. Yvor Winter, *Forms of Discovery* (1967), 185.
56. Laurence Lerner, 'Poetry as the Play of Signifiers', *Essays in Criticism*, 35 (1985), 3. 246.
57. Nicholas Tredell, '*Tristram of Lyonesse*: Dangerous Voyage', *Victorian Poetry*, 20 (1982), 2. 97.
58. Tredell, 104fn.
59. Tredell, 107.
60. B. Dobree (ed.) *Swinburne: The Penguin Poets* (1961), 12.
61. Susan E. Lorsch, 'Algernon Charles Swinburne's "Evening on the Broads": Unmeaning Landscape and the Language of Negation', *Victorian Poetry* 18 (1980) 91–6. Reprinted in *Where Nature Ends* (1983).
62. Rosenberg, 145.
63. Fletcher, 192.
64. Arthur Symons, *Figures of Several Centuries* (1916), 161. Symons also wrote on Swinburne in *Studies in Strange Souls* (1929).

# 2 Swinburne and romantic authority

David G. Riede

When Swinburne began writing poetry in the latter half of the nineteenth century, he was confronted with the difficult problem already faced by such older contemporaries as Tennyson, Browning, and Arnold – in the aftermath of the Romantic movement, with its high ideals and still higher ambitions for poetry, how was the poet to live up to his high calling? In a time of confusion and uncertainty, a period that quite self-consciously thought of itself as an age of transition, how was the ambitious poet to find coherent themes for what Wordsworth called the 'high argument' of his prophetic song? Tennyson and Browning had both begun their careers with abortive attempts at prophetic utterance, at visionary song, and had both soon realized that the illimitable ambitions of Romanticism were no longer reasonable in a sadder but wiser age. The problem, as Arnold saw it, was that a world of uncertainties left one without any single unified and coherent faith, and consequently without any possible grounds for authoritative utterance. From Arnold's point of view Tennyson, Browning, Clough, and even Keats suffered from 'multitudinousness', a failure to find and follow a unified and unifying 'Idea of the world.' From this point of view, it was an age unpropitious to the muse, an age of 'unpoetrylessness'.[1] And from this point of view, Swinburne agreed – in his essay on Arnold he denounced the poetry characteristic of an age of transition in phrases that seem to apply to much of Arnold and Clough, and to the Tennyson of *In Memoriam*. Not poetical, he said are,

> the small troubles of spirits that nibble and quibble about beliefs living or dead; so are not those sickly moods which are warmed and weakened by feeding on the sullen drugs of dejection; and the savour of this disease and its medicines is enough to deaden the air of poetry. Nothing which leaves us depressed is a true work of art. We must have light though it be lightning, and air though it be storm.
>
> (*Works*, 14:98)

As the passage suggests, Swinburne believed, emphatically, that the poet must speak without vacillation or hesitation, that he must speak powerfully and authoritatively. But where was he to find the faith that would provide him with passionate intensity? Swinburne was certainly not oblivious to the age he had been born into. As a poet, he acknowledged that he had been born into what he called the 'Church of Tennyson' (*Letters*, 1:97), but despite his great respect for Tennyson's powers, he could see that the Church of Tennyson had no available doctrine. Indeed, when Tennyson rose to the bardic mode with 'The Higher Pantheism', Swinburne's response was not only a merciless parody, but also a passing dismissal of the oracle as a 'gabble and babble of half-hatched thoughts in half-baked words' (*Letters*, 2:86).

Unaided by the contemporary high priests of poetry, Swinburne looked back to the Romantics. A Victorian heretic, Swinburne turned from the Church of Tennyson, declaring himself a member of the 'Church of Blake and Shelley' (*Letters*, 3:14). He evidently saw in his Romantic assumptions a way to transcend the unpropitious historical moment, a way to continue in the high prophetic mode. Following the examples of Blake and Shelley rather than those of Wordsworth and Coleridge, Swinburne sought an authority that would consist of three distinct but interwoven assumptions: first, that imaginative separation from and rebellion against conventional pieties is itself a source of power; second, that mastery of poetic forms and harmonies is in effect a sign and seal of authoritative power; and third, that visionary poets speak to one another across the ages in a tradition that transcends time and historical circumstances as it keeps in view a realm of eternal truths and unchanging laws. It is consequently not surprising that his early critical masterpiece and manifesto was on William Blake, and that his first concern in *William Blake: A Critical Essay* was to establish Blake's authority, to urge that far from being mad Blake 'spoke with authority; not in the least like the Scribes of his day' (*Works*, 16:56). For Swinburne, the great poet remains a bard and prophet who stands apart from and above his time, outside of history, to speak with an authority greater than the scribes of the passing day can muster. But of course, despite his echo of the New Testament (Matthew 7.29), Swinburne did not believe in God – whence, then, the authority? It is clearly a fundamental problem for a prophet to lack a divine word – indeed, as William Kerrigan has pointed out, after the word of God lost its authority, after Milton, 'The new "poet-prophet", defining his prophetic tradition with increasing eccentricity, spoke his fiery words from the margins of culture.'[2]

The Romantic poet-prophet in fact may gain his authority precisely by seeking the margins of culture, by rebellion against the prevailing ideology of his time and place. Blake and Shelley, Swinburne said, had been 'born and baptized into the church of rebels' (*Works*, 16:55). Their authority, and Swinburne's own, would come in part precisely by rejecting and rebelling against received doctrines, by insisting on the autonomy of the imagination to construct its own 'truths'. Like Blake, Swinburne would supplant conventional Christian faith with faith in the divine human imagination. And still more like

Shelley, Swinburne would combine the high prophetic mode with radical skepticism. As Shelley asks of the heavenly powers he has invoked at the end of 'Mont Blanc',

> . . . what were thou, and earth, and stars, and sea,
> If to the human mind's imaginings
> Silence and solitude were vacancy?

so Swinburne, after a seemingly visionary glance into the secrets of life and death in 'The Lake of Gaube', asks:

> Whose vision has yet beholden
> The splendour of death and of life? (*Poems*, 6:282)

And as Shelley asserts in *Prometheus Unbound* that 'the deep truth is imageless', so Swinburne answers his own question in 'The Lake of Gaube' with an affirmation that affirms only skepticism:

> Deep silence answers; the glory
> We dream of may be but a dream.

Like Shelley, and like the Blake whom he somewhat misunderstood, Swinburne would find his power and authority in a kind of Romantic Agnosticism, or Agnostic Romanticism, that would define itself in opposition to or rebellion against any dogma that held itself to be beyond the questioning powers of the imagination, and that would make the making and unmaking power of poetry its only idol. But as I will want to argue, even this idol, unquestioned by Swinburne, is not immune to the corrosive powers of reason and skepticism. The attempt to retain the iconoclastic authority of Romanticism is an attempt, of course, to preserve the authority of Romantic icons.[3]

Neverthless, we can and should realize that Swinburne's Romantic authority is in part, and paradoxically, an authority achieved by rebellion against authority – like Blake and Shelley, Swinburne is born and baptized into the church of rebels, and his strength will be that of the Promethean, the strength of resistance. Yet this very fact makes it imperative that the work of art define itself not in transcendence of its historical moment, but in a historically situated rebellion against specific ideological targets – it must, that is, define itself in terms of the historical moment. And here we must recognize that Swinburne's authority in his early works, especially in the first series of *Poems and Ballads*, is not metaphysical, but ideological and political. *Poems and Ballads* was of course written and published as a direct affront to Victorian cultural assumptions, to a hypocritical ideological structure that Swinburne defined in *Notes on Poems and Reviews* as an 'overshadowing foliage of fictions, [an] artificial network of proprieties'. The rebellious author's authority comes from a recognition of received assumptions, of society's common beliefs, as 'false consciousness', as *mere* ideology. As Michel Foucault has argued repeatedly and at length, the way for an artist to challenge the prevailing discourse of power is by transgressing the allowable limits of that discourse – and Swinburne's explicitly erotic and blasphemous language in *Poems and Ballads*, and for that matter in *Chastelard* and *Atalanta in Calydon*, was nothing if not transgressive. According to Foucault's 'A Preface to Transgression', transgressive language defines the limits and boundaries of thought by showing where they are broken. It subsequently finds itself in an existential void, beyond the speakable, but this is celebratory, an affirmation, since recognition of the void 'does not restore us to a limited and positivistic world, but to a world exposed by the experience of its limits, made and unmade by that excess which transgresses it.'[4] But alas, despite Foucault's usual emphasis on the need to historicize, we are here once again in an essentially familiar Romantic position, not simply judging ideological perspectives by observing a clash of ideologies, but attempting to transcend earthly discourse altogether – as Wittgenstein once pointed out, this recognition of the boundaries of thought 'satisfies a longing for the transcendent, because in so far as people think they can see the "limits of understanding", they believe of course that they can see beyond them.'[5]

Nevertheless, even though no metaphysical power or transcendent authority is to be found in a romanticization of transgression, it would seem indisputable that Swinburne did achieve at least a politically powerful discourse of transgression in *Poems and Ballads* – the extraordinary public outcry is sufficient testimonial. In fact the hostile but in some ways astute comments of John Morley's contemporary review help to locate Swinburne's transgressions in their historical time and place. Morley almost seems to anticipate Foucault in his assertion that one effect of poetry is 'to recall to the minds of men the bounds that have been set to the scope of their sight and sense', but he remarks that the poet seeing these bounds can either seek to inspire a 'true poetic awe' of 'solemn rapture' at the immensity that lies beyond, or he can 'jeer and mock' at human limitations 'like an unclean fiery imp from the pit.' (*Hyder*, 29) At least from Morley's Victorian point of view, Swinburne, a jeerer and a mocker, is lacking in true Romantic awe – his poetry has the power to show the bounds of thought, but certainly not to transcend them, and consequently not to threaten them, not to threaten received faith and prevailing assumptions. Yet if Swinburne's poetry were the ineffectual whining and puerility that reviewers called it, it could not have gained so much attention from men like Morley in the first place. Though it lacked transcendent authority, it *did* have an ideological power at least to put contemporary critics on the defensive. As a 'fiery imp from the pit', Swinburne at least adopts the position and prestige of the 'Satanic School' of poetry.

What gave Swinburne's work this power, it has been repeatedly suggested, is its undeniable status as art based on the sheer 'authority of his craftsmanship', (*McGann*, 206) Simply because the work is too good to be ignored, it takes its place within a tradition of reputable and even venerated works. In a recent article on Swinburne and Baudelaire, Richard Sieburth put the case strongly:

> Obscenity is more or less tolerated as long as it remains the specialized, subterranean province of pornography; while the sacred disorders of poetry are in turn safely exiled, in Vigny's phrase, to the ivory tower. The refusal of Baudelaire and Swinburne to observe the segregation of high and low, pure and impure, sacred and obscene may in part account for the tenor of the attacks on their work: their poetry is perceived as dangerously 'dirty', not because it reads like crude smut, but precisely because its technical mastery so clearly designates it Art with a capital A.[6]

Technical or artistic mastery, indeed, is the basis of poetic authority that Swinburne himself most consistently and persistently insisted upon. The great essay on William Blake, from its opening Baudelairean epigraph on, insists that the authority to speak on matters of art belongs exclusively to artists themselves, those trained in the laws and the mysteries of their craft. 'Artists alone', he says at one point, 'are finally competent to deliver sentence by authority' (*Works*, 16:153). As a quotation from the essay will indicate, Swinburne's aestheticism offers not a mere escape from social concerns in a sterile art for art's sake, but a powerful source of Romantic authority. He argues at length that

> the laws and the dues of art it is never permissible to forget. It is in fact only by innate and irrational perception that we can apprehend and enjoy the supreme works of verse and colour; these as Blake indicates with a noble accuracy, are not things of the understanding; otherwise, we may add, the whole human world would appreciate them alike or nearly alike, and the high and subtle luxuries of exceptional temperaments would be made the daily bread of the poor and hungry; the *vinum daemonum* which now the few only can digest safely and relish ardently would be found medicinal instead of poisonous, palatable instead of loathsome, by the run of eaters and drinkers; all specialities of spiritual office would be abolished, and the whole congregation would communicate in both kinds. All the more, meantime, because this 'bread of sweet thought and wine of delight' is not broken or shed for all, but for a few only – because the sacramental elements of art and poetry are in no wise given for the sustenance or the salvation of men in general, but reserved mainly for the sublime profit and intense pleasure of an elect body or church – all the more on that account should the ministering official be careful that the paten and chalice be found wanting in no one possible grace of work or perfection of material. (*Works*, 16:85–86)

The first point that must be made about this long and dense passage is that its almost flippantly snobbish tone should not be taken lightly as mere whimsy – the passage is offensive, deliberately offensive, to the Philistine, and its very tone establishes not a desire for a separate peace but a declaration of intellectual warfare. Further, in its rebellious defiance of conventional views, in its insistence on formal perfection, and in its adherence to the 'laws and dues of art' the passage combines the three fundamental assumptions of Swinburne's conception of romantic authority. The analogy to a church, moreover, is not simply anti-Christian parody, but is meant seriously to set forth the claims of a counter-church. Indeed, James Russell Lowell had recognized that *Poems and Ballads* had been an affront not only to the Christian Church, but to the prevailing intellectual institution or 'church', of poetry. According to Lowell, 'The true Church of poetry is founded on a rock, and I have no fear that these smutchy back-doors of hell shall prevail against her.' (*Hyder*, xxiii) And one might also be reminded of Hopkins's famous notion that the first transgressive song was Satan's, a song that built a 'countermusic and countertemple and altar'.[7] Swinburne's verse is thematically transgressive; its very mastery and the aesthetic theory that justifies it are more transgressive still. But what is particularly disturbing here is a dissonance between Swinburne's Romantic rebelliousness and the forms in which he chooses to express it – the intellectual democrat is now talking of an elect body, an aristocracy of chosen spirits, *born* superior to the mass of mankind. This dissonance, I think, gives us the opportunity to slip from inside Swinburne's own Romantic ideology and judge it from a distanced perspective, to begin to see its limitations, those which it cannot transgress because it cannot recognize. We can see, for example, that the Romantic rebellion within the literary establishment was in fact in the process of consolidating its own establishment along clear class lines – Swinburne's aestheticizing, his insistence on innate tact and taste and his insistence on the importance of a learned tradition place him very much in the development, traced by Raymond Williams, of the social and class significations of terms like 'literature' and 'culture' in the nineteenth century.[8] Further, the whole idea of a 'church' is disturbing, especially when we recall Swinburne's repeated use of the idea – particularly of his claim to have been a member of the church of Blake and Shelley.

But in order fully to appreciate this paradoxical institutionalization of rebellious artistry, it is necessary to examine what Swinburne referred to as the 'laws and dues of art', the laws that must be served and obeyed. It is these laws, after all, and this church, that must provide the ultimate sources of authority in Swinburne's writing. The first law, of course, is fidelity to the technical demands of flawless workmanship, but the dogma of the Swinburneian church (akin of course to the apostolic dogmatism of Catholicism and High Anglicanism) is the inherited tradition. Swinburne made the point in terms of Blake's mythmaking:

> A single man's work, however he may look to inspiration for motive and material, must always want the breadth and variety of meaning, the supple beauty of symbol, the infectious intensity of satisfied belief, which grow out of creeds and fables native to the spirit of a nation, yet peculiar to no man or sect, common yet sacred, not

invented or constructed, but found growing and kept fresh with faith (*Works*, 16:236–237).

What is notable in this passage is that the emphasis is not on craftsmanship or individual inspiration, but on a living body of belief, and a sustaining principle of faith. It is true that Swinburne speaks here only of 'creeds and fables', not of absolute truths, that he does not speak of dogma at all. Still, he does insist on shared faith, not rebellion, and throughout the study of Blake and all of his other writings he insists on *law*, not mere individual creativity. As Jerome McGann has said, Swinburne 'is against meanings, not order, precepts, not law'. As a poet, he conceives his function to be the representation of a law and order which has continually to be rediscovered and recreated by each person. Like Blake and Mallarmé, he neither can nor will lay down the law: in such matters, as Shelley had said, 'each to [himself] must be the oracle.' (*McGann*, 65) Yet the quotation from *William Blake* indicates clearly that each must seek oracular assurance from some source beyond the self. The point that becomes increasingly clear is that though Swinburne could gain a measure of polemical authority by outraging the authorities, by masterful transgression in his early works, he was not likely to rest satisfied with a mode of writing that could only transgress law, not express it, only parody faith, not join in it.

Indeed, it is clear that Swinburne took the idea of a Church of poets quite seriously, that his doctrine was the sacred scripture of poetry canonized in the great tradition, and that his god was Apollo, understood as a personification of the living power of poetry, of 'man's live breath'. As a practical matter this faith is evident already even in his earliest poetry, which gains its resonance and much of its effect by alluding to or echoing earlier generations of poets from Aeschylus and Sappho through Shakespeare and Shelley. *Atalanta in Calydon*, for all its passionate pessimism, for all its apparent nihilism, is at least an affirmative work to the extent that in echoing the forms of Greek tragedy it is recurring to the authoritative beginnings of the western tradition. By appropriating the high style of Greek tragedy, Swinburne seeks to achieve what Mikhail Bakhtin says all works in the high literary style seek, an 'association with the past, the source of all authentic reality and value.' Such works attempt to gain authority of a kind by deliberately removing themselves from the sources of confusion and despair in the present. Indeed, Bakhtin's description aptly suggests why a poet might imitate such models to avoid a 'multitudinous' present: such works 'withdraw themselves, so to speak, from the present day with all its inconclusiveness, its indecision, its openness, its potential for re-thinking and re-evaluating. They are raised to the valorized plane of the past, and assume there a finished quality.'[9] In a similar way, the defiance of *Poems and Ballads* gains its power by echoing the themes and even the rhythms of an ancient tradition in such poems as 'Sapphics' and 'Hendecasyllabics', and by attempting, for example, to recapture the very voice and passions of Sappho in the blasphemous 'Anactoria'. In 'Anactoria', in fact, Swinburne has Sappho affirm the power of song to transcend time and change, to fulfil the natural world with the undying breath of immortal song so that the singer will be 'one . . . /With all high things for ever' (*Poems*, 1:65). Even in the deeply personal poem 'The Triumph of Time', Swinburne demonstrates a practical desire to invest his words with power by joining it to the songs of all high singers through an extraordinary allusiveness that catches up the rhythms and diction and themes of earlier singers. As Cecil Lang has pointed out, the poem alludes to *Hamlet, A Midsummer Night's Dream, Wuthering Heights*, Jaufré Rudel, the *Iliad*, and Plato's *Republic*, 'not to mention Genesis, Isaiah, Job, Ecclesiastes, the Synoptic Gospels, the Pauline Epistles, and many others.'[10] And as has often been pointed out, in the succeeding years the faith in poetry implicit in *Poems and Ballads* emerges as an explicit creed that is most economically stated in Swinburne's comments on 'The Last Oracle', a poem that celebrates Apollo as

> older than Time or any God born of Time, the Light and the Word incarnate in man, of whom comes the inner sunlight of human thought or imagination and the gift of speech and song, whence all Gods or ideas of Gods possible to man take form and fashion – conceived of thought or imagination and born of speech or song (*Letters*, 3:137).

Obviously Swinburne, like Blake and Shelley, has transferred divinity from the heavens to the human mind, the imagination, but just as obviously he finds power not solely in the individual mind, but in the cosmic Apollonian song passed down and amplified from generation to generation of singers. The ways in which Swinburne explored and exploited this myth in such later poems as 'Thalassius', 'On the Cliffs', 'By the North Sea', and 'A Nympholept' have been discussed at length elsewhere, and need not detain us here. I merely want to point out that by seeking authority in an immemorial tradition Swinburne was providing an apostolic succession of poet-priests and a canonical body of texts for his 'church of rebels', that there is an unsettlingly dissonant conservatism providing apparent authority for supposed rebelliousness.

Not surprisingly, the contradictory impulses inherent in the idea of a 'church of rebels' emerge most clearly in Swinburne's political verse, where his Republicanism calls for rebellion against established authority even as his poetic form constantly seeks to establish its own authority. Not content with the power to outrage the British Philistine, Swinburne wanted to be the spokesman and prophet of a higher and truer 'Idea of the world' than any then current; he wanted not only to defy lawful authorities, but to express the higher law of a higher authority. He wanted to speak with authority, and not as the scribes of the day. Indeed, his pertinent comment to William Rossetti is well known – after the aestheticism of the early works he wanted to go on to something he could believe in: 'After all,' he wrote, 'in spite of jokes and perversities – malgré ce cher Marquis et ces foutus journaux – it is nice to have something to love and to believe in' (*Letters*, 1:195). Consequently it is not surprising that from the mid-sixties his poetry increasingly seeks to express not rebellion against law, but law itself. In *Erechtheus*, and especially in *Songs before Sunrise*, he wanted to establish a basis of genuine authority, not simply to question authority by transgressing it. As McGann has argued persuasively and at length, the extraordinary formal complexity of *Erechtheus*, its interweaving of 'divine, natural, and human worlds' in an intricate metaphorical web and echo system, is designed to transcend the temporal world by embodying cosmic law:

> The work's realities are not its characters at all, or its gods, or even nature. All these are metaphors to Swinburne, veils of vision. The most real, most material and visibly present phenomenon in the play is law – a vast, organic order made manifest with all the passion of disciplined music. (*McGann*, 126)

In this sense the dominant theme of Swinburne's middle and late works is not 'liberty' at all, but law, a source of absolute authority.

The ways in which Swinburne attempted to establish the authority to sing in such an extraordinarily high prophetic strain can best be seen in the initiatory poems to *Songs before Sunrise*, since in these poems especially he needed to convince his audience that he was a prophet worth listening to. In certain very obvious ways these poems establish their singer within the radical tradition of Blake and Shelley. In 'The Eve of Revolution', for example, a Blakean visionary protests against priest and king, urging us to cast off our own 'mind forged manacles':

> Priest is the staff of king,
> And chains and clouds one thing,
> And fettered flesh with devastated mind.
> Open thy soul to see,
> Slave, and thy feet are free;
> Thy bonds and thy beliefs are one in kind,
> And of thy fears thine irons wrought
> Hang weights upon thee fashioned out of thine own thought.
> (*Poems*, 2:15–16)

And in the same poem he even more insistently takes the stance of the Shelleyan prophet of 'Ode to the West Wind', repeatedly establishing himself as the 'trumpet of a prophecy' with the oft-reiterated line, 'I set the trumpet to my lips and blow.' Finally, in a more exclusively Swinburneian mode, he places himself within a tradition of voices echoing eternal truth down the ages so that he can 'take the trumpet from [his] lips and sing', knowing that he is joining in an enduring chorus

Of refluent antiphones
More tender-tuned than heart or throat of dove,
Soul into soul, song into song,
Life changing into life, by laws that work not wrong.

(*Poems*, 2:24)

The Swinburneian position is that harmony with the song of the tradition is harmony with the very nature of things, and is therefore harmony with 'laws that work not wrong.'

The grounds of Romantic authority are perhaps even more emphatically declared and enacted in the volume's opening poem, entitled simply 'Prelude'. 'Prelude' self-consciously creates an authoritative persona for the volume, one who turns from the playthings of youth – and of *Poems and Ballads* – to more serious matters. He turns from 'Such tendrils as the wild Loves wear', from 'the fierce flute whose notes acclaim/Dim goddesses of fiery fame' (*Poems*, 2:6) from a world of transient pleasures in general, to eternal, unchanging verities:

But weak is change, but strengthless time,
To take the light from heaven, or climb
The hills of heaven with wasting feet.
Songs they can stop that earth found meet,
But the stars keep their ageless rhyme;
Flowers they can slay that spring thought sweet,
But the stars keep their spring sublime;
Passions and pleasures can defeat,
Actions and agonies control,
And life and death, but not the soul.

Because man's soul is man's God still . . .

(*Poems*, 2:7)

The persona leaps from time to eternity, transcending death and change, transcending history. Significantly, in these political poems in which Swinburne was to grapple directly with issues of the day, he assumes a bardic position that is outside of history, that conveys authority, but eliminates immediacy, and perhaps even relevance to the present historical moment. But he has at least found a faith that enables him to avoid the poetical vice of the present historical moment, to avoid the poetry of Arnoldian or Tennysonian vacillation. His persona, at least, 'builds not half of doubts and half/ Of dreams' (*Poems*, 2:5). Yet the faith is not in a transcendent God, but in 'man's soul' as God, and this soul is removed from time, as we might expect, by Swinburne's belief in a trans-historical communion of visionaries:

And each from each takes heart of grace
And spirit till his turn be done,

And light of face from each man's face
In whom the light of trust is one;
Since only souls that keep their place
By their own light, and watch things roll,
And stand, have light for any soul.

(*Poems*, 2:8)

The poem not only thematically expresses Swinburne's ideas of Romantic authority – the rebellion against conventional faiths, the insistence on masterful song, the transcendent power of bardic song – but it also *enacts* Romantic authority by echoing the poems of Blake, Shelley, and the young Coleridge:

For what has he whose will sees clear
To do with doubt and faith and fear,
Swift hopes and slow despondencies?
His heart is equal with the sea's
And with the sea-wind's, and his ear
Is level to the speech of these,
And his soul communes and takes cheer
With the actual earth's equalities,
Air, light, and night, hills, winds, and streams,
And seeks not strength from strengthless dreams.

(*Poems*, 2:4)

The opening lines echo Blake's echo of Jesus' rejection of merely natural and temporal ties in 'To Tirzah': 'Then what have I to do with thee?' But more significantly the stanza, and the poem as a whole, catches up the thematic concerns and to some extent the diction and rhythms of Shelley's 'Ode to Liberty' and Coleridge's ode to freedom, 'France: An Ode'. Indeed, this should not be surprising, since Swinburne saw those poems as among the greatest achievements of the two poets he regarded as the supreme romantic lyricists, and what is more, he saw Shelley's ode as explicitly following in the tradition of Coleridge's: 'it was but natural that Shelley himself should pay such tributary homage as he did with not more loyalty than justice' (*Works*, 15:341). No doubt Swinburne in 'Prelude' is similarly aligning himself within the romantic tradition, paying 'tributary homage' to both Coleridge and Shelley.

What is a little disturbing, about this reliance on a high poetic tradition to call for radicalism is the implicit contradiction: continuity with the past provides authority for breaking with the past. This problem can be resolved, of course, by insisting that revolution is not so much a break with the past that has invested the present with authority as a return to the true origins of authority in a more distant past. Not surprisingly, Swinburne follows the example of Shelley's 'Ode to Liberty' by following the spirit of liberty all the way back to Republican Athens, which became his model for the combination of law and true freedom in *Erechtheus*, and again in 'The Eve of Revolution':

> But where for us began
> The first live light of man
> And first-born fire of deed to burn and leap,
> The first war fair as peace
> To shine and lighten Greece,
> And the first freedom moved upon the deep,
> God's breath upon the face of time
> Moving, a present spirit, seen of men sublime;
>
> There where our east looks always to thy west,
> Our mornings to thine evenings, Greece to thee,
> These lights that catch the mountains crest by crest,
> Are they of stars or beacons that we see?
> Taygetus takes here the winds abreast,
> And there the sun resumes Thermopylae;
> The light is Athens where those remnants rest.
>
> (*Poems*, 2:12–13)

Once again, the poem not only describes a return to origins, but enacts it, echoing the description of the signal beacons in the opening passage of Aeschylus' *Oresteia*, the trilogy celebrating the founding of the free city of Athens. As Hannah Arendt and others have argued, such a return to origins, and to a 'true' tradition is a common authorizing strategy of revolutionists,[11] but in providing authority it also provides restraints, limits on the revolution – because it must remain within the prescribed limits of the rediscovered 'true' laws, the revolution hardens into a new establishment. And this, I think, returns us to the whole paradox of a 'church of rebels', and institutionalization of rebellion. Swinburne's authority for revolutionary thought turns out to be a church of poets, ranging from Hugo, Landor, Shelley, and Coleridge all the way back to Sappho and Aeschylus, and his governing principle turns out not to be unlicensed freedom, but a law of eternal harmony, a law epitomized in the harmony of eternal poetry.

The tendency of this high literary tradition, as such recent critics as Raymond Williams, Terry Eagleton, Jerome McGann, and Frank Lentricchia have argued, is to remove poetry from politics altogether – as Lentricchia puts it, 'all writing, but especially the self-conscious literary sort with its overdeveloped sense of ancestry, has a marked disposition to suppress its material condition.' And in a passage that more exactly catches the spirit of Swinburne's beacons across the ages, Lentricchia notes that 'Our transcendent giants of the sophomore survey speak only to one another, above the differences of time and society; Milton to Wordsworth, Wordsworth to Stevens, and so on.'[12] The danger of such a removal from historical actualities is especially great for a poet with a political agenda – words come to replace not only actualities, but even thoughts. It is only a short step from Swinburne's tradition-bound republicanism in *Songs before Sunrise* to his faith in the tradition in such hide-bound conservative poems as the later 'Athens: An Ode'. Indeed, Raymond Williams, tracing the 'increasing specialization of literature' has noted that it leads to, among other things, the 'development of the concept of "tradition" within national terms',[13] a tendency that helps to explain Swinburne's rapid movement from a tradition-bound but cosmopolitan republicanism to the English jingoism of such poems as 'The Armada'. Lang admirably described Swinburne's political transformation in his introduction to *The Swinburne Letters:*

> The republican-turned-'English Republican' became English first and last, and remained republican only by a semantic sophistry that would be as much at home in *1984* as in *Through the Looking-Glass*. 'People nowadays seem to forget . . . ,' he wrote to his mother in 1886, 'that the first principle of a Republican is and must be Unity (without which liberty can only mean license – or pure anarchy – or pretentious hypocrisy) . . . ' (1:xxviii)

In Swinburne's early republican poetry, as for example in 'Hertha', the principle of unity had been all-inclusive, had drawn all things into harmony, but the principle later became not inclusive, but exclusive: 'Whether the first principle of an Irish peasant, an Abyssinian, a South African ought to have been unity seems not to have occurred to him' (*Letters*, 1:xxix). I am not, however, at present concerned with the appalling consequences of a narrowly defined tradition in Swinburne's politics, but I want to note that the principle of unity, of adherence to a unified tradition, also had appalling consequences for Swinburne's poetry. Once it is determined that authority comes from an established body of texts in a certain high literary style, it becomes necessary to define that body, to form a canon of, in effect, sacred scriptures. But the issue is not only what works are to be included in this unified tradition, but also, perforce, what works, and what styles are to be excluded. Or, to put it in Swinburne's own terms, once a 'church' has been established, even if it is a 'church of rebels', a certain 'elect body' must be determined, and those who do not belong must be excommunicated. The most direct result of such ways of thinking in Swinburne may, perhaps, be his failure in later life to experiment with new forms of thought and expression, his tendency to follow in his own tradition and so to repeat the forms of his earlier poetry at times almost to the point of self-parody. But Swinburne's faith in an Apollonian tradition of poets had other, less obvious consequences, positive as well as negative.

In the first place, the institutionalization of a 'church of rebels', as Swinburne explicitly says in *William Blake*, establishes the poet in the role of high priest, and establishes what Arnold would have called the 'grand style' as an authoritative and priestly language. In his later essay on 'Wordsworth and

Byron' Swinburne defined this style as eternal and transcendent: it is 'the sovereign style, the eternal and universal dialect, of imagined and impassioned poetry' (*Works*, 14:217) and it obeys 'the high and unwritten laws of great poetic style. . . . laws of no man's making, . . . laws wherein the God of song shows himself mighty' (*Works*, 14:238). Even a church of rebels, understood in this way, is in essential respects tending to extreme conservatism. As Bakhtin has argued 'such ideas as a special "poetic language," a "language of the gods," a "priestly language of poetry" ' reflect a poetic language at its stylistic limits that 'often becomes authoritarian, dogmatic and conservative, sealing itself off from the influence of extraliterary social dialects.'[14] Most obviously, the dialect of the gods defined as 'man's live breath' slights woman's live breath and the dialects of all those whose education does not instil in them a poetic tradition reaching back to the classics. In the nineteenth century, of course, this means in practical terms that the 'elect body or church' able or entitled to profit from the 'sacramental elements of art and poetry' consists solely of privileged men who have been educated in the public schools and the great universities. Indeed, according to one contemporary of Swinburne's who was working at the limits of poetic style, the craftsmanship that establishes authority is an exclusively male quality. The most ostentatiously priestly poet of the age, Gerard Manley Hopkins, once asserted that 'the artist's most essential quality, masterly execution . . . is a kind of male gift and especially marks off men from women.'[15] Even though Swinburne traced the origins of the great tradition back to Sappho, even though he several times remarked that 'great poets are bisexual; male and female at once' (*Works*, 14.305), even though he was chastized by the manly critics of his age as a kind of poetic hermaphrodite, the tendency of Swinburne's reliance on a classical tradition that had become an exclusively male inheritance was to cut his most ambitious verse off from the expression of what might be called a female point of view. Indeed, Swinburne himself bought into the age's notion that poetry ought to be, as he said, 'the sustenance of men', ought to be 'neither puerile nor feminine, but virile.' On these grounds he was, not surprisingly, scornful of Robert Buchanan's assertion that study of the classics tends to 'emasculate' the student, and his sarcasm on the point impugns the masculinity of his less than erudite critic, and seems to praise that of the great classically trained English poets – Milton, Marlowe, Jonson, and so on (*Works*, 16:372–373).

But the high tradition not only excludes female voices; it attempts to raise itself above the flux of history and the immediacy of the present altogether, with the result that the politically committed verse ends up as ineffectually aesthetic. It cannot both speak authoritatively and speak of and to the concerns of the day. As Swinburne asserted in *William Blake*, the authoritative works of the priestly dialect are explicitly denied to the masses, 'otherwise . . . the whole human world would appreciate them alike, and the high and subtle luxuries of exceptional temperaments would be made the daily bread of the poor and hungry.' It may be argued that these aestheticist comments were made before Swinburne turned explicitly to the poetry of his political faith, but my argument is simply that the stylistic tendencies of even Swinburne's most ardently republican verse confine the works to a high style, a dialect incapable of expressing or addressing the immediate concerns of precisely the disenfranchised many that republicanism seeks to serve. If only because the high style must be maintained to give the poet bardic or priestly authority, *Songs before Sunrise*, as McGann has said, 'never involves itself emotionally with occasions, people, and historical realities', but presents a profoundly idealized republicanism, in a dialect that is therefore 'characteristically Swinburneian, one might even say aesthetic' (*McGann*, 238).

The result of Swinburne's dehistoricizing tendency, of his attempt to achieve authority by a romantic assertion of the priestly authority of the poet, is a fundamental contradiction of the core of his poetics. He insists, in proper romantic fashion, on the organic vitality of poetry and of the poetic tradition. For him poetry is a man's *live* breath, and great poetry has 'the one invaluable quality of actual life' (*Works*, 16.57), has 'the infinite blessing of life; the fervour of vital blood' (*Works*, 16.94). Yet cutting itself off from the living present, subsisting in a dialect conscientiously sealed off from the multitudinous voices of Victorian society, the poetry is cut off from the life that, for example, Bakhtin sees in the novel's 'semantic openendedness, a living contact with unfinished, still-evolving contemporary reality (the openended present).'[16] The high poetic style of romantic authority paradoxically attempts to attain eternal life by cutting itself off from mortal life. As Swinburne himself said, when Blake rose to 'prophesy,' when he 'spoke with authority' and 'not in the least like the scribes of his day,' he spoke an 'oracular vapour,' which the public, not surprisingly, 'had no mind to inhale' (*Works*, 16.55–6). What Swinburne aimed for in his poetry was a language of authority and power, a univocal language that could not be weakened by give and take with alien discourses. Such a highly crafted language, in harmony with the great tradition, would have the force of law, would not merely reflect or echo the multitudinous, conflicting, vacillating voices of contemporary society. But arguably, at least, uprooting his poetry from the living present left Swinburne with a language of the gods that was more 'oracular vapour' than 'man's live breath'.

Nevertheless, I do not mean simply to concede to the anti-Swinburneian notion that Swinburne's work is a mere haze of words, founded on literature and not life. Instead I want to emphasize that Swinburne was employing what may have been the only strategy available to a Victorian poet who wanted to speak authoritatively, yet to speak not of absolute dogma, but of doubts, who wanted to speak as a prophet, but as an agnostic prophet. Under such circumstances, the authority must come from the language itself, not the content, from the medium, not the message. Consequently romantic authority must come from a mastery of craft that would enable the poet to communicate even uncertainties in tones of certainty, and as Bakhtin argues, this can only be done by writing within a 'world of poetry' that is removed from the world of actualities. Indeed, Bakhtin's description of such a 'world of poetry' seems to epitomize the conditions Swinburne sought to fulfil in order to write forceful poetry in an 'unpoetical' age:

> The world of poetry, no matter how many contradictions and insoluble conflicts the poet develops within it, is always illumined by one unitary and indisputable discourse. Contradictions, conflicts and doubts remain in the object, in thoughts, in living experiences – in short, in the subject matter – but they do not enter into the language itself. In poetry, even discourse about doubts must be cast in a discourse that cannot be doubted.[17]

Bakhtin's description better suits the *aspirations* of such poetry as Swinburne's than any possible achievement, but it does admirably sum up what the poet must at least aim for if he wants to claim authority. And of course the emphasis falls clearly on poetic craftsmanship within a well defined tradition – falls clearly, that is, on the grounds of authority on which Swinburne insisted both in theory and in practice. The most important conclusion to draw at this point, I think, is that despite the conservative and even exclusionary tendencies of Swinburne's romanticism, it provided him with an 'Idea of the world' that enabled him to speak with the force that he thought poetry must have. And from within his romantic ideology he *did* write works that had and continue to have tremendous power – *Atalanta in Calydon, Poems and Ballads, Erechtheus, Songs before Sunrise, Tristram of Lyonesse*, and many of the late nature poems all succeed with admirable force in presenting a subject matter full of 'contradictions and insoluble conflicts' within a 'unitary and indisputable discourse.' The prophet without dogma can still at least *seem* to speak according to 'high and unwritten laws', and lacking any other god, the style itself can affirm 'laws wherein the God of song shows himself mighty.' Though we can of course now see that romantic authority has no absolute metaphysical sanction, we should still recognize that it has tremendous rhetorical force.

Nevertheless, after recognizing Swinburne's very great achievement, I still want to ask whether the romantic assumptions that enabled him to write with such force may not have been limiting as well. As I have already suggested, his tendency to follow in his own tradition, to reverberate his own forms and motifs, and to follow his own prescriptive laws, may have led him, especially late in life, to the excesses of antiphonal representations that have opened him up, with some justice, to the charge that his poetry is often a mere haze of words. And of course the conservative tendencies inherent in his idea of a priestly language, and the failure to check that language against existent historical actualities, led him into both bad politics and bad verse. But one wonders also what might have been if Swinburne had not self-consciously limited himself to a certain poetic role as bard, if he had not so completely cut himself off from other voices, other forms. One source of poetic authority, of course, is consistency within the author's canon, and Swinburne's comments on Blake show that he was well aware of this by the late 1860s. He claimed there that it 'is true of all poets and artists worth judging' that they are consistent, 'For what are we to make of a man whose work deserves crowning one day and hooting the next?' (*Works*, 16:151). Looking back at the extraordinarily rich and diverse work of the beginnings of Swinburne's career, and at the increasing narrowness of his outlook and even of his poetic style in subsequent years, I am at least tempted to wonder if his desire to achieve an authoritative voice and an authoritative canon did not contribute to his failure to develop in the rich and diverse ways that once seemed possible. The early experimental novels, for example, demonstrated a genius for forms of thought and writing that were much more in touch with the historical moment and the complexities of contemporary thought and discourse than any of his subsequent poetry. Swinburne never lost interest in these novels, but when he finally managed to print *A Year's Letters* in 1875, he significantly did so under a female pseudonym, Mrs Horace Manners – as if he were afraid that association with the work would undermine the virile authority of his more strictly canonical work. The wonderful burlesques of his early years, too, show a sense of humour that continues to surface in his letters, but finds no place in the later works of the mature bard. Further, the thoughtful, innovative criticism that culminated in *William Blake* increasingly became dogmatic and assertive, no longer in any sense experimental or searching, as Swinburne became more and more assertive about the poet's authority to judge in matters of art, and more and more convinced of his own place as a poet and therefore of his own authority. In short, one wonders whether the romantic ideology that enabled Swinburne to be perhaps the last romantic bard, may not also have been constricting and confining, may not have cost the world a major novelist, a powerful satirist, a still more influential critic, and a more richly diverse poet. The ideal of a high romantic church gave Swinburne power and authority but may have led to the excommunication of those elements of his genius that would have gained from more direct contact with an excitingly multifarious age.

## Notes

1. Howard Foster Lowry (ed.), *The Letters of Matthew Arnold to Arthur Hugh Clough* (1932), 97, 130, 126.
2. William Kerrigan, *The Prophetic Milton* (Charlottesville, Virginia, 1974), 14.
3. Or to adopt Jerome McGann's way of putting it, Romantic rhetorical power, the

Romantic polemic, 'is that it will not be polemical; its doctrine that it is non-doctrinal, and its ideology that it transcends ideology.' Cf. *The Romantic Ideology* (Chicago, 1983), 70.

4. Donald F. Bouchard and Sherry Simon (trans.), *Language, Counter-Memory, Practice: A Critical Investigation* (Ithaca, 1977), 32.
5. G. H. Von Wright (ed.) and Peter Winch (trans.), *Culture and Value* (Oxford. 1980), 15e.
6. Richard Sieburth. 'Poetry and Obscenity: Baudelaire and Swinburne', *Comparative Literature*, 36 (1984), 345.
7. Christopher Devlin, S. J. (ed.), *The Sermons and Devotional Writings of Gerard Manley Hopkins* (1959), 201.
8. Raymond Williams, *Marxism and Literature* (Oxford, 1977), 46–51.
9. Caryl Emerson and Michael Holquist (trans.), M. M. Bakhtin, *The Dialogic Imagination: Four Essays* (Austin, 1981), 18.
10. Cecil Y. Lang (ed.), *The Pre-Raphaelites and Their Circle* (2nd ed. Chicago, 1975), 514.
11. See Hannah Arendt, *Between Past and Future: Eight Exercises in Political Thought* (1961, repr. New York, 1977), 141.
12. Frank Lentricchia, *Criticism and Social Change* (Chicago, 1984), 125, 127. See also Williams, *Marxism and Literature*; McGann, *The Romantic Ideology*; and Eagleton, *Criticism and Ideology: A Study in Marxist Literary Theory* (1976).
13. Williams, 48.
14. *The Dialogic Imagination*, 287.
15. Claude Colleer Abbott (ed.), *The Correspondence of Gerard Manley Hopkins* (1935), 133. For a discussion of the male tradition of classicism see Walter J. Ong, *Interfaces of the Word: Studies in the Evolution of Consciousness and Culture* (Ithaca, 1977), 22–34.
16. *The Dialogic Imagination*, 7.
17. *The Dialogic Imagination*, 286.

# 3 Swinburne, Shelley, and *Songs before Sunrise*

Terry L. Meyers

From its earliest reviews *Songs before Sunrise* has been seen by critics as deeply influenced by Shelley. Given the volume's revolutionary fervor and the history of Swinburne's dedication to Shelley before and, indeed, after its publication, it is not surprising to discover such a careful critic as Georges Lafourcade drawing attention to the 'numerous reminiscences or resemblances'[1] of Shelley in the book or Newton Arvin positing Shelley as 'godfather'[2] to Swinburne's offspring. The anonymous *Westminster Review* writer who reviewed *Songs before Sunrise* upon its first appearance[3] used Shelley as a kind of quick benchmark for the volume, finding in Swinburne similarities of lyricism, style, and enthusiasm that have occurred to critic after critic down the decades.

But despite the quickness of critics to see the affinities that do exist, the influence Shelley has on the volume is carefully prescribed by Swinburne, and Shelley's voice is only one among a number of voices in the larger chorus calling for the freedom of Man. Swinburne's engagement with Shelley during the 1850s and the 1860s shows that even as he consciously modelled himself on Shelley in his earliest apprenticeship and liked to see Shelleyan comparisons with himself drawn in several areas, he was also careful to establish a distance between himself and this one among several of his admired elder singers, especially in the area of Shelley's optimistic hopes and assumptions of melioration.

To date Swinburne's first reading of Shelley with absolute certainty may now be virtually impossible, though it seems reasonable to assume that it came at Eton, for, as Swinburne noted, 'Epipsychidion' had been special to him 'ever since boy-hood' (*Letters* 5:224). Georges Lafourcade speaks with seeming authority when he dates the discovery to the winter of 1851–2 (*Lafourcade*, I:89).[4] Certainly if he had read Shelley before writing one of his earliest poems, 'The Triumph of Gloriana,' on the occasion of Queen Victoria's visit to Eton, 4 June 1851, there is no trace of a Shelleyan influence. And Shelley's antipathy to religion seems not to have had an immediate effect on Swinburne, for his religious faith shines through his letters from Germany in 1855 and was probably not dissolved until his exposure to his friends' skepticism at Oxford. Though biographers find it impossible to isolate a simple origin for Swinburne's enthusiasm for liberty, and especially Italian liberty, Humphrey Hare seems close to the truth when he locates Swinburne's college friend John Nichol as bringing about the crystallization of 'those vague libertarian emotions which had been burgeoning in that excitable mind, the fading Jacobinism of Sir John [Swinburne] at Capheaton, the enthusiasm for Shelley, Landor, and Hugo, the lectures of Signor Saffi.'[5] Saffi, Swinburne's tutor in Italian, figures in *Lesbia Brandon*, as Herbert Seyton's tutor: Herbert 'learnt the teacher's language rapidly and roughly enough, and his politics in much the same fashion: as fast as he picked up words, he gathered up opinions' (*Hughes*, 106).

Despite the relative obscurity of Swinburne's life at Oxford, it is clear that especially in the course of 1856–7 Swinburne threw himself into a dedication to Shelley that is reflected in 'Shelley' and in the saturation of such poems as 'The Temple of Janus' and 'Song' ('O Love! sole winged power') with Shelleyean ideas and techniques.[6] Though the impact of Dante Gabriel Rossetti and his crew all but effaced Shelley's influence in Swinburne's poems for a space in 1857, his apostasy was far from complete. Within eight days of acquiring a copy of Browning's famous essay on Shelley,[7] Swinburne, on 22 May 1858, was reading the essay to members of the Old Mortality and in the discussion afterwards directing attention to Browning's (and Swinburne's) struggle with the question of how Shelley's character as a man and his character as a poet reflected each other:

> Mr. Swinburne in the chair, Browning's essay on Shelley . . . was read. It illustrated very forcibly the peculiar merits and defects of the author's style: as well as his intense appreciation of Shelley's excellence both as a man and as a poet. Several interesting questions were naturally suggested by this essay, among others that of the amount of correspondence we may expect to find between the writing and the life of a great poet and the inference we draw from the one regarding the other.[8]

The question is one that attracted Swinburne's attention a number of times, probably for personal reasons, and never more interestingly than when he hesitated about William Michael Rossetti's quotation from Shelley's 'Defence of Poetry' on the title-page of his defence of *Poems and Ballads:*[9]

> 'Let us for a moment stoop to the arbitration of popular breath. Let us assume that Homer was a drunkard, that Virgil was a flatterer, that Horace was a coward, that Tasso was a madman. Observe in what a ludicrous chaos the imputations of real or fictitious crime have been confused in the contemporary calumnies against poetry and poets' – SHELLEY.

Clearly, the words cut near to the bone in an area that Swinburne was particularly interested in, for Swinburne fancied that many parallels existed between himself and Shelley, between his values and Shelley's. Throughout his letters and other works Swinburne frequently uses Shelley as a kind of comparison for himself even in biographical matters, in his being born, for example, an aristocrat and having gone to Eton and Oxford (and having been sent down from Oxford).[10] Perhaps most revealing of Swinburne's pressure to identify with Shelley is his having adjusted his age when, having almost drowned, he thought of Shelley: ' "I reflected with resignation that I was exactly the same age as Shelley when he was drowned." '[11] Swinburne at the time was thirty-one.

The evidence from the 1860s suggests Swinburne continued his personal dedication to Shelley. The one exception, when Swinburne confessed about 1866 to admiring Byron more than Shelley,[12] seems to pale beside other evidence. Indeed, when Swinburne was encouraged by Mazzini in March, 1867 not to 'lull us to sleep with songs of egotistical love and idolatry of physical beauty . . . [ but to] Give us a series of "Lyrics for the Crusade" ' (*Letters*, 1:236n), his immediate reaction was to cast himself as a poet in the Shelleyan mode: 'I have had a letter from Mazzini on my poems, especially the Cretan Ode, which has given me (though not wholly worthy of it) the same delight it would have given to Shelley, had the Fates sent him such a tribute' (*Letters*, 1:232–233). Hugo and Whitman, of course, must be considered the most immediate models for *Songs before Sunrise* (*Letters*, 1:268), but Shelley was crucial too to the germination of the volume. Indeed, Swinburne in the first months of 1869 was deeply involved with Shelley, even to the point of scouting out the minutiae of Shelley's text and subjecting them to close analysis.[13]

Of the critical estimations of Shelley's influence on *Songs before Sunrise* perhaps the most expressive and concise is that of Samuel Chew who succinctly indicates the themes and influences on the volume:

> Swinburne was proud of the epithet 'our younger Shelley' bestowed upon him by some of his admirers. Nowhere is the influence of Shelley so apparent as in the 'Songs.' The devotion to Italy, the aspirations towards intellectual and political freedom, the hatred of priests and kings, the emphasis upon reason as the highest intellectual expression of the human spirit and upon love as the highest emotional expression of the same, the thought of love as the moving spirit of the universe, the mystical tinge imparted to the ideas – all these motives are Shelleyan; and it is appropriate that the sonnet 'Cor Cordium', in honor of Shelley is inserted among the 'Songs.'[14]

Chew's perceptions are acute and true, and yet one needs to be a bit cautious in delineating the influence. Already, in *Atalanta in Calydon*, Swinburne had manifested his resistance to Shelley's optimism by evoking it only to rebut it.[15] This is not to say that Shelleyan diction, images, and doctrines are not present in *Songs before Sunrise*, for they are, and in ways that deserve notice and elaboration. Yet these allusions are often occasional in nature, choices of strategy for a local effect or affiliation. What is equally significant is Swinburne's apparent delimiting of Shelley's political idealism and optimism.

Shelley's verbal and imagistic influence enters the volume with the 'Prelude' and helps inform the Swinburneian myth that leads to such poems later in *Songs before Sunrise* as those addressed to individuals, 'Armand Barbes', 'To Walt Whitman in America', 'Eurydice (to Victor Hugo),' and, of course, the sonnet to Shelley, 'Cor Cordium.' Jerome J. McGann has clarified how, evoking the continuing and immortal influence of the works and deeds of men who have lived before, Swinburne must have seen 'himself as one more avatar in the endless generations of Brahma/Apollo, one more mirror in which the One was again incarnate', (*McGann*, 80), as Swinburne's linkings in the 'Prelude' demonstrate:

> No blast of air or fire of sun
> Puts out the light whereby we run
> With girded loins our lamplit race,
> And each from each takes heart of grace
> And spirit till his turn be done
> And light of face from each man's face
> In whom the light of trust is one;
> Since only souls that keep their place
> By their own light, and watch things roll,
> And stand, have light for any soul.
>
> (*Poems* 2:8)

Clearly Shelley's exposition of the dying nightingales in *Prometheus Unbound* is not far away:

> Another from the swinging blossom
> Watching to catch the languid close
> Of the last strain, then lifts on high
> The wings of the weak melody,
> Till some new strain of feeling bear
> The song, and all the woods are mute.[16]
>
> (II.ii.30–35)

The same process of evocation – and reanimation – is clear in 'Adonais' where the sort of poetic fealty Swinburne himself is famous for is evoked in powerful images of conflagration: not only do the famous (Chatterton, Sidney, Lucan) live and shape human history, but so do 'many more, whose names on Earth are dark,/But whose transmitted effluence cannot die/So long as fire outlives the parent spark' (406–9). Like Keats, and Shelley, and, indeed, Swinburne, the poets become that 'Light', 'Beauty', 'Benediction', and 'Love' that 'Burns bright or dim, as each are mirrors of/The fire for which all thirst' (478–85).

Given this history of eager and accepted influence, it is not surprising that when Swinburne sets trumpet to lip in 'The Eve of Revolution' he evokes the Shelleyan trumpet in 'Ode to the West Wind.' Indeed, to emphasize the point, Swinburne evokes Shelley as one of the poets who are the 'known and unknown fountain-heads that fill/Our dear life-springs of England' (*Poems*, 2:20) and who constitute the 'latter watch-fires' (*Poems*, 2:19) of Freedom. Yet what is most intriguing about 'The Eve of Revolution' is the apparently studied lack of verbal or imagistic parallels. William Michael Rossetti was moved to evoke two of Shelley's most central odes, those to Liberty and Naples, in speaking his enthusiasm for 'The Eve of Revolution,'[17] but in these poems so close in situation, in thought, and even in form, the echoes and allusions are few and spare. Indeed, what remains most striking is the sense of an opportunity for allusion and for incorporation forgone, a chance for Swinburne to have evoked Shelley as predecessor in a powerful and striking way, a chance declined.

The process of poetic incorporation of Shelley, and yet delineation of his limits, is clear in 'Hertha', where the allusions recall Shelleyan myth and yet emphasize Swinburne's distance from them. One stanza of 'Hertha', for example, depends obviously on the Book of Job, but also importantly on Shelley. Hertha asks mankind,

> What is here, dost thou know it?
>         What was, hast thou known?
> Prophet nor poet
>         Nor tripod or throne
> Nor spirit nor flesh can make answer, but only thy mother alone
> (*Poems* 2:74)

The debt here is clearly to Shelley's 'Hymn to Intellectual Beauty' and Shelley's sense of futility in the face of pressing, essential questions:

> No voice from some sublimer world hath ever
>         To sage or poet these responses given –
>         Therefore the names of Demon, Ghost, and Heaven,
> Remain the records of their vain endeavor.
> (25–8)

Swinburne's evocation emphasizes subtly the differences between the two poets' perceptions of this force greater than mankind. Shelley's perception is tentative, partial, and longing, with the poem cast in the shape of a prayer; Swinburne's is total and absolute, with the poem cast in the revelatory assertions and paradoxes of traditional religion and mystic truth. His evocation also reminds the reader of the poem that poets too are limited in their ability to articulate the ineffable, even more limited than Shelley might acknowledge (and Shelley was keenly aware of a poet's weaknesses as well as a poet's power).

A number of the other poems in *Songs before Sunrise* show borrowings from Shelley. Swinburne commented that his 'Hymn of Man' occupied 'the outworks of *Prometheus Unbound*' and outblasphemed 'Queen Mab' (*Letters* 2:120, 87) and McGann has commented that 'the entire poem is instinct with Shelley and Blake' (*McGann*, 197). Certainly Swinburne's celebration of the power of man's thought (*Poems*, 2 100–01) derives from *Prometheus Unbound* (IV, 141–46; 394; 412–22). 'A New Year's Message' cites as an epigraph a line from 'To Emilia Viviani' to manifest Swinburne's fulfilment with love,[18] and several of the images depicting the arrival of a new year derive from similar revivals in *Prometheus Unbound* (IV, 179, 234–35) and 'To Jane: The Invitation' (5). 'Mater Triumphalis' too recalls Shelleyan images from 'Ode to the West Wind' and, again, *Prometheus Unbound*. But, interestingly, in the very poem where one might expect to find an especially intense influence from Shelley, one finds again an opportunity forgone. The very absence of compelling verbal or imagistic echoes in 'Cor Cordium' suggests Swinburne's careful and precise resistance to some of the doctrines of his admired god of song for reasons that become clearer in the relationship of Shelley to the 'Epilogue' of *Songs before Sunrise*.

Though its concluding tone has not been much remarked, the 'Epilogue' makes *Songs before Sunrise* close on a mixed, muted and even subtly negative note. If the sunrise these songs prelude is certain and inevitable, the optimism of this concluding poem is not as unalloyed as it might be. To be sure, several of the imagistic links between Swinburne and Shelley in the poem are forceful and positive ones, for example the precipitant fall 'from their star-like stations/Far down the night in disarray' (*Poems*, 2:228) of 'The suns of sunless years whose light/And life and law were of the night.' Clearly the ancestry of these images includes *Paradise Lost* (III, 396) as well as Shelley's 'Ode to Liberty':

> When like Heaven's Sun girt by the exhalation
>         Of its own glorious light, thou didst arise,
> Chasing thy foes from nation unto nation
>         Like shadows.
>
> (159–62)

But also striking in both the 'Epilogue' and Shelley's 'Ode' are the similarities of ambiguity and hesitation that mark both poems. Indeed the similarity of the concluding images of drowning suggests that Swinburne had the 'Ode' in mind as he wrote. Shelley hears liberty near him, but can only pose a question about its final arrival:

> I hear the pennons of her car

Self-moving, like cloud charioted by flame;
Comes she not, and come ye not,
Rulers of eternal thought,
To judge, with solemn truth, life's ill-apportioned lot?
(259–63)

The end of the 'Ode to Liberty' is abrupt and despairing as the 'Spirit of that mighty singing / To its abyss was suddenly withdrawn' (271–72). The image of drowning makes the link with Swinburne palpable. Over the song 'closed the echoes far away / Of the great voice which did its flight sustain,/ As waves which lately paved his watery way / Hiss round a drowner's head in their tempestuous play' (281–85). Swinburne's having almost drowned, and having done so with thoughts of both Shelley's fate and *Songs before Sunrise*[19] flashing through his head, drives home the link as he images himself in the 'Epilogue' swimming out to sea to meet a dawn that it is conceivable may not come, that he will not see. Indeed, Swinburne transfers Shelley's image of drowning to the earth, and does so in a way that is at once affirmative and hauntingly pessimistic that, if the dawn comes for no man, 'Let earth's self in the dark tides drown.' Elaborated over two stanzas and concluding with a possible vision of a dead world's being gone, being replaced by 'The sole sun on a worldless sea' (*Poems* 2:236), the tone, even more than at the end of the 'Ode to Liberty', gives the reader pause.

This complex relationship between Shelley and Swinburne in *Songs before Sunrise* can perhaps best be seen in the uncertainty Swinburne felt about some of Shelley's doctrines. Though both poets were radical, Shelley's absolute and optimistic faith in revolution, social, political, and individual, was not so compelling to Swinburne, doubtless for reasons that have as much to do with Victorian social and political history as with other matters. Not that Swinburne wanted to repudiate revolution. Indeed, he recognized as much as any man the power of power and its use in political and violent agitation. But Swinburne took a slightly less sanguine view of the perfectibility of Man and the course to Liberty than did Shelley.

Shelley's views are instinct throughout his works, whether his love poems or his political poems. Perhaps the most useful statement of his central doctrines comes from Mary Shelley:

> Shelley believed that mankind had only to will that there should be no evil, and there would be none . . . That man could be so perfectionized as to be able to expel evil from his own nature, and from the greater part of the creation, was the cardinal point of his system. And the subject he loved best to dwell on was the image of One warring with the Evil Principle, oppressed not only by it, but by all – even the good, who were deluded into considering evil a necessary portion of humanity . . . he hoped to induce some one or two [readers of *Prometheus Unbound* ] to believe that the earth might become . . . [ideal], did mankind themselves consent.[20]

This attitude and expectation are manifest even in such a work as the 'Ode to

Liberty' where man has 'on his own high will, a willing slave, . . . enthroned the oppression and the oppressor' (244–45). If man will but heed the poet's commands, 'human thoughts might kneel alone, / Each before the judgement-throne / Of its [man's] own aweless soul, or of the Power unknown!' (231–33). In the pragmatic (by comparison to *Prometheus Unbound* and 'The Ode to Liberty') 'The Revolt of Islam', we can see Shelley work out the length and the cost of the battle for liberty and his emphasis on man's being able to will his freedom. The general direction of the work is clear in the preface:

> It is a succession of pictures illustrating the growth and progress of individual mind aspiring after excellence, and devoted to the love of mankind; its influence in refining and making pure the most daring and uncommon impulses of the imagination, the understanding, and the senses; its impatience at 'all the oppressions which are done under the sun'; its tendency to awaken public hope, and to enlighten and improve mankind; the rapid effects of the application of that tendency . . .[21]

The emphasis on the central power and role of human will builds throughout the poem. The guards of the oppressive tyrant have dedicated themselves to ill, 'And for its hateful sake their will has wove / The chains which eat their hearts' (1644–45). In the midst of battle, Laon's troop revives itself by 'deliberate will' (2411). In the speech to the mariners, Laon again exhorts them to use their will:

> 'This need not be; ye might arise, and will
> That gold should lose its power, and thrones their glory;
> That love, which none may bind, be free to fill
> The world, like light; and evil faith, grown hoary
> With crime, be quenched and die . . .'
>
> (3334–38)

The arrival of liberty is instantaneous with the realization of truth, as in the case of Laon's effect on women: ' "They looked around, and lo! they became free!" ' (3553).

The ultimate triumph is clear even in the disastrous end of the narrative. Even with the return of the tyrant with allies, the slaughter of the masses, and the reimposition of the yoke, Cyntha's faith that freedom will finally win is clear. The ultimate triumph is cast in terms of death and regeneration, of autumn and spring, and is certain because of the existence of eternal absolutes to which Laon and Cythna are the ' "chosen slave" ': ' "Virtue, and Hope, and Love, like light and Heaven, / Surround the world" ' (3667–68). Though doomed to die, Laon and Cythna themselves, like the nightingales of *Prometheus Unbound*, will leave an inspiration for the world to follow:

> 'The good and mighty of departed ages
> Are in their graves, the innocent and free,

Heroes, and Poets, and prevailing Sages,
    Who leave the vesture of their majesty
    To adorn and clothe this naked world; – and we
Are like to them – such perish, but they leave
    All hope, or love, or truth, or liberty,
Whose forms their mighty spirits could conceive,
To be a rule and law to ages that survive.'

(3712–20)

Shelley's belief in the inevitability of liberty, his sense of movement towards it even in the midst of disaster, and his conception of martyrs living on spiritually to inspire their followers are all tenets that, of course, inform Swinburne's conception of liberty in *Songs before Sunrise*. And yet Swinburne's myths of the perfectibility of man and the nature of liberty are more complex, ambiguous, and inconsistent than Shelley's. Swinburne's plethora of different but contiguous myths with their ambivalence seeks to qualify the dogmatism and doctrinaire certainty for which Swinburne faulted Shelley, as in his gently sardonic sketch of Shelley's beliefs:

> In politics, Shelley looked steadfastly forward to the peaceful and irreversible advance of republican principle, the gradual and general prevalence of democratic spirit throughout Europe, till the then omnipotent and omnipresent forces of universal reaction should be gently but thoroughly superseded and absorbed.
>
> (*Works*, 14:195)

By assuming a number of personæ within *Songs before Sunrise*, by seeing liberty and the struggle for it from a number of points of view, Swinburne assembles a multivalent, largely consistent view of the whole process, staking his faith on the event, yet leaving open a number of ways to anticipate and image it, and leaving room for that very real emotion associated with revolution – agonizing doubt and despair.

Swinburne's openness to a multiplicity of imaging is clear in his presentation of the figure of Liberty in *Songs before Sunrise*. Though anthropomorphized to some small extent, Shelley's power of liberty, consistently imaged throughout his works, remains essentially a platonic absolute or form, and is associated with other eternal, unchanging absolutes. Swinburne, on the other hand, works comfortably with a startling range of personifications, from that of the Jehovah-like in 'Quia Multum Amavit' and 'Mater Triumphalis' to that of the courtly lover, in 'The Pilgrim,' and even to that of the femme fatale, again within 'Mater Triumphalis'. The most sustainedly erotic presentation of Liberty comes in 'The Oblation':

All things were nothing to give
    Once to have sense of you more,
        Touch you and taste of you sweet,

Think you and breathe you and live,
Swept of your wings as they soar,
Trodden by chance of your feet.

(*Poems* 2:221)

Though unlike, each of these imagings is also analogous one to the other, an imaging from a different perspective, from a different point of view. Swinburne expands the narrowness of a single hypothesis, and does so by positing a series of over-lapping metaphoric respresentations (the technique, if not the doctrine, is, of course, parallel to Shelley's habitual workings of similes one after the other, as in the 'Hymn to Intellectual Beauty').

The same multiplicity of possibility is true of Swinburne's vision of how and when Liberty for mankind will arrive. Were we to ask whether liberty is inevitable, whether our devotion can speed it, whether time alone determines its arrival, or whether man can will it into existence, Swinburne's response in each instance would be 'yes', for these questions do not involve contradictions among themselves. Each of his presentations of liberty is true, though they may differ one from the other, from the one that is inevitable ('To Walt Whitman in America'; 'Christmas Antiphonies'; 'On the Downs') to the one that is god-like and that will bestow or grant liberty largely on its own initiative ('Ode on the Insurrection in Candia') or that demands and uses the sacrifice and submission of humans to help her ends ('The Halt before Rome'). Like Shelley, Swinburne stresses in several of his poems the importance of man's will, his being the co-author of his own oppression, the rousing effect of a single figure, the continuing generations of heroes, the contagious nature of liberty – all optimistic, perfectibilian doctrines dear to Shelley, though not totally acceptable to Swinburne.

But that the Shelleyan view of will as all powerful is but one of a multitude of possible attitudes is suggested by one of its early appearances as a response to the question in 'A Watch in the Night':

Master, what of the night? –
Child, night is not at all
Anywhere, fallen or to fall,
Save in our star-stricken eyes.
Forth of our eyes it takes flight,
Look we but once nor before
Nor behind us, but straight on the skies;
Night is not then any more.

(*Poems* 2:29)

There are eighteen other responses to the question, each reflecting the view of the particular person speaking. Each is true to the situation in some sense, but no one of them is totally and completely true. This particular, insistent sense of will as all powerful does repeat itself throughout the volume, in 'The Eve of

Revolution', in 'A Marching Song', in 'The Hymn of Man,' in 'Monotones', for example. And yet within the volume this Shelleyan voice is a muted voice, one among a chorus. The book is permeated at once with hope and fear, with faith and doubt, with calm and anxiety. This multiplicity of feeling and tone represents, of course, the complexity of historical movements toward the attainment of liberty and the views from a multiplicity of personæ. It is a voice informed by more history than Shelley's, or, rather, more history subsequent to Shelley's hope and fears. It is a Shelleyan voice, matured and muted, made multitudinous and multivalent. And finally, it is a voice that depends implicitly on our recognizing that Shelley took pride of place in Swinburne's pantheon of poets, of gods, not for his actual political penetration or pragmatic effect so much as for his powers of spontaneous, lyrical music that supersedes political content or revolutionary fervor.[22]

## Notes

1. Georges Lafourcade, *Swinburne: A Literary Biography* (1932), 200.
2. Newton Arvin, 'Swinburne as a Critic', *Sewanee Review*, 32 (October, 1924), 405.
3. *Westminster Review* (American Edition) 95 (April, 1871), 275.
4. It should be noted, however, that H. S. Salt claimed that Swinburne's youthful reading at Eton as well as at home was so restricted that neither Byron nor Shelley was then available to Swinburne. Salt's testimony must carry some weight – he was, after all, the son-in-law of Swinburne's Eton tutor, J. L. Joynes, had access to the checkout records of the library in Joynes' house, and had talked to Swinburne about his Eton days (see 'Swinburne at Eton', *TLS*, 2 Dec. 1919, 781; *Memories of Bygone Eton* (1928), 125; *Company I have Kept* (1930), 47). Nevertheless, it seems to me more likely that Salt may simply have been elaborating the well-known story of Swinburne's promising – and keeping the promise – not to read Byron until he was 21 (*Lafourcade*, 1:89).
5. Humphry Hare, *Swinburne: A Biographical Approach* (1949), 19. In an unpublished letter in the Edith S. and John S. Mayfield Collection at Georgetown University, Swinburne implies John Nichol's major responsibility for his republican faith.
6. 'Shelley' appeared as a miniature book in 1973 (Worcester, Mass: Achille J. St. Onge) and appears also in 'Shelley: A Poem by Swinburne', *Keats-Shelley Journal*, 24 (1978), 171–2. 'The Temple of Janus' is in the British Library (Add. Mss. 40888); 'Song' is in the Rutgers University Library.
7. See lot 926, *Catalogue of the Library of Theodore Watts-Dunton, Esq.* (Sotheby, Wilkinson and Hodge, March 13, 14, 15, 17, 1917). The book had Swinburne's signature and the date 13 May, 1858. Swinburne's interest in Shelley may have been stimulated just at this time too by another friend, Edwin Hatch, who may be the author of an essay on Shelley published in early March in *Chambers's Journal* (see *Letters*, 1:19n).
8. Quoted in Gerald C. Monsman, 'Old Mortality at Oxford' *Studies in Philology*, 67 (1970), 367.

9. *Swinburne's Poems and Ballads: a Criticism*. For Swinburne's squeamishness, see *Letters*, 1:205. One suspects that the quiet deletions from Shelley's statement – Lord Byron as peculator, Raphael as libertine, and Spenser as Poet Laureate – were studied.
10. See, among many possible citations, *Letters*, 1:256; 2:284; 3:234.
11. Edmund Gosse, *Portraits and Sketches* (1912), 24.
12. Sigma (Julian Osgood Field), 'Personalia', *Blackwood's Magazine*, 174 (September, 1903), 306.
13. Swinburne's correspondence is replete with discussions of Shelleyan matter: his 'Notes on the Text of Shelley' was published in *The Fortnightly Review* in May, 1869. See *Works*, 15, 348–97.
14. Samuel Chew, *Swinburne* (1929), 119–20.
15. See my 'Shelley's Influence on *Atalanta in Calydon*', *Victorian Poetry*, 14 (1976), 150–4.
16. Citations from Shelley are from *Shelley: Poetical Works*, ed. Thomas Hutchinson, corrected by G. M. Matthews (1970), given hereafter with the line numbers.
17. Roger W. Peattie, ed., *Selected Letters of William Michael Rossetti* (1990), 253.
18. Richard Garnett's *Relics of Shelley* added this line to the poem in 1862. Since the next two lines were published only in 1876, Swinburne read and meant the line literally.
19. Gosse, *Portraits and Sketches*, 24.
20. *Shelley: Poetical Works*, 271, 274.
21. *Shelley: Poetical Works*, 32.
22. For further elaboration, see my 'Shelley and Swinburne's Aesthetic of Melody', *Papers on Language and Literature*, 14 (1978), 284–95, and 'Swinburne's Conception of Shelley', *The Pre-Raphaelite Review*, 3 (1980), 36–47.

# 4 Swinburne and the dramatic monologue

Nicholas Shrimpton

Did Swinburne write dramatic monologues? Reading his poems the answer seems obvious. On more than a dozen occasions he chose to work, sometimes with the greatest distinction, in the form of verse (spoken, dramatically, by a person not to be identified with the poet, frequently but not always to an internal auditor and on a particular occasion) which is now widely accepted as the most distinctive and original of Victorian poetic genres. Defending *Poems and Ballads* (1866) in *Notes on Poems and Reviews*, Swinburne himself insisted that his book was 'dramatic, many-faced, multifarious' (*Works* 16.354). The 'Hymn to Proserpine', spoken by a Roman of the fourth century AD, 'Laus Veneris', spoken by a thirteenth-century German knight, and 'The Leper', spoken by a poor French scribe of the early fourteenth century, would need to feature in any adequate anthology of this important genre.

Reading Swinburne's critics, on the other hand, such simple confidence rapidly disappears. Harold Nicolson, for example, classifying the contents of *Poems and Ballads, First Series* in his 1926 life-and-works of Swinburne, identified only three poems ('Félise', 'The Leper', and 'At Eleusis') as dramatic monologues. Other – seemingly obvious – examples Nicolson placed elsewhere. The 'Hymn to Proserpine' belonged, in his view, to the 'Poems on Death and Mortality'. 'Laus Veneris' was a 'Poem of Passion'.[1]

More damagingly, many critics have cast doubt on Swinburne's own description of his early poems as 'dramatic'. C. K. Hyder, for example, argued in 1970 that this public defence had 'more logic than candour' to it. As powerful evidence of this disingenuousness, he cited the private letter to W. M. Rossetti of 28 September 1866 ('I have proved Dolores to be little less than a second Sermon on the Mount') and the subsequent letter of 9 October 1866, with its logic-chopping insistence on the impossibility of proving that poems are *not* dramatic. Hyder's conclusion was that, 'while the objectionable poems indisputably are dramatic, they are also rooted in Swinburne's convictions and sensibility' (*Hyder* xxi; *Letters* 1.186, 192–8). The 'dramatic' quality of the poems, in other words, may be a mere subterfuge, or convenient mask, for the expression of inconveniently controversial impulses and opinions.

By the strict criteria of Ina Beth Session's celebrated definition of the dramatic monologue, with its seven essential characteristics of speaker, audience, occasion, revelation of character, interplay between speaker and audience, dramatic action, and action which takes place in the present, it has always been possible to argue that Swinburne's poems are imperfect or merely 'formal' approximations to the genre[2]. Those rigorously formalist standards gave way in 1957, with the publication of Robert Langbaum's *The Poetry of Experience*, to a more inward and affective analysis of the form. Thereafter monologues would tend to be discussed in terms of the interplay, in the reader's experience of the poem, between 'sympathy' and 'judgement'. But for Swinburne's (supposed) monologues these new criteria proved even more awkward than the old formalist tests. Put less sympathetically, Hyder's comments can readily become the claim that Swinburne fails to achieve the depth of characterization, and ironic detachment from his speakers, which are the hallmarks of the true dramatic monologue. All sympathy and no judgement, articulated in voices stylistically industinguishable from Swinburne's confessional mode, they fall incompetently between the two stools of sincerity and fiction.

If these poems, then, are not genuinely 'dramatic', what are they? Jerome McGann, in 1972, suggested the subtler notion of artistic 'impersonality' as the appropriate description of Swinburne's practice. Eliot's term (here reinforced by Keats) indicates a poetic discourse which is more than simply confessional but less than fully dramatic. Swinburne is,

> . . . protesting against standards of criticism based upon the standards either of ethics or of Romantic sincerity. He wants his work to be judged aesthetically . . . the values upheld in poetry are beyond the poet's own personal attitudes . . . Swinburne wants to refine himself out of existence on principle. He is the supreme 'chameleon poet.'
>
> (*McGann* 210)[3]

There is nothing either disingenuous or incompetent about such a mode. But it is not in any specific way the mode of the dramatic monologue. In these terms no distinction can be made, on generic grounds, between 'Laus Veneris' (spoken by a thirteenth-century German knight), 'Dolores' (spoken, according to *Notes on Poems and Reviews*, by an unidentified 'man . . . foiled in love and weary of loving . . . seeking refuge in . . . fierce and frank sensualities') (*Works* 16.360), and such apparently confessional poems as 'August', 'The Sundew', 'A Leave-Taking', or even the directly autobiographical 'Dedication' to Edward Burne Jones ('. . . my gift is single, / My verses, the firstfruits of me') (*Poems* 1.293). We must agree, if only on grounds of narrative theory, that all these poems are 'impersonal', uttered by a fictive 'implied author' who is not the private person Algernon Charles Swinburne. But that necessary agreement is a blunt instrument if we are engaged in a generic enquiry which requires discrimination between relative degrees of fictiveness.

Thaïs Morgan, in an article published in 1984, seemed to restore the category of the dramatic to the discussion of Swinburne's early poetry. Her title was 'Swinburne's Dramatic Monologues: Sex and Ideology', and her argument began with an insistence that Swinburne was 'deliberately working with the dramatic monologue as a genre'. Reductive readings of his early poems as 'the fictionalized autobiography of a sexually and socially maladjusted individual' were, very properly, dismissed. Instead, Morgan showed how Swinburne 'reconstructed' the voices of Sappho, Tannhäuser, and the pagan Roman of the 'Hymn to Proserpine' in order to expose 'the deep contradictions he finds in Victorian moral and religious values'.[4] The thematic argument was powerfully sustained. But in strictly generic terms it took away with one hand what it gave with the other. These Swinburne poems, Morgan suggested, were not autobiographical. They did not, that is, simply expose details of his private life or aspects of his psyche. But they were, in her analysis, polemical, and were so in the service of causes in which Swinburne deeply believed. Behind a thin mask, or subterfuge, in other words, we find a direct expression – not, it is true, of the poet's personality – but of the poet's opinions.

What Morgan called 'the skill of aesthetic distancing that critics readily find in the dramatic monologues of Browning and Tennyson'[5] normally means something rather more than this. It is, of course, important not to exaggerate Langbaum's notion of objective 'judgement', and Langbaum himself was careful to reject the idea that 'dramatic monologues are more or less like Browning's "My Last Duchess", and that most dramatic monologues being rather less like it are not nearly so good'.[6] His stress was much more on the concept of 'sympathy', and on the way in which dramatic monologues offered the possibility of understanding, or experiencing, unfamiliar phenomena from within. None the less, his theory had in the end to insist on the necessity of both 'disequilibrium between sympathy and judgement' and 'particular perspective'[7] if the dramatic monologue was to retain a distinct identity as a genre. Browning's 'Rabbi Ben Ezra', for example, was in his view,

> . . . a dramatic monologue by virtue of its title only; otherwise it is a direct statement of a philosophical idea, because there is no characterization or setting. Because the statement is not conditioned by a speaker and a situation, there is no way of apprehending it other than intellectually; there is no split between its validity as somebody's apprehension and its objective validity as an idea.[8]

There is, as Langbaum puts it in a subsequent discussion of the same poem, a 'lack of a particular perspective; the statement is not conditioned by a particular person in a particular time and place, the poem is not located or anything in it seen . . . these are maxims put forward as universally applicable'[9] Langbaum, as it happens, accepts several Swinburne poems, including both 'Anactoria' and the 'Hymn to Proserpine' as authentic dramatic monologues.[10] But, in Thaïs Morgan's more detailed analysis, Swinburne seems to use Sappho and his Roman pagan in a sympathetic manner more akin to Browning's Rabbi Ben Ezra, or to Byronic role-playing, than to true dramatic impersonality. Sappho, for example, steps out of her 'particular time and place' to make an anachronistic attack on Christianity. Such characters, Morgan argued, 'are ironic masks, calculated to take the publicly prudent but privately prurient Victorian reader unaware'[11]. For a mask to qualify as 'ironic' (saying one thing but meaning another), it must presumably be transparent.

So it is perhaps not surprising to find recent critics celebrating Swinburne as the deconstructor of the High-Victorian dramatic monologue, or at least of its claims to dramatic objectivity. Ekbert Faas, in a book which argues that the monologue was originally understood as a mode of psychological enquiry, concludes that, 'where Browning and Tennyson had opted for the disguise, Swinburne spoke out more directly', courageously manifesting his own 'authorial morbidity'[12]. Critics of the generation of Ina Beth Sessions had seen the specifically dramatic qualities of the monologue as the source of our pleasure in such poems. Faas sees them as a form of bad faith, and praises Swinburne for the cynical shallowness with which (in Faas's view) he uses them. Less tendentiously, Alan Sinfield identifies the dramatic monologue as neither simply dramatic nor simply confessional. Instead it occupies an extensive and various space intermediate between the two modes, which Sinfield calls (echoing Käte Hamburger) 'feigning' or 'the feint':

> If there is a heavy apparatus of circumstantial detail which establishes for the speaker a world which we know is not the poet's, then the feint begins to approximate to fiction. If, alternatively, the speaker is relatively unlocated in time and place so that there is little beyond the title, say, to remind us that it is not supposed to be the poet speaking, then the feint is closer to the poet's 'I'.[13]

Sinfield finds Swinburne interesting because he demonstrates one extreme of this wide range of possibilities – the point at which the feint is used merely for 'oblique self-expression',[14] almost merging with 'the poet's "I" '. *Poems and Ballads, First Series* is made up, in Sinfield's view, of 'various attitudes endorsed to varying degrees; they are all aspects of Swinburne but none has the authority of a final personal utterance'.[15] The dramatic quality of the poems is, in this reading, of real but strictly negative importance, saving Swinburne from the limitations and inconvenience of explicit commitment.

We are left, then, with a puzzle. Here is a substantial body of poems which were described as 'dramatic' by their author, and seem, intuitively, to belong to the great Victorian genre of the dramatic monologue. Yet in the eyes of sensitive and well-informed twentieth-century critics they do so either (at worst) dishonestly, or (at best) in the most marginal and tenuous of ways. Can feints at the very margin of confession be enjoyed in the same way as 'Ulysses' or 'Andrea del Sarto'? Are transparent masks properly to be understood as dramatic monologues at all?

Some of the blame for this uncertainty must be borne by Swinburne. He did, unquestionably, muddy the generic waters, though more by over-simplification than by direct deceit. In 1902, in the 'Dedicatory Epistle' prefaced to the first collected edition of his poems, he glanced back at the critical reception of *Poems and Ballads, First Series*, and in particular at the,

> . . . censors who insisted on regarding all the studies of passion or sensation . . . in it as either confessions of positive fact or excursions of absolute fancy. There are photographs from life in the book; and there are sketches from imagination. Some which keen-sighted criticism has dismissed with a smile as ideal or imaginary were as real and actual as they well could be: others which have been taken for obvious transcripts from memory were utterly fantastic or dramatic . . . In my next work (*Songs before Sunrise*) it should be superfluous to say that there is no touch of dramatic impersonation or imaginary emotion.[16]
>
> (*Poems* 1, vi–viii)

In very broad terms this is true. But the attractive simplicity of this contrast between the two volumes cannot be sustained in detail. The opinions expressed in *Songs before Sunrise* are undoubtedly sincere. But two of the most important poems in which they are articulated rely heavily upon 'dramatic impersonation'. The first part of 'Tiresias' is spoken (like the monologue of the same title which Tennyson was to publish fourteen years later) by the blind Theban seer. 'Hertha' is, throughout, a dramatic poem uttered by the Germanic earth goddess.

The over-simplification was, understandably, still more extreme in the vexed circumstances of 1866. Aided and abetted by William Michael Rossetti, Swinburne sheltered from the critical storm by giving the impression that he could claim dramatic status for the whole of *Poems and Ballads, First Series*:

> With regard to any opinion implied or expressed throughout my book, I desire that one thing should be remembered: the book is dramatic, many-faced, multifarious; and no utterance of enjoyment or despair, belief or unbelief, can properly be assumed as the assertion of its author's personal feeling or faith. Were each poem to be accepted as the deliberate outcome and result of the writer's conviction, not mine alone but most other men's verses would leave nothing behind them but a sense of cloudy chaos and suicidal contradiction. Byron and Shelley, speaking in their own persons, and with what sublime effect we know, openly and insultingly mocked and reviled what the English of their day held most sacred. I have not done this.
>
> (*Works* 16.355)

Read carefully, this paragraph says the same thing as the 'Dedicatory Epistle' – that it is impossible for the reader to know, with certainty, which poems are dramatic and which are confessional. But it is put in a way which suggests much more, and Swinburne's detailed examples re-inforce this general implication. In 'Anactoria', Swinburne points out, he is speaking as Sappho: 'I have striven to cast my spirit into the mould of hers, to express and represent not the poem but the poet'. (*Works* 16.359). 'Laus Veneris' is uttered from a point of view so distinctively medieval that, 'Once accept or admit the least admixture of pagan worship, or of modern thought, and the whole story collapses into froth and smoke' (*Works* 16.365). 'Dolores' expresses, 'that transient state of spirit through which a man may be supposed to pass, foiled in love and weary of loving, but not yet in sight of rest', and the poem is, 'like *Faustine*, so distinctly symbolic and fanciful that it cannot justly be amenable to judgement as a study in the school of realism'. Indeed, 'Dolores' is specifically identified as 'monodrama':

> The next act in this lyrical monodrama of passion represents a new stage and scene. The worship of desire has ceased . . . the spirit . . . dreams now of truth discovered and repose attained . . . 'Hesperia,' the tenderest type of woman or of dream . . . This is the myth or fable of my poem; and it is not without design that I have slipped in, between the first and the second part, the verses called *The Garden of Proserpine*, expressive. . . of that brief total pause of passion and of thought, when the spirit . . . thirsts only after the perfect sleep.
>
> (*Works* 16.361–2)

We know from Swinburne's letter of 9 October 1866 that William Michael Rossetti suggested this classification to him, and that he was at first reluctant to adopt it ('I should not like to bracket "Dolores" and the two following as you propose'). But the same letter goes on to identify a still more extensive monodrama:

> I ought (if I did) to couple with them in front harness the 'Triumph of Time' etc., as they express that state of feeling the reaction from which is expressed in 'Dolores.' Were I to rechristen these three as trilogy, I should have to rename many earlier poems as acts in the same play.
>
> (*Letters* 1.197)

Swinburne compromised, adopting Rossetti's insufficient trilogy of 'Dolores', 'The Garden of Proserpine', and 'Hesperia' for the purposes of *Notes on Poems and Reviews*, but doing nothing to the text of subsequent editions of *Poems and Ballads, First Series* to identify either this, or the larger monodrama incorporating 'The Triumph of Time' and 'many earlier poems', to readers of his verse. Also left obscure in the text was the strongly 'dramatic' reading of 'Félise' offered in Swinburne's letter to Ruskin of 21 March 1866:

> A young fellow is left alone with a woman rather older, whom a year since he violently loved. Meantime he has been in town, she in the country; and in the year's lapse they have had time, he to become tired of her memory, she to fall in love with his . . . 'Sech is life,' as Mrs Gamp says . . .
>
> (*Letters* 1.160)

None of this is, strictly speaking, dishonest – even the compromise with William Michael Rossetti's suggestion of a monodramatic trilogy may represent a genuine change of mind. It misleads by over-simplifying ('He becomes ineffective through mere over-emphasis,' as J. W. Mackail observed of Swinburne's literary criticism in general),[17] and in particular by failing to distinguish sufficiently between one kind of dramatic poem and another. 'Anactoria', 'Laus Veneris', 'Dolores', 'Faustine', 'Hesperia', and 'Félise' are all dramatic in one sense, though it is the 'weak' sense better suggested by Jerome McGann's term 'impersonal'. But they are all dramatic in different ways and to different degrees. 'Laus Veneris' is a dramatic monologue. 'Faustine' is not, and Swinburne's self-defensive stretching of the term 'dramatic' to cover both categories has damaged our ability to enjoy those poems in which he does, genuinely, work as a monologuist.

Precise discrimination between different kinds of 'dramatic "I" poems' is a comparatively recent critical achievement, and it is one which is immensely helpful to the reading of Swinburne. Ina Beth Sessions, in 1947, identified 'imperfect', 'formal', and 'approximate' versions of the dramatic monologue and Alan Sinfield, thirty years later, pointed to the way in which the 'feint' occupied an extensive territory between 'the poet's "I" ' and 'fiction'. But the specific identification of the subdivisions of that territory was really begun in two articles published in the mid-1970s. In 1976 Ralph W. Rader distinguished four separate categories: 'the expressive lyric', in which 'the poet speaks in his own person out of the stimulus of a real situation'; the 'dramatic lyric', in which the poet 'simulates as dramatically present to a lyric actor a significant experience of the real world which is in its origin a memory but which, as reconstructed, stands free of memory'; the 'mask lyric', in which the 'poet speaks through an actor who is registered almost overtly as an artifical self'; and finally the dramatic monologue, in which the 'poet simulates the activity of a person imagined as virtually real whom we understand as we would an "other" natural person, inferring from outward act and expression to inward purpose'.[18] A year before, A. Dwight Culler had supplied a fifth category by reminding us of the significance of the term which Swinburne, prompted by William Michael Rossetti, used in *Notes on Poems and Reviews*: 'monodrama', a form in which the poet (originally with the help of music) traces successive phases of fluctuating passion, representing 'the motions of the soul'.[19] Though the precise boundary between the categories will, in particular cases, sometimes be uncertain, the five terms 'expressive lyric', 'dramatic lyric', 'monodrama', 'mask lyric', and 'dramatic monologue' provide an indispensable tool for understanding the work of a post-Romantic poet like Swinburne.

Though the map of this territory may be modern, in other words, the landscape itself is not. Even if one disregards the ancient roots of the dramatic monologue in prosopopoeia, complaint, and dramatic epistle, and treats it as a form significantly re-invented by Tennyson and Browning in the 1830s,

Swinburne came to it at a late and sophisticated stage in its history. By the time Swinburne began to write them, both 'monodrama' and 'dramatic monologue' were established terms, the latter first used as a section heading in George W. Thornbury's *Songs of the Cavaliers and Roundheads*, 1857. He purchased Browning's key statement on 'dramatic' or 'objective' poetry, the 1852 'Essay on Shelley', in May 1858 and read it to the Old Mortality a week later.[20] Defending Meredith's poems in a letter to the *Spectator* of 7 June 1862, he picked out for praise that moving dramatic monologue, 'The Old Chartist', and drew attention specifically to two characteristics much stressed by later formalist critics of the genre, vividness of characterization and dramatic impersonality:

> . . . the 'Old Chartist,' equal to Béranger for completeness of effect and exquisite justice of style, but noticeable for a thorough dramatic insight, which Béranger missed through his personal passions and partialities.
>
> (*Letters* 1.53).

And his deep understanding of the particular way in which Browning's dramatic monologues function would be made abundantly clear, thirteen years later, in a long section of his essay on George Chapman,

> . . . he flashes at once the whole force of his illumination full upon the inmost thought and mind of the most infamous criminal, a Guido Franceschini or a Louis Bonaparte, compelling the black and obscene abyss of such a spirit to yield up at last the secret of its profoundest sophistries . . . thanks to this very quality of vivid spiritual illumination we are able to see by the light of the author's mind without being compelled to see with his eyes, or with the eyes of the living mask which he assumes for his momentary impersonation of saint or sophist, philosopher or malefactor; without accepting one conclusion, conceding one point, or condoning one crime.
>
> (*Works* 12. 147–8)

The process is one of 'exposition by soliloquy and apology by analysis' (*Works* 12.149), and the one reservation about Browning's achievement which Swinburne expresses is a subtle perception of a possible failure of dramatic objectivity,

> . . . we may doubt . . . whether the perception of good or evil would actually be so acute in the mind of the supposed reasoner; whether, for instance, a veritable household assassin, a veritable saviour of society or other incarnation of moral pestilence, would in effect see so clearly and so far.
>
> (*Works* 12.148)

Parodying a Browning monologue in 'John Jones', or a Tennyson monologue in 'Disgust: A Dramatic Monologue', Swinburne showed once again just how thoroughly he grasped their assumptions and procedures.[21]

This impressive analytical grasp of the nature of the dramatic monologue went hand in hand, in Swinburne's early career, with a good deal of practical experiment. His unpublished imitations of the monologues collected in William Morris's 1858 volume, *The Defence of Guenevere*, were a key part of his apprenticeship as a poet. 'The Day before the Trial' is, unashamedly, a pendant to Morris's title poem, in which King Arthur is made to reveal his mixed feelings about the trial of his wife: part fear and pain, part jealous resentment, and part the puzzlement of an *homme moyen sensuel* at the maidenly purity which enabled Launcelot (in this King Arthur's generous understanding, at least) 'to see/ The White Sangreal borne up in air' (*Lafourcade* 2.53). Swinburne, in effect, completes the triangle begun by Morris, adding the voice of Arthur to those of Guenevere and Launcelot.

The three poems spoken by the troubadour Jaufré Rudel, also very early work, take the romantic longing of Browning's 1842 monologue of the *amor de lonh*, 'Rudel to the Lady of Tripoli', and move it towards both Morrisian stylistic monotony (the 'medieval' use of single rhyme, sometimes for as many as five lines in a stanza), and a Swinburneian interest in the pathology of obsessive, disappointed love.[22] The historical speaker, and the occasions on which he speaks, are firmly established, though the internal audience (Rudel's servants in the first poem) becomes less clear as the troubadour approaches death. The result is a vivid evocation of what Swinburne, in his speech to the 1866 Anniversary Dinner of the Royal Literary Fund, would call, 'that fierce monotony of tenderness, that bitter absorption of life, which has made the heathenish love of Provencal fighters and singers a proverb to this day'.[23] Returning to the topic some years later in 'The Triumph of Time', Swinburne would abandon the monologue format but incorporate three stanzas of tribute to Rudel, the fellow-sufferer through whose analogous experience he had previously approached the problem dramatically.

'The Queen's Tragedy', written in 1859, is once again, as Lafourcade charmingly puts it, Morris 'légèrement swinburnisée' (*Lafourcade* 2.64). But what the younger poet has here taken from Morris is not just some tricks of style, but an ambitiously broad definition of dramatic setting. As in Morris's poems on topics from Froissart, we hear a voice speaking from a real, rather than idealized, Middle Ages of arbitrary violence, deranging passion, and incongruous beauty. This is a cultural rather than merely individual *Einfühlung* – a sympathetic seeing-from-within of the consciousness of an era.[24] The poem attempts, that is, to enter the emotions of people who lived, in the opinion of Aesthetic Movement medievalists, more authentically than the inhibited human beings of the nineteenth century. The speaker is fully imagined as distinctively medieval, the occasion is highly specific, and the internal audience is cleverly used. The poem even offers the involuntary self-revelation of the classic Browning monologue, as the bereaved Queen's plans to build a church are shown to be motivated by a sensual wish for an erotic reunion with her dead husband.

All these poems are juvenilia, suppressed by Swinburne and printed only posthumously. What they show is that by the early 1860s he was fully at home, both in theory and in practice, with the dramatic monologue. Coming to the form with the examples of (amongst others) Tennyson, Browning, Meredith, Morris, and Baudelaire before him, he could pick and choose his models. His first choice was Morris. But the important point is the variety of available practices. Morris himself mixes a Browningesque interest in criminal behaviour, with a Tennysonian taste for elegant rather than roughly colloquial expression, and a willingness, as Ekbert Faas points out, to engage the reader of a monologue like 'The Wind' in 'psychological processes without allowing him the analytical distance usually provided by the genre'.[25] Swinburne carries something of this into his own mature work in the genre, and his combination of a broadly Tennysonian manner with Browningesque topics of actual human criminality and perversity may be one reason why reviewers found his poems so shocking. Critics who had remained untroubled by the justification of murder in 'Porphyria's Lover', or by the necrophiliac gloating of Thornbury's Browningesque 'The Succory Water' ('Death has tricked Justice! Cut her boddice lace, / Bring water; beautiful devil, how she's shaped!'),[26] found Swinburne's verse immoral.

Just as important as this sense of a range of possible manners within the genre of the dramatic monologue, is the awareness – inevitable for an intelligent poet of Swinburne's generation – of the existence of a wide range of cognate forms, each dramatic to a different degree. Swinburne writes dramatic lyrics, monodrama, mask lyrics, and dramatic monologues, and mixes them without warning. G. W. Thornbury, by contrast, had carefully assembled the more shocking poems in his *Songs of the Cavaliers and Roundheads* (1857) under the specific sub-heading 'Dramatic Monologues'. Other texts which were, in strict generic terms, just as much dramatic monologues could safely be left in Thornbury's 'Miscellaneous' category. Swinburne's decision to leave everything in the miscellaneous category was what subsequently allowed him to imply, in self-defence, that all his poems were dramatic in the same way. But it was also, I suspect, what had most disturbed the critics in the first place, and thus made self-defence necessary.

The expressive lyric (the poem, like 'Tintern Abbey', in which, in Rader's words, the poet 'speaks in his own person out of the stimulus of a real situation',[27] and of which our reading is enriched rather than pedantically diminished by biographical information) is a rare bird in *Poems and Ballads, First Series*. Only the 'Dedication, 1865', the elegy for Landor, and the *hommage* to Victor Hugo belong clearly in this category, though a few poems such as 'The Sundew' and 'A Leave-Taking' hover between it and the dramatic lyric.

That second form is, however, of considerable importance. Though the search for the Dark Lady of 'The Triumph of Time' is a legitimate occupation for Swinburne's biographers, readers of the poem do not need her name. Nor, on the other hand, do they need to take refuge (with T. S. Eliot) in the assumption that the text is so impersonal as to be somehow semantically void. 'The Triumph of Time' is a dramatic lyric, a poem in which, in Rader's formulation, the poet 'simulates as dramatically present to a lyric actor a significant experience of the real world which is in its origin a memory but which, as reconstructed, stands free of memory'.[28] Langbaum had pointed out how the dramatic lyric, 'in which the poet discovers his idea through a dialectical interchange with the external world', differed from the traditional longer lyric in which, 'the poet sets forth his already formulated idea either epigrammatically or logically'.[29] Swinburne's poem has this sense of dramatic immediacy and direct address ('Before our lives divide for ever,/. . . I will say'). But it also has that quality of an artificial reconstruction of personal experience which Rader, in a later article, suggests was well caught by Wordsworth's remark that in 'With Ships the Sea Was Sprinkled Far and Nigh', 'I am represented . . . as casting my eyes on the given scene'.[30] Swinburne, likewise, is represented (by Swinburne) as uttering words which are manifestly fictive – the initial sense that the utterance is taking place in real time, for example, is rapidly undermined. But the text simultaneously insists that the origin, or motive, of these words is authentic. The dramatic lyric, an intermediate form, is not an imaginative entry into another person like the dramatic monologue, but rather an imaginative standing back from the self.

Several other poems in the volume are also of this kind. Gosse, loyal to Swinburne's suggestion of a more wholeheartedly dramatic format, tried to read 'Faustine' as a full dramatic monologue:

> A gladiator in whose arms the Empress has lain the night before stands up in the arena about to die and denounces her cruelty and pitilessness.
>
> (Quoted in *Lafourcade* 2.455)

The tense of the verbs forbids such an interpretation. Faustine is a modern woman who reminds the modern speaker of the historical Faustina, who once (past tense) 'loved the games men played with death' (*Poems* 1.108), and now (present tense) leads him to speculate about the persistence of moral and biological types through time. That modern speaker is Swinburne, or more precisely a reconstructed voice which is less inconveniently referred to as 'Swinburne' than by any other name. 'Félise', too, is a dramatic lyric. Swinburne's letter to Ruskin in March 1866 (quoted above) suggests an elaborately novelistic situation. If he had given us a title which identified the speaker rather than the person addressed, and perhaps (in Sinfield's words) a little more 'circumstantial detail',[31] we would have a striking dramatic monologue of modern domestic life. He does neither, and we are left with a dramatic lyric at the more 'dramatic' end of its own generic spectrum.

Three of the dramatic lyrics in *Poems and Ballads, First Series* were retrospectively classed by Swinburne, though possibly only on the prompting of W. M. Rossetti, as a 'monodrama'. Conventionally dismissed as a subterfuge, the term is actually a genuinely interesting one. Monodramas can, of course, have named speakers who are not the poet. What distinguishes them from dramatic monologues is the fact that they are concerned, not with the idiosyncracies of individual character, but with universal emotions of which the named or unnamed speakers are convenient representatives. More particularly, they display sequences, or successive phases, of passion. Tennyson's 'Oenone', *Maude* (retitled, *Maud, A Monodrama* in 1875), 'Locksley Hall', and *In Memoriam*, are picked out by Dwight Culler as outstanding mid-nineteenth-century specimens of the form.[32] M.W. MacCullum, in 1925, suggested that Meredith's *Modern Love* was another.[33] Swinburne knew all of these poems, heard *Maude* from the lips of the laureate in 1858, and defended *Modern Love* in the *Spectator* four years later. His own 'lyrical monodrama of passion', if on the authority of *Notes on Poems and Reviews* one chooses to read it as such, traces the successive emotions of an unnamed speaker from the 'fierce and frank sensualities' of 'Dolores', through the exhausted longing for death of 'The Garden of Proserpine', to the ideal love of 'Hesperia' (*Works* 16.360–2). As such, it deserves comparison with the distinguished examples by Tennyson and Meredith, and judgement in its own appropriate terms. Alternatively, and with equal authority, one can read the three poems as they stand in *Poems and Ballads, First Series* – that is as dramatic lyrics. Taken as monodrama, their speaker both is and is not Swinburne in the sense that he is offered as the generalized representative of (supposedly) universal emotions. Taken as dramatic lyrics, their speaker both is and is not Swinburne in the slightly different sense that the form involves an objective standing back from the self.

With the next generic category, the mask lyric, we move much closer to the dramatic monologue and, consequently, come face to face with the real problem of Swinburne's practice. The mask lyric, in Rader's words, is the form in which 'the poet speaks through an actor who is registered almost overtly as an artificial self'.[34] This is that feint on the very boundary of confession, or transparent mask, which is sometimes assumed to be the characteristic – or even the only – mode of Swinburne's dramatic writing. Mask lyrics certainly occur in *Poems and Ballads, First Series*. Swinburne wrote them skilfully, and with relish. But he also wrote dramatic monologues, and the distinction is necessary if we are to do justice to his achievement. Swinburne wrote mask lyrics, not inadvertently or as an incompetent gesture towards the full dramatic monologue, but by a deliberate act of choice.

The greatest example of the mask lyric in the 1866 volume is, of course, 'Anactoria', and the kind of mask chosen is itself significant. Swinburne speaks through the lips of a great poet of a previous culture. He does, in other words, precisely what Edward Fitzgerald had chosen to do in his supposed 'translation' of *The Rubáiyát of Omar Khayyám*, published in 1859 and discovered by the Rossetti circle in 1861. Swinburne combines, adapts and expands upon the fragments of Sappho, in the same way that Fitzgerald had combined, adapted and expanded upon the originally separate *rubais* or quatrains of Omar, and to the same end: the expression, under a thin disguise, of shocking views. Fitzgerald's mask lyric itself had a precedent in Matthew Arnold's *Empedocles on Etna*. Here the fragments of the Greek poet-philosopher, Empedocles, were combined, adapted, and expanded in a manner which led Arnold's friend J. C. Shairp to formulate a good, brief definition of the mask lyric. Observing the process of composition in 1849, Shairp observed that Matt, 'was working at an "Empedocles" – which seemed to be not much about the man who leapt into the crater – but his name and outward circumstances. . . used for the drapery of his own thoughts'.[35] Browning's poem 'Rabbi Ben Ezra', published in 1864, almost certainly as a deliberate riposte to the *Rubáiyát*, was a further contribution to this remarkable sequence, or dialogue, of mask lyrics. Arnold's Greek poet, Fitzgerald's Persian poet, Browning's Jewish poet, and Swinburne's Greek poetess are all used for the drapery of their authors' own thoughts, but in ways which make subtle use of their intertextual relationships.

It is important not to underestimate the dramatic quality of 'Anactoria', and Swinburne's mask is more substantial than we sometimes allow. The male poet is, for a start, speaking as a woman, and attempting to register the 'otherness' of female sexuality in ways which go far beyond the exploration of feminine emotional experience in such cross-gendered Browning monologues as 'A Woman's Last Word' or 'Any Wife to Any Husband'. More particularly, Swinburne is speaking as Sappho, at least to the extent to which his poem implicitly demonstrates the inadequacy of an existing tradition of Sapphic adaptation by other (male) poets. From Catullus's Latin translation, denounced in *Notes on Poems and Reviews* as 'colourless and bloodless, puffed out by additions and enfeebled by alterations' (*Works* 16.357), to such modern poems as Southey's monodrama 'Sappho' (1793), Tennyson's 'Fatima' (published in 1832 with an epigraph from Sappho's second fragment), or Matthew Arnold's dramatic monologue 'A Modern Sappho' of 1849, the imitations seem tepid by the side of 'Anactoria'. None of the modern poems, for example, allows any hint of homosexuality, and Arnold's domesticated, bourgeois setting ('Nothing stirs on the lawn but the quick lilac shade')[36] shows just how far the convention had moved from the real extremity and shock of the Sapphic. Swinburne's poem, by contrast, insists that Sappho cannot be assimilated to the polite assumptions of a male, nineteenth-century, North West European, middle-class, Christian heterosexual.

If, in all these ways, 'Anactoria' approaches the genre of the dramatic monologue, the penultimate term in that list reminds us that it does not get there. In order to stress the fact that Sappho was not a Christian, Swinburne makes her – anachronistically – anti-Christian. At the same time he both exaggerates the imagery of suffering in her account of erotic experience into something more full-bloodedly sado-masochistic, and provides a decidedly post-Romantic meditation on the mutability of Nature and the persistence of art:

> For never Muse has bound above thine hair
> The high Pierian flower whose graft outgrows
> All summer kinship of the mortal rose
> And colour of deciduous days . . .
>
> (*Poems* 1.63)

The marvellous transposition of 'mortal' (more normally associated with days) and 'deciduous' (normally a characteristic of roses) goes beyond Romantic Elizabethanism, and into the intellectual environment of the mid-nineteenth century, with the scientific precision of that second adjective. Swinburne rectifies a current distortion of Sappho. But his correction is, characteristically, an over-correction, carrying him beyond an objective interest in the character of a Greek poet of the seventh century BC to the expression of urgently personal and modern concerns. His Sappho may, as a consequence, be less unlike the original than the Sappho of some other English poets. But she remains, in Shairp's phrase, the drapery of Swinburne's own thoughts, and the poem is a powerful example of mask lyric.

*Poems and Ballads, First Series* contains numerous examples of Swinburne's use of the voice of other poets, whether in free translations such as 'Love at Sea' (Gautier's 'Barcarolle'), or in direct imitations of a poetic manner like the Villonesque 'A Ballad of Burdens' or the Chaucerian 'St. Dorothy' (where the hero, Theophilus, is an anti-Tannhäuser, converted from the cult of Venus to Christianity). Such texts are not dramatic monologues or mask lyrics, since neither the character of the original poet nor the distinctive thought of the imitator is at issue. Instead they are pastiche in the spirit of Chatterton, another writer's ideas or poetic manner being transmitted, more or less faithfully, and without implicit comment. The only other true mask lyrics, in fact, beside 'Anactoria' and its pendant 'Erotion', are the paired poems with which the collection opens. William Michael Rossetti, in his *Criticism* of the volume, carefully pointed out that 'A Ballad of Life' and 'A Ballad of Death' are, 'Italian canzoni of the exactest type, such as Dante, Cavalcanti, Petrarca, and the other medieval . . . poets of Italy have written'.[37] Their form, that is, suggests that they are utterances of the fourteenth, fifteenth, or early sixteenth century. Their content makes that location more specific. Even without the sub-titles which Swinburne tried unavailingly to add in 1876, they are clearly addressed to Lucretia Borgia (1480–1519) by a poet who is a member of her court.

Students of Swinburne's manuscripts can give this mask the name of

Tebaldeo Tebaldei, the fictitious hero of an unfinished prose story of the early 1860s. Set in the court of Lucretia Borgia, 'The Chronicle of Tebaldeo Tebaldei' was probably written for an imitation of Boccaccio, to be called the *Triameron*. Readers merely of *Poems and Ballads* can make no such attribution, but can – in principle at least – sense that the style of the poem is that of the real poets of Lucretia Borgia's court: Pietro Bembo, Ercole Strozzi and, above all, that near-namesake of Swinburne's fictitious hero, Antonio Tebaldeo. A late Petrarchist, 'nearer', in John Scott's judgement, 'to Baroque extravaganza than to the chaste muse of Petrarch',[38] he represents a wholly appropriate voice for the expression of courtly love in its self-indulgent decadence. But Swinburne's two poems are mask lyrics, not translations or dramatic monologues. 'A Ballad of Life' and 'A Ballad of Death' are not based on a particular original text, and invite no retrospective judgement on the views expressed by 'Tebaldeo'. Instead they are the drapery of Swinburne's thoughts, going beyond the extravagant erotic sycophancy of Bembo, Strozzi, or Tebaldeo to a paradoxical moral inversion which is distinctively of the later nineteenth century:

> Then Fear said: I am Pity that was dead.
> And Shame said: I am Sorrow comforted.
>     And Lust said: I am Love.
>
> (*Poems* 1.2)

At the same time, Petrarch's division of the *Canzoniere* into the poems written before and after Laura's death is here exaggerated into an opportunity for the display, in 'A Ballad of Death', of a Baudelaireian corpse sensation, plucking out 'beauty . . . from actual carrion', as Swinburne put it in his praise of Baudelaire's 'Une Charogne' (*Works* 13.421).

With the 'Hymn to Proserpine' we might at first sight seem to be in the same generic category of the mask lyric. The anti-Christian views expressed are very much Swinburne's, and the confident prediction that the new religion will itself in turn be the victim of historical change has a distinct air of nineteenth-century hindsight. But here, in fact, we have crossed the line into the true dramatic monologue. This poem is consistently spoken by a pagan of the fourth century AD. Swinburne is not using his speaker as a mask for his own opinions, but is sympathetically exploring an alien position. As in 'Laus Veneris', the crucial distinction is one of tone. Like Swinburne, both Tannhäuser and the Roman pagan hold values which are not those of the Judaeo-Christian tradition. But they do so in a very different spirit from the confident anti-theism of a nineteenth-century unbeliever. In the case of 'Laus Veneris' this is obvious enough. Tannhäuser chooses Venus, but is tortured by his choice. So strongly is his thinking shaped by the medieval world view, the monotheistic ideology, in which he has grown up, that even when he rejects Christ he can figure his Epicurean alternative only as the Christian Hell:

Night falls like fire; the heavy lights run low,
And as they drop, my blood and body so
    Shake as the flame shakes, full of days and hours
That sleep not neither weep they as they go.

(*Poems* 1.13)

As Swinburne himself observed, 'Once accept or admit the least admixture of pagan worship, or of modern thought, and the whole story collapses into froth and smoke' (*Works* 16.365). The modern thinker can observe the ethical torment of this medieval speaker objectively, with compassion and relief.

In the case of the 'Hymn to Proserpine' the crucial difference of tone is best shown by the contrast with the 'Hymn of Man' in *Songs Before Sunrise* (1871). Swinburne linked the poems in his 'Dedicatory Epistle', describing them as, 'the death-song of spiritual decadence and the birthsong of spiritual renascence' (*Poems* 1.xvi), and the sub-title of the 'Hymn of Man' ('During the Session in Rome of the Oecumenical Council') makes the connection obvious. The Oecumenical Council of 1869, which (notoriously) defined the infallibility of the Pope, was only the twentieth such council in the history of the Christian Church. At the First, at Nicea, in 325 AD, Christianity became *de facto* the religion of the Roman Empire. The Second, at Constantinople in 381, completed the Nicene Creed and declared it to be the Catholic faith. A decade later, the tolerance of paganism which had persisted through most of the fourth century ceased. Theodosius closed the temples and banned all forms of pagan cult in 391. The sanctuary of Demeter at Eleusis was destroyed by Alaric in 395.

Swinburne offers us two poems, one a dramatic monologue, the other a dramatic lyric, which survey the history of Christianity as an institutional religion from opposite ends. The 'Last Pagan' (as Swinburne described him in a letter to Lady Trevelyan in December 1865) (*Letters* 1.11) speaks, under the shadow of the First and Second Oecumenical Councils, in a tone of defiant despair. Echoing the dying words of Julian the Apostate in 386 AD ('Vicisti, Galilaee') to register the extent of the Christian triumph, and quoting Epictetus to declare his Stoic beliefs, he mourns the advent of a religious era which he sees as cruel, inhibiting, and dogmatic. He does, of course, predict the eventual passing of Christianity, and does so with a sense of historical relativism which can sound anachronistically Paterian. But Pater's account of the relative spirit was itself derived from the pre-Socratic philosopher Heraclitus,[39] and the tone of the prediction is far from triumphant. The Roman pagan cannot know when the Galilean will, like the 'throned Cytherean' (*Poems* 1.71) he has displaced, in turn be rejected, and he worships Proserpine, goddess of death, not the more vital 'Cytherean' (Venus) or Demeter. There is, of course, an anti-Christian point to such worship, since the death which Proserpina offers is a merciful extinction ('death is a sleep') (*Poems* 1.73). It is not, in other words, that promise of eternal torment for the damned which prompted the ethical objection to Christianity, held by so many Victorian unbelievers. But Swinburne's Roman remains, none the less, a voice of defeat, the representative of the 'spiritual decadence' which had failed to prevent the rise of Christianity. He lacks the positive humanism and the evolutionary understanding of the speaker of the 'Hymn to Man', who is able – by contrast – to see the doctrinal declarations of the Twentieth Oecumenical Council (and presumably the 'Syllabus of Errors' appended to the Papal encyclical *Quanta cura* in 1864, which condemned pantheism, naturalism, moderate rationalism, latitudinarianism, socialism, and even Bible societies) as the desperate defensive measures of a Christian Church in full retreat. The modern thinker can sympathize with the Roman pagan, but is not obliged to share his sense of defeat. As in 'Laus Veneris', the tone of the utterance is to be judged objectively, and the poem is a dramatic monologue.

Several other texts in *Poems and Ballads, First Series* fall, in whole or in part, into this generic category, some of them clearly enough – the central section of 'Before the Mirror', for example, or the victim's speech in 'Les Noyades' (where the reactionary, anti-Republican political status of the speaker complicates any suggestion of simple authorial identification). William Michael Rossetti, in his *Criticism* noted that 'Les Noyades' and 'The Leper' had a 'sort of unlike likeness' to such Browning monologues as 'Johannes Agricola', 'Karshish', and 'The Bishop orders his Tomb at St. Praxed's', in their common interest in 'out-of-the-way subjects', though Swinburne went beyond Browning in his combination of 'moral and physical repulsiveness'.[40] 'The Leper' in particular shows how powerfully Swinburne could use the monologue as developed by Browning and Morris – in its first draft, 'A Vigil', this poem was derivatively Morrisian[41] – for an imaginative entry into the experience of criminality or moral perversity. The long speeches by the heroine in 'Phaedra' obviously operate in the same area, though the fact that the internal auditors also speak makes this poem technically a dramatic fragment.

'Itylus', though consistently spoken by Philomela to Procne, is perhaps best described as monodrama, since this exquisite expansion of a traditional conception of the nightingale's voice is representative rather than individual. 'At Eleusis', on the other hand, is a dramatic monologue, and an important one. Often dismissed, perhaps because of a nervous feeling that it is somehow too close to the Homeric 'Hymn to Demeter' to count as an original poem (Rutland condemns it as 'an exercise', and both he and Lafourcade suggest that it is, in manner, merely a derivative imitation of Landor's *Hellenics*)[42], it is a striking text, both in its own right and as a necessary counterpart, within the volume, to the 'Hymn to Proserpine'.

'At Eleusis' is spoken entirely by the goddess Demeter, or, more precisely, by the old nurse Doso at the moment when she finally reveals herself to be the goddess Demeter. As well as a speaker very decidedly not the poet, it has internal auditors, and an intensely dramatic occasion. If in no other way, Swinburne has transformed the material of the Homeric Hymn into an original text by thus allowing Demeter to tell the story – that is, by making it into a dramatic monologue.

Speaking as a god, Swinburne can here address positively the issues handled in a more negative and fatalistic spirit in the 'Hymn to Proserpine'. The Latin names Proserpina and Ceres become the Greek Persephone and Demeter, registering a shift back in time to the beginning, rather than the end, of classical paganism. The poem depicts, in fact, the moment of divine revelation which initiates that key component of ancient worship, the Eleusinian Mysteries. With these words Demeter, mother of 'Proserpine', and goddess of Nature, fertility, and the physical cycle of life and death, begins the religious practice which will eventually be betrayed by the despairing 'spiritual decadence' of the fourth century AD. But in 'At Eleusis' the mood is serene and triumphant. That same practice, it is implied, could be fruitfully reconstituted in the reverently scientific humanism of late Victorian England.

In three poems, in other words, Swinburne traces the birth, death, and renascence of his preferred system of belief, and those poems are closely linked. The Roman of the 'Hymn to Proserpine', one remembers, is, as the 'Last Pagan', speaking after the destruction of the great Temple of Demeter at Eleusis in 395 AD. Indeed, if one wished to give him a name, I suspect it should be Claudian, the last great representative of the classical tradition in Latin poetry, and a defiant pagan, whose unfinished epic the *Raptus Proserpinae* was probably written as a direct response to the sack of the sanctuary at Eleusis. And the loving, female 'earth', the 'motherless mother of men', of the 'Hymn of Man' (*Poems* 2.94) points us back very directly to Swinburne's delicate re-creation of the thwarted maternal tenderness of the Homeric 'Hymn to Demeter' in 'At Eleusis'.

Deprived of her daughter Persephone, the grieving Demeter tells us how she took on the form of an old woman in order to nurse Triptolemus, the infant son of Celeus and Metaneira. Loving this adoptive, human child with the fierceness of her own, baffled maternal emotions, she secretly sought to make him divine by burning out his mortality in the household fire. His mother, Metaneira, was afraid and interrupted them,

> . . . the flame
> Writhed once all through and died, and in thick dark
> Tears fell from mine on the child's weeping eyes,
> Eyes dispossessed of strong inheritance
> And mortal fallen anew.
>
> (*Poems* 1.213–14)

Thus far 'At Eleusis' is a late Romantic poem about the longing to escape from the fallen condition of mortality. But Swinburne moves on confidently from such thwarted longing to the recommendation of a positive humanist belief, a religion contentedly based in the physical world:

> Dividing earth and reaping fruits thereof
> In fields where wait, well-girt, well-wreathen, all

The heavy-handed seasons all year through.

(*Poems* 1.214)

Tennyson, writing a dramatic monologue spoken by Demeter (which although composed nearly twenty years later is probably at least in part a riposte to Swinburne), contrives to give the subsequent return of Persephone from the underworld a Christian implication.[43] Swinburne omits it, concentrating instead on man's life as something confined to this world, and on Demeter as the appropriate symbol of such a conception. Swinburne's Mother Nature, indeed, comes in her grief to reject her fellow gods with anti-theistic intensity:

I set my lips against the meat of gods
And drank not neither ate or slept in heaven.

(*Poems* 1.211)

Walter Pater, in an essay on 'The Myth of Demeter and Persephone' written nine years after the publication of 'At Eleusis', and still the best (implicit) commentary on Swinburne's poem, spells out the significance of the myth for a sceptical intellectual of the later nineteenth century. Reminding us of the way in which Charles Newton's excavations of the small Temple of Demeter at Cnidus in the late 1850s had reawakened interest in the topic, he suggests that for the early Greeks,

> all . . . that related to the earth in its changes, the growth and decay of all things born of it – was covered by the story of Demeter, the myth of the earth as a mother. They thought of Demeter as the old Germans thought of Hertha, or the later Greeks of Pan, as the Egyptians thought of Isis . . . thus naming together in her all their fluctuating thoughts, impressions, suspicions, of the earth and its appearances.[44]

Pater's essay goes on to warn how this 'primitive cosmical myth'[45] gradually hardened into a sense of these gods as autonomous personalities. Tactfully, he does not mention the similarly distinct, unsymbolic personality of the Judaeo-Christian god, but then he scarcely needs to. Instead he ends his essay with an assertion of the relevance of the earliest phase of Greek religion 'for us, at the present day'. The myth of Demeter and Persephone 'arose naturally out of the spirit of man, and embodied, in adequate symbols, his deepest thoughts concerning the conditions of his physical and spiritual life'.[46]

'At Eleusis', in other words, is no mere 'exercise', but a poem which articulates some of the key beliefs of Swinburne and his circle. It is, none the less, not a mask lyric but an authentic dramatic monologue. The stiff, deliberately awkward verbal manner (designed to *sound* like the literal translation of an ancient text, though it actually adapts the material, rather than translates the words, of the Homeric Hymn) suggests the irrecoverably distant context of the utterance. The views expressed are a disturbing mixture of human emotions and austerely divine detachment. The poet is not a god, though he here speaks as one for the duration of the poem, as Browning had done in 'Artemis Prologizes' and as Tennyson would do in 'Demeter and Persephone'. In the gap between a sympathetic dream of divine omniscience, and a sober judgement on our actual mortal condition, dramatic objectivity arises.

And in Swinburne's case, that gap is precisely what the plot of his poem, simultaneously, enacts. The infant Triptolemus does not become divine. 'Eyes dispossessed of strong inheritance', he remains, like the reader, in our condition of confined perception, the world of language. Here, as in the later 'Hertha', speaking as a god, sympathetically entering a divine perspective, can help us to understand our humanity. But the 'judgement' with which, at the end of the poem, we consciously relinquish this temporary status is what confirms that (distinctively secular) understanding and makes it vivid. Swinburne not only writes dramatic monologues competently, deliberately, and with an understanding of their difference from other forms. He also, on occasion, exploits their distinctive characteristics with exceptional subtlety.

## Notes

1. Harold Nicolson, *Swinburne*, 1926, 108–9.
2. Ina Beth Sessions, 'The Dramatic Monologue', *PMLA* 62, 1947, 503–16.
3. For T. S. Eliot's 'Impersonal theory of poetry' see his essay 'Tradition and the Individual Talent' in the *Sacred Wood*, 1920. For Keats's account of the way in which 'the camelion Poet . . . has no Identity' see his letter to Richard Woodhouse, 27 October 1818.
4. Thaïs E. Morgan, 'Swinburne's Dramatic Monologues: Sex and Ideology', *Victorian Poetry* 22, 1984, 175–95.
5. Morgan, 176.
6. Robert Langbaum, *The Poetry of Experience, The Dramatic Monologue in Modern Literary Tradition*, London, 1972, 76.
7. Langbaum, 140.
8. Langbaum, 105–6.
9. Langbaum, 140.
10. Langbaum, 93.
11. Morgan, 177.
12. Ekbert Faas, *Retreat into the Mind, Victorian Poetry and the Rise of Psychiatry*, 1988, 189, 199.
13. Alan Sinfield, *Dramatic Monologue*, 1977, 25.
14. Sinfield, 62.
15. Sinfield, 61.
16. The 'Dedicatory Epistle' was published in 1904, but its reference to the 'thirty six years since my first volume of miscellaneous verse' suggests composition in 1902.
17. J. W. Mackail, *Swinburne*, 1909, 12.
18. R. W. Rader, 'The Dramatic Monologue and Related Lyric Forms', *Critical Inquiry* 3, 1976–7, 131–51.
19. A. Dwight Culler, 'Monodrama and the Dramatic Monologue', *PMLA* 90, 1975, 381.
20. See Gosse in *Works* 19.39; the *Catalogue of the Library of Theodore Watts-Dunton, Esq.*, Sotheby, Wilkinson and Hodge, March 13–17, 1917, Lot 926; and

G. C. Monsman, 'Old Mortality at Oxford', *Studies in Philology* 67, 1970, 367.

21. 'John Jones', a parody of Robert Browning's 'James Lee' (1864) was published in *The Heptalogia*, 1880. Swinburne subsequently changed the title to 'John Jones's Wife' to reflect Browning's own change of title to 'James Lee's Wife' (1868). 'Disgust: A Dramatic Monologue' was published in E. Gosse and T. J. Wise, eds., *Posthumous Poems by Algernon Charles Swinburne*, 1917, and is a parody of Tennyson's 'Despair: A Dramatic Monologue' (1881).
22. The first two poems of this sequence were published in 1925 in *Works* 1.74–7, under the joint title 'The Death of Rudel', with the second poem sub-titled 'At Tripoli'. The third poem, which Swinburne refers to, in his letter to Edwin Hatch of 17 February 1858, as both 'The Golden House' and 'Rudel in Paradise' (*Letters* 1.16), was published in T. J. Wise, *A Swinburne Library*, 1925, 245–6, as 'Rudel in Paradise'.
23. T. L. Meyers, 'Swinburne's Speech to the Royal Literary Fund, May 2, 1866', *Modern Philology* 86, 1989, 197–8.
24. Langbaum, 79.
25. Faas, 17.
26. George W. Thornbury, *Songs of the Cavaliers and Roundheads, Jacobite Ballads, &c.*, 1857, 153.
27. R. W. Rader, 'The Dramatic Monologue and Related Lyric Forms', *Critical Inquiry* 3, 1976–7, 150.
28. Rader, 150.
29. Langbaum, 53.
30. R. W. Rader, 'Notes on Some Structural Varieties and Variations in Dramatic "I" Poems and Their Theoretical Implications', *Victorian Poetry* 22, 1984, 105.
31. Sinfield, 25.
32. Culler, 379–81.
33. M. W. MacCullum, *The Dramatic Monologue in the Victorian Period*, Warton Lecture 16, Oxford, 1925,18.
34. R. W. Rader, 'The Dramatic Monologue and Related Lyric Forms', *Critical Inquiry* 3, 1976–7, 150.
35. F. L. Mulhauser, ed., *The Correspondence of Arthur Hugh Clough*, 1957, 1.270.
36. C. B. Tinker and H. F. Lowry, eds., *Arnold, Poetical Works*, 1950, 19.
37. W. M. Rossetti, *Swinburne's Poems and Ballads, A Criticism*, 1866, 31.
38. John A. Scott, 'Lyric and Pastoral Poetry: Italy' in A. J. Krailsheimer, ed., *The Continental Renaissance*, 1971, 140.
39. See the quotation from Plato's *Cratylus* used as an epigraph to the 'Conclusion' to *The Renaissance, Studies in Art and Poetry* (1873); *The Works of Walter Pater*, New Library Edition, 10 vols., 1910, 1.233.
40. W. M. Rossetti, 49.
41. 'A Vigil' has been published in T. J. Wise, *A Swinburne Library*, 1925, 2, and in *Lafourcade* 2.63–4.
42. See W. R. Rutland, *Swinburne, A Nineteenth Century Hellene*, 1931, 273 and *Lafourcade* 2.462.
43. See Tennyson's 'Demeter and Persephone' (1889), especially 11.126–51.
44. Walter Pater, 'The Myth of Demeter and Persephone', originally given as two lectures in 1875, and published in the *Fortnightly Review*, January and February 1876. Reprinted as an essay in two parts in *Greek Studies, A Series of Essays* (1895); *The Works of Walter Pater*, New Library Edition, 10 vols., 1910, 7.97.
45. *ibid*, 7.120.
46. *Ibid*, 7.151.

# 5 The Algernonicon, or thirteen ways of looking at *Tristram of Lyonesse*

Rikky Rooksby

Swinburne's *Tristram of Lyonesse* is a difficult poem to deal with in a short space. A symphony of verbal echoes, it cries out for a concordance as does no other work by Swinburne, though (alas) we do not have even a scholarly edition of it. It is as densely woven as a tapestry, and to draw out one thread – be it a theme, an image, a word – is quickly to find the hand of commentary unpicking the whole poem. This is impractical. So here are thirteen ways of looking at *Tristram*, any one of which will serve for lengthier explorations into one of Swinburne's greatest achievements.

## I

Consider the following quotation from Swinburne's poetry:

> Mockeries and masks of motion and mute breath,
> Leavings of life, the superflux of death –
>
> What should I do to follow? yet I too,
> I have the heart to follow
>
> Not love but hate, thou bitter God and strange
>
> 'Hast thou no sword? I would not live till day;'
>
> From hills that first see bared the morning's breast
> And heights the sun last yearns to from the west,
> All tend but toward the sea
>
> A little time, O Love, a little light,
> A little hour for ease before the night.

Most readers could be forgiven for thinking that these lines come from 'Anactoria', 'Itylus', 'Hymn to Proserpine', 'In the Orchard', 'The Garden of Proserpine', and one of the shorter lyrics of *Poems and Ballads* (1866); that is, from a volume whose quality and historical significance are unquestioned. In fact, all the above are from *Tristram of Lyonesse* (*Poems*, 4: 10, 12, 84, 51, 54, 87). It is hardly surprising that the first should be so reminiscent, since when he started the poem in December 1869 Swinburne remarked that the verse was 'modelled . . . after my own scheme of movement and modulation in "Anactoria" ' (*Letters*, 2: 74). Nevertheless, these echoes strongly remind us that although *Tristram* is nominally a Putney volume (which until recently was tantamount to saying unread and unreadable) its genesis is in the 1860s when Swinburne's creative powers were at their height. In this respect *Tristram* is quite unlike any of the other volumes of poetry Swinburne published after 1879. It straddles the great sea-change of his life like the colossus of Rhodes, having more in common, stylistically and thematically, with his earlier work than has been acknowledged.

This granted, it can be plausibly argued that *Tristram* has a unique centrality in Swinburne's poetic canon, linking the fiery romanticism of *Poems and Ballads* with the intense absorption in landscape and seascape that typifies the best of his later poetry. It is striking, for example, to recall his fervent wish of February 1870, writing to Rossetti, that 'by the grace of the Devil I hope to make the copulative passages of the poem more warm and provocative of sinful appetite than anything my chaste Muse has yet attempted.' (*Letters*, 2:90). This could easily be Swinburne limbering up for ten more stanzas of 'Faustine' or 'Dolores'.

## II

If the centrality of *Tristram of Lyonesse* is accepted, what can be said of its status amongst the Putney volumes? There were ten books of poetry published between 1880 and 1904, and they include a handful of fine poems. The reputations of 'On the Cliffs', 'Thalassius', 'By the North Sea', 'Evening on the Broads', 'Past Days', 'To a Seamew', 'In Memory of John William Inchbold', the Auvergne elegy for Richard Burton, 'Loch Torridon', 'A Nympholept', and 'The Lake of Gaube' are now established. But despite these achievements, despite the satirical wit of *The Heptalogia*, and the compressed simplicity of *The Tale of Balen*, during the Putney years *Tristram of Lyonesse* is pre-eminent.

As Sir Edmund Gosse remarked, 'the one epic of a great poet should, of course, have made its undistracted appeal to the public in a single, handsome volume' (*Works*, 19:231). Never were three words quite such a liability to a poet as the 'and Other Poems' attached to its title. Swinburne wrote gleefully to William Bell Scott:

> I have just sent to the publishers the biggest book of verse – bar Bothwell – that ever I launched on the devoted heads of the public . . . I expect 'the Mothers of England' to rally round me on the publication of a volume in which, out of a total of one

> hundred poems, between forty and fifty are devoted to the praise of little children: though I cannot expect the approbation of the British Matron for certain passages – or indeed for one entire canto – of the leading poem, 'Tristram of Lyonesse'
> (*Letters*, 4: 267–68)

This meant that in the first edition *Tristram* occupied a mere 169 pages out of 361. None of the shorter poems can be counted as having any special poetic merit, and by publishing *Tristram* in this manner Swinburne (and Watts-Dunton, if the idea were his) did one of his major works a grave disservice.

This particular incident highlights something of the relationship between *Tristram* and the later poetry as a whole. It is instructive to ask what would be lost if, by some queer change such as wiped out the dinosaurs, posterity had been robbed of all Swinburne's Putney poetry, of the 'enormous length' of 'sea-serpents in verse' and 'mastodons of metre' (*Hyder*, 200), with the exception of *Tristram*? To lack the poems cited above would be a tragedy indeed. But if we had *Tristram* we would still have a pretty good understanding of the essence of the later Swinburne. I am suggesting that one way to approach *Tristram* is to see it as a compendium, an 'Algernonicon', of the later poetry, and, to some degree, of the earlier too.

Before pursuing this in more detail, consider how much of the dead wood of the Putney poetry *Tristram* avoids. Apart from one charming enough reference (72), there are no children or babies and, save one fleeting allusion in the 'Prelude' (9), no Shakespeare. Not only does *Tristram* stand free of Bardolatry and the pitter-patter of the crèche, it is also undeformed by most of the other tedium of Swinburne's later verse – the dull effusions about England, English history, English institutions, odes to Eton, sonnets about Nell Gwyn and Sir William Gomm, poems about the Channel Tunnel, vague musings on death, grandiloquent elegies, and unnecessary poems about Elizabethan plays and dramatists. In *Tristram of Lyonesse* we have the essential later Swinburne.

## III

A careful reading of *Tristram* shows the extent to which Swinburne united in it so many of his most central preoccupations and techniques. For example, Swinburne was extremely fond of antiphonal effects and contrasts in his poetry. This is very evident in the poems of a late volume like *A Century of Roundels*, where many of the roundels engage in antiphonal response as they debate their themes.[1] We may see antiphony throughout *Tristram*, and until we consciously grasp just how much Swinburne echoes his own phrasing the lyric intensity of the style is apt to overwhelm our sense of the poem's structure. The most obvious examples of this kind of antiphony are the way the 44-line apostrophe to Love in the 'Prelude' is answered by one of similar length on Fate in canto 9, and cantos 1 and 9 describe sea-voyages of very different situation and emotion. The poem contains three dramatic monologues spoken by each of the major characters, and each of these contrasts with the others in both tone and content. Iseult's monologue in canto 5 is intercut throughout by the antiphonal responses of the storm and the sea in the darkness. There are striking verbal echoes too. The difference in the relationship of Tristram to each of the women is rendered by the contrast between 'And their four lips became one burning mouth' (38) and the markedly cooler 'And their two hearts were as one trembling lyre' (67). Similarly, in canto 1 Swinburne casts an ominous anticipatory shadow over Tristram and Iseult as they approach the fateful moment of the drinking of the potion, by stressing how this is 'the last time',

> The last hour of their hurtless hearts at rest,
> The last that peace should touch them, breast to breast,
> The last that sorrow far from them should sit,
> This last was with them, and they knew not it. (36)

As we will see later, this is a vivid instance of Swinburne's concern with the fact of the irrevocable, an unavoidable feature of linear time in contrast to cyclical time. This passage is dramatically echoed in canto 8 in a 20-line sequence structured by the words 'the last time', culminating with 'The last wherewith love's eyes might yet be lit, / Came, and they could but dream they knew not it.' (113)

*Tristram* is also typical of the later poetry in the importance it places on the response to landscape and seascape. Many of the very best of Swinburne's later poems fall into this category, a category not so well expressed in his poetry before 1879, however much it is fiercely present in an early prose work like *Lesbia Brandon*. Both the narrator and Tristram celebrate the life of Nature, from the memorable and compact evocation of 'the wind-hollowed heights and gusty bays / Of sheer Tintagel' (13) and the Cornish wood near the sea in canto 2, to the Northumbrian moorland and coast described in canto 6. But unlike 'By the North Sea'. Swinburne seems not so intent on pressing the theme of erosion, despite the fate of the chapel at the very end. He is closer to the ecstatic enjoyment of the natural world typified by poems like 'A Nympholept' and 'Loch Torridon'.

This ecstatic response is most obviously expressed through Tristram's two encounters with the sea, in cantos 4 and 8, expressing an experience that informs other later poems like 'In Guernsey', 'Off Shore', 'A Swimmer's Dream', 'The Lake of Gaube', and 'A Midsummer's Holiday'. Swimming, like drink, prams, and the birch, is a feature of Swinburne's poetry that his less sympathetic critics often put to parodic use. But we know that one of Swinburne's most powerful early experiences was of being thrown into the sea by his father, and the ontological nature of the experience of swimming is evident in a letter like this, written at 52:

> I ran like a boy, tore off my clothes, and hurled myself into the water. And it was but for a few minutes – but I was in Heaven! The whole sea was literally golden as well as green – it was liquid and living sunlight in which one lived and moved and had one's being. And to feel that in deep water is to feel – as long as one is swimming out, if only for a minute or two – as if one was in another world of life, and one far more glorious than even Dante ever dreamed of in his Paradise.
> (*Letters*, 5:275)

The references to Paradise and Heaven go beyond the mere expression of pleasure and enthusiasm. For Swinburne, the encounter with the sea seems a recovery of a unity of being and connection with life, and this is embodied in *Tristram*.

Tristram's first immersion is precipitated by pursuit and the threat of imprisonment and death. His dive off the cliff in canto 4 is analogous to the swimmer's dive in 'The Lake of Gaube':

> So Tristram one brief breathing-space apart
> Hung, and gazed down; then with exulting heart
> Plunged: and the fleet foam round a joyous head
> Flashed, that shot under, and ere a shaft had sped
> Rose again radiant, a rejoicing star,
> And high along the water-ways afar
> Triumphed (71)

Here is a classic example of Swinburne's ability to subordinate the couplet to his own requirements and not allow it to develop the rocking-horse rhythm Keats deplored in the Augustans. Brief seconds of tense decision, and the pause between decision and action, are built into the verse by punctuation, and the delaying of the main verbs to the start of each line, so that an extra emphasis is put upon the physical actions. Especially mimetic is the sense of Tristram drifting in an expanse of water, created by 'high along . . . afar'.

Tristram's dawn swim in canto 8 is more significant, marking as it does the last stage in his spiritual maturing. Waking to contemplation of his solitude and seeing the sea in the first light, Tristram enjoys an epiphanic moment, or what is known to some psychologies as a 'peak-experience', in which his perceptions are heightened, his mind being

> . . . rapt abroad beyond man's meaner kind
> And pierced with love of all things and with mirth
> Moved to make one with heaven and heavenlike earth
> And with the light live water. (126)

It is important to note that where Swinburne's later poems celebrate such experiences, the transcendence they record does not mean a leaving behind of the things of earth, hence the phrase 'heavenlike earth'. This phrase was to be later echoed in 'A Nympholept' when its speaker says 'Heaven is as earth, and as heaven to me / Earth' (*Poems*, 6:140). Consciousness is lifted out of its usual limits to an ecstatic experiencing of the unity of all life. A generation who are coming to the universities in the 1990s inspired by the vision of Gaia, the biosphere as one living system, may well be more impressed by this than by the aridity of a notion like the 'prison-house of language'. In such passages as this, Tristram exhibits the attainment of a higher innocence that takes him beyond the ego. He has already enjoyed a sense of relationship with the greater forces of life in canto 3:

> The heart of the ancient hills and his were one;
> The winds took counsel with him, and the sun
> Spake comfort; in his ears the shout of birds
> Was as the sound of clear sweet-spirited words (61)

In his encounter with the sea at dawn the language of sexuality is used by Swinburne as a powerful metaphor for spiritual unity. The sea is a bride who 'on her bare bright bosom . . . takes the young sun . . . / Home to his place with passion' (126) and Tristram 'Struck strongly forth with amorous arms made wide / To take the bright breast of the wave to his' (127). The imagery implies a real encounter with the Other – both in the physical sense of the elements and those levels of being which, though part of the Self, are beyond the ego and therefore experienced as 'Other'. In recent years critics have been ready to praise Swinburne for the un-Victorian willingness with which he jettisons anything that might resemble belief in a transcendent dimension, and extolls instead a naturalistic vision of humanity's place as material creatures in a material cosmos. Kerry McSweeney, for example, has written of the poem's major theme as, 'the dignity and grandeur of a wholly naturalistic vision of human existence.'[2] However, Swinburne's language admits of the possibility of a reading that sees another dimension to the world that goes beyond physical realities alone.

To see some of the more striking experiences of Tristram and Iseult in a new light we might go to the mescalin essays of Aldous Huxley, or to Swinburne's own glorious description of Blake as a visionary:

> All this was not a mere matter of creed or opinion, much less of decoration or ornament to his work. It was . . . his element of life, inhaled at every breath with the common air, mixed into his veins with their natural blood . . . About his path and about his bed, around his ears and under his eyes, an infinite play of spiritual life seethed and swarmed or shone and sang . . . Even upon earth his vision was 'twofold always'.
>
> (*Works*, 16:90–91)

Unlike Blake, Swinburne did not 'see' angelic spirits. But the poetry of *Tristram* suggests 'an infinite play of spiritual life' in the natural world, in the elements he constantly anthropomorphizes, and the reader of Swinburne needs to acknowledge that what impels the imagery of Tristram's dawn swim – 'Between the live sea and the living sun' (128) – is not literary in origin. To my knowledge no-one has yet entertained us with lysergical speculations about the contents of the potion made 'Out of live roots and life-compelling flowers' (18), of the kind which have featured in the critical history of *Alice in Wonderland*. But I do not think Blake's famous dictum about the cleansing of the doors of perception is inapplicable when it comes to understanding Tristram's renewed joy in being alive and part of the one life of earth. Stripped though it may be of a theology, a dogma, a church, or a holy book, the emotion that many of Swinburne's landscapes or seascapes are 'filled full of' is a religious one.

## IV

This naturally leads to *Tristram of Lyonesse*'s overwhelming focus on the experience of unity. For once in Swinburne's poetry the forces of death, frustration, failure, division and impermanence, do not have the field to themselves. Even by the end of the first canto the lovers have fused in the irrevocable kiss by which 'their four lips became one burning mouth', just as Tristram finds unity with Creation in his dawn swim. Fearless meeting with the natural world and human love are the two major keys that unlock this experience in the soul. In both cases the human consciousness seems to become aware of its bond with the underlying unity of all things, as referred to in the 'Prelude's' second line, 'The light that has the living world for shade', and in the antiphonal sequence of canto 9, where Fate is

> The power beyond all godhead which puts on
> All forms of multitudinous unison,
> A raiment of eternal change inwrought
> With shapes and hues more subtly spun than thought,
> Where all things old bear fruit of all things new
> And one deep chord throbs all the music through,
> The chord of change unchanging (133)

These lines might be profitably compared with some chapters in a text like the *Tao Te Ching* to show how they can be interpreted as having a meaning which goes beyond materialism without violating Swinburne's implacable anti-theism and his general agnosticism. Fate as 'change unchanging' 'beyond all godhead' might be illuminated by such sayings as 'Tao is a thing that is both invisible and intangible. Intangible and invisible, yet there are forms in it' or,

> There is a thing inherent and natural,
> Which existed before heaven and earth.

Motionless and fathomless,
It stands alone and never changes;
It pervades everywhere and never becomes exhausted.
It may be regarded as the Mother of the Universe . . .
If I am forced to give it a name,
I call it Tao, and I name it as supreme.[3]

*Tristram of Lyonesse* is a celebration of the power of romantic love to create in the individual life a state of affairs which mirrors the unity of the macrocosm. In canto 1, for instance, Tristram's song sets Iseult, as yet innocent of love, wondering about 'that sweet wonder of the twain made one' and the attainment of 'one thought and one vision and one song' (33). The potion takes them into a state of being that is in truth the undiluted experience of how things are, how the universe is to those who are not blind. To adapt a proverb from Blake, a fool sees not the same ocean that a wise man sees. As canto 2 begins, we meet the lovers, 'eyes made great and bright', haunted by an inner music 'singing in their ears', with the consequence that,

Nought else they saw nor heard but what the night
Had left for seal upon their sense and sight,
Sound of past pulses beating, fire of amorous light,
Enough, and overmuch, and never yet
Enough (40)

This unity is given full sensual expression in the account of their love-making, a sequence that by the standards of Victorian poetry is unusually explicit, and, for Swinburne, unusually free of the sado-masochistic feelings which colour sexual activity in a poem like 'Anactoria'. The second canto ends significantly just as another sexual act is about to take place, thus again demonstrating the impulse to unity.

Time has passed and the lovers are separated when Tristram delivers his monologue in canto 3. But he is moving towards a deeper awareness of his experience with Iseult and its wider implications:

'All these and we are parts of one same end;
And if through fire or water we twain tend
To that sure life where both must be made one,
If one we be, what matter? (56)

It is because of the importance of recurring key-words like 'twain' and 'one' that *Tristram* would be well served by a concordance. By contrast with this experience of unity, and the way that both Tristram and Iseult are, in their own ways, led to a fuller appreciation of the unity of all life, one of the gloomiest moments is provoked by their parting at Joyous Garde, where they 'fell separate' and 'saw the skies / Dark with their deep division' (113). Words like 'separate' and 'division' take on a specially horrible resonance in the context of a poem that is a hymn to the opposite.

Tristram and Iseult are not the only figures in the poem whose lives incarnate the theme of the unity of life. We must also examine Swinburne's highly individual deployment of the story of Merlin and Nimue.

## V

In *Under the Microscope* Swinburne had expressed forthright opinions concerning Tennyson's Vivien:

> The Vivien of Mr. Tennyson's idyl seems to me, to speak frankly, about the most base and repulsive person ever set forth in serious literature. Her impurity is actually eclipsed by her incredible and incomparable vulgarity – ('O ay', said Vivien, 'that were likely too'). She is such a sordid creature as plucks men passing by the sleeve. (*Works*, 16:408)

Swinburne's Nimue is not much less than a goddess. He introduces in canto 1 'the heavenly hands of holier Nimue . . . of lovelier blood and breath', a woman who 'could pass between the quick and the dead'. Her function as a power of feminine beneficence, restoring the lost unity of being, much as the sea does for Tristram, is enshrined in a lovely speech by Tristram in canto 6. Iseult has asked him about the fate of Merlin, and his reply is a single inclusive sentence of 46 lines that is one of the most memorable in the whole work. Merlin is presented by Swinburne as enjoying a trance-like state of communion with the natural world and the forces of life that flow through it. He is neither alive nor dead, but in a 'strange rest' which has greatly extended his awareness. Unlike Tennyson's Merlin, fondly overcome by female wiles and caught in a magical imprisonment, Swinburne's wizard is to be envied. The timelessness of this state is aptly rendered by the sheer length of the sentence and its many rich clauses, a grammar that allows Swinburne to melt the seasons one into another without the strong break that a full stop might create. It is a grammar of boundlessness, just as Merlin's mind is unconstrained in its awareness. Despite the initial metaphor of a "sleep" for his condition, a long sequence of verbs – 'takes . . . hears . . . feels . . . knows . . . hears . . . hears' – makes it quite plain to the reader that Merlin is not insentient. The sense of harmony and beauty throughout also leaves us with the impression of a state of being of almost unutterable fullness, even though it might appear inactive. Beneath Merlin's feeling of 'ambient change' is a deeper dimension; for he,

> . . . knows the soul that was his soul at one
> With the ardent world's, and in the spirit of earth
> His spirit of life reborn to mightier birth
> And mixed with things of elder life than ours (98).

Surely this implies more than the idea that humanity projects its own mind onto a 'designified' landscape? The poetry is telling of an encounter between that mind and a life beyond the ego's usual perception. It is also worth noting the shift of tenses here. The past tense of 'was' is important, for it indicates that Merlin has 'died' to his old self but at the same time undergone a rebirth to a higher state of awareness. He hears the cosmic song from 'the mystic mouth of Nimue', the song of the greater life – 'the life thereof / Part of that life that feeds the world with love' (99), just as the potion filled the ears of Tristram and Iseult with a music such 'As hearing he grows god and knows it not' (39). The lines that describe the relationship of Merlin and Nimue could just as easily apply to the lovers:

> Yea, heart in heart is molten, hers and his,
> Into the world's heart and the soul that is
> Beyond or sense or vision (99)

Here is the ideal of love whose loss Swinburne had lamented in 'The Triumph of Time', stated without irony. The implicit association of the two couples is brought out in canto 9 when the dying Tristram remembers some of his most numinous memories, clinging hard,

> Only to dreams of joy in Joyous Gard
> Or wildwood nights beside the Cornish strand,
> Or Merlin's holier sleep here hard at hand
> Wrapped round with deep soft spells in dim Broceliande. (140)

Pauline Fletcher was quite right to suggest that 'Merlin's sentient trance might be compared with the experience described in A Nympholept',[4] for like the speaker in that poem Merlin can quite authentically say 'And nought is all, as am I, but a dream of thee' (*Poems*, 6:140). Thus *Tristram* is once again directing us back to a poem like 'The Triumph of Time' and forward to the later land and seascape lyrics. Far from being a patch of local Arthurian colour thrown in to give Tristram and Iseult something to chat about while they take a breather from howling 'in melodious couplets to the accompaniment of winds and waves' (*Works*, 19:240), Swinburne's Broceliande envisions the central theme of *Tristram*: the attainment of a unity 'mixed with things of elder life than ours'. Approached in this way, it seems inadequate to say that Nature in Swinburne is merely alive with the projections of the human imagination, that 'all of nature is alive with man's life'.[5]

It is welcome, therefore, after seeing Swinburne's later lyrics defoliated by interpretations that reduce their meanings to statements about solipsism, designification, and the undermining of 'quasi-theological hypostatizations',[6] and despite McSweeney's firm 'Swinburne is not a pantheist in any meaningful sense of the word',[7] that Anthony Harrison should re-plant the 'pantheistic vision'[8] of *Tristram of Lyonesse* in the groves of Academe, just when post-structuralist readings appeared set fair to do away with a Swinburne who had any relation with 'extra-linguistic reality'.[9] Arguing the case for Swinburne's 'mystical organicist philosophy',[10] Harrison is well aware of the importance of Tristram's Broceliande speech, since 'the virtue of their love assures both Tristram and Iseult immortality in myth, as well as an organically envisioned afterlife similar to that of Merlin and Nimue.'[11] He sees the state of Tristram and Iseult after their deaths as 'much the same'[12] as Merlin and Nimue. For a hint from Swinburne that this is so we need only reflect on these lines describing Merlin as,

> More deep asleep in green Broceliande
> Than shipwrecked sleepers in the soft green sea
> Beneath the weight of wandering waves. (98)

At the end of the poem Tristram and Iseult become just such two 'shipwrecked sleepers', yet Merlin is 'more deep asleep' than they and lives still. As in some ways 'A Nympholept' is a poem that requires interpretation in the light of its last line, so we need to keep Tristram's Broceliande speech in mind because it may offer a key to the interpretation of the conclusion of canto 9.

## VI

Unity's great enemy is death. Insofar as it is also preoccupied with death, *Tristram* is representative of a large number of later poems in which Swinburne struggled to reconcile faith and scepticism. Where in his early verse he had been confident enough to write poems like 'The Garden of Proserpine', where humanity's lot at death is 'Only the sleep eternal / In an eternal night' (*Poems*, 1:172), with the passing of years Swinburne takes a less dogmatic stance. In many of the later elegies – and this is true of *Tristram* – the poetry is fuelled by the tension caused by Swinburne's being unable intellectually to give his assent to what his instincts and feelings are telling him. As a result, as I have argued elsewhere about 'Loch Torridon', his most profound 'statements' about the nature of death are in the form of images and symbols, not philosophical dicta.[13]

*Tristram* is no exception. Death is raised as a theme in the 'Prelude', and Swinburne's ambivalence is immediately apparent in his use of the paradox which states that the lovers are led to the 'lifeless life of night' (6). Why bother using the word 'life'? The fame of Tristram and Iseult will offer a kind of immortality, as the calendar of the famous exemplifies. Swinburne is confident that the dead have 'peace'. But his doubt is evident in the very real question 'If these things and no more than these things be / Left when man ends or changes, who can see?' (10). Similarly, in the ninth canto, no sooner has he pronounced of death that 'No vigils has that perfect night to keep, / No fever-fits of vision shake that sleep' (134), than he adds 'Nor if they wake'.

Nowhere is Swinburne's ambivalence about death more apparent than in the closing verse paragraph. Much commentary on these closing lines seems to claim the kudos of a 'tough-minded' annihilationist position, yet does so in phrases that remain subtly consoling. Francis Sypher writes 'death is for them not a separation, but a consummation and a release from bondage. In losing this life, they will find the "lifeless life of night" '.[14] Margot Louis, writing of the 'peace of dissolution', says that 'at the end, the lovers, swallowed up by the sea, enjoy a rest beyond love or life'.[15] Riede says of them that 'their souls, troubled in life, are finally at rest';[16] and McSweeney comments that 'they find quiet in the silent void of death'.[17] In each case, it is implied that the lovers 'find' or 'enjoy' or have a 'release' into something, when in fact, from the annihilationist point of view, they have simply ceased to be; the word 'they' itself is inadmissible.

Swinburne's own language commits exactly the same ontological tautology. The closing lines of *Tristram* are peppered with 'their', 'they' and 'them'. He repeatedly makes statements like 'their sleep / Hath round it like a raiment all the deep' (149) where the metaphor can only imply something still in being that the sea can surround. The same problem afflicts 'Gave them deliverance to perpetual rest' (148) – deliverance 'to' can only be to something else, not to nothing at all. Even 'perpetual rest' suggests something that continues forever. The same analysis applies equally to the noble ending.

> But peace they have that none may gain who live,
> And rest about them that no love can give,
> And over them, while death and life shall be,
> The light and sound and darkness of the sea. (151)

It may be objected that these are merely figures of speech by which we talk about the dead. But whatever the poetry is trying to denote must be balanced against the ambiguities and the emotive connotations of such language as surreptitiously keeps the lovers before our attention in a unity ('they', 'them') that has seemingly survived extinction. Since the notion that acts of interpretation must be confined by our knowledge of what the author intended, or by consonance with his or her known beliefs, has long been abandoned, it must be allowed that this is a reading of the poem that does not do violence to it. Richard McGhee felt able to say of Tristram and Iseult that 'they find perfect marriage only when they die',[18] and Harrison concludes that death is 'what permanently allows the unity they have experienced transiently in their love-making and that Tristram perceives as the dominant fact of nature'.[19] To insist that the poetry be read only in its usual figurative sense, so that we read it as meaning that the lovers are no more, is to foreclose a debate which is a source of fruitful tension in Swinburne's poetic universe.

## VII

The question about the nature of death can be seen in a new light not only by viewing it in the context of Merlin and Nimue, or Swinburne's own ambivalence, but also through the two concepts of time that inform *Tristram of Lyonesse*. Linear time is represented by the narrative, by the succession of events that lead the lovers through various experiences that culminate in their deaths. It is the dimension of normal life, where things are won but also lost; it allows for the ecstasy of loving and the pain of parting, and is where the 'wound of living' (11) is felt. We have already seen how Swinburne emphasizes the irrevocability of certain events in the linear dimension, for example in his use of the phrase 'the last time', exploiting the pathos of the reader's knowing what the lovers cannot know, that 'This last was with them, and they knew not it' (36).

By contrast, there is the world of cyclical time, of renewal, of the seasons and the elements. It is cyclical time that Merlin seems to have become a part of in Broceliande, and perhaps Tristram and Iseult enter it when they die – or maybe it would be more accurate to say that they exist in both spheres of time, and death is simply the leaving of the linear dimension. When we first meet the lovers in canto 1 they are already together. There is not a 'time' in the poem when they are not, though Swinburne could have chosen to start his story with Tristram's voyage to Ireland. This signifies their participation in the cyclical world of time. As McGann wrote:

> His method of thought turns all sequential processes of beginnings, middles, and ends into self-contained circles. This is why he characteristically talks about the 'life' of Tristram and Iseult in spatial rather than temporal terms: their essential life never changes, never needs to be sought for and found. (*McGann*, 141)

The Prelude's Calendar can be seen as a harmonization of cyclical time (the months of the year) with the linear time (the humans associated with them). More than this, with the privileging of cyclical time it becomes difficult to find a place in *Tristram* for the absolute stasis of annihilation. Instead, the poem stresses the 'day and night of things alternative' (5).

## VIII

At an immediate level, Swinburne's concern with time shapes such features of style as his repetitious diction, antiphony, paradox, and description. With regard to the last, early critics like Gosse complained about the lack of action. But this was in accord with Swinburne's stated intention to write 'not in the epic or romantic form of sustained or continuous narrative, but mainly through a succession of dramatic scenes or pictures with descriptive settings or backgrounds' (*Poems*, 1:xviii). The function of the descriptive passages is not merely decorative but to embody something of Swinburne's concern to find an intersection of cyclical time with linear time where, in the words of Oliver Elton, as in a 'true romance . . . the conception of time is abolished altogether' (*Hyder*, 230). What this means is that there is a strong drive in the poem towards the kind of intensity of experience – be it physical, sexual, aesthetic or spiritual – in which the sense of time is obliterated.

This is the purpose of such an extraordinary piece of description as that devoted to Iseult's 'unimaginable' eyes, which starts with a five-line simile evoking the colours of a wave and continues,

> So glowed their awless amorous plenilune,
> Azure and gold and ardent grey, made strange
> With fiery difference and deep interchange
> Inexplicable of glories multiform;
> Now as the sullen sapphire swells toward storm
> Foamless, their bitter beauty grew acold,
> And now afire with ardour of fine gold. (14)

Iseult's eyes have virtually become a world in themselves, and within a page of the story's getting underway narrative event has given way to rhapsody which desires only to remain within contemplation of beauty, not to go anywhere. Swinburne was primarily a lyric poet, and the essence of lyricism is the longing to overwhelm the ego's boundaries, either through becoming lost in subjective emotion or by being overwhelmed by an experience coming from without, such as beauty. To help create this effect of being overwhelmed, Swinburne makes good use of polysyllabic words like 'unimaginable', 'inextricable' and 'inexplicable', using them as a diction of what cannot be put into words. They signify not so much by what they denotatively mean, but by their effect as a clatter produced by someone kicking at the gates of infinity.

*Tristram*'s descriptive passages are therefore often not decoration but a contemplation of supreme values. In such passages, linear time is temporarily held at bay, and ecstatic absorption – of Tristram and Iseult in each other, or of Tristram with the sea, or of the reader in the poem – assuages the 'wound of living'. The poem constantly aspires to a transcendence of dulled feelings and perceptions in the inexpressible, as the endings of the first two cantos demonstrate, breaking off as they do in a way which is reminiscent of Jean Delville's picture of Tristan and Isolde burning up in a radiance of light.[20]

## IX

The impulses to unity, transcendence, to an ecstatic experience of the one life immanent in linear and cyclical time, are all linked through the extensive use of musical images and metaphors throughout *Tristram of Lyonesse*. If the sea is to be imagined sounding all through it, then superimposed on the crashing surf must be an unearthly music. The very order of things in *Tristram* is spoken of as music, life and death being 'The sweet twain chords that make the sweet tune live', and Love the force that 'keeps all the choir of lives in tune' (5), and Fate 'that keeps all the tune of things in chime' (133), while underneath all is 'The chord of change unchanging'. Canto 1 begins 'About the middle music of the spring' (13), Tristram is renowned for his skill as a harpist and singer, sings three songs in the course of the story, and teaches music to Iseult. The poem resounds with 'sea-music' (69), 'morning and the moon / Alternative in music' (113), 'the wind's clarion and the water's chime' (126); the battle of Tristram with Palamedes is a 'tempestuous tune' and a 'mighty music' (47), Merlin enjoys the mystic song of Nimue, and Iseult of Brittany's first sight of Tristram strikes her like 'a song out of the graves of years' (63). In the first intensity of their love, Tristram and Iseult are able to hear the 'choral thunders of the quiring spheres' (40). As everything in the poem aspires to unity of being, so all existence expresses the music of being.

## X

If all this is true, in what sense, if any, is *Tristram of Lyonesse* a tragedy? Neither Tristram nor Iseult is destroyed by a tragic flaw. The real tragic figure is Iseult of Brittany, who is unable to experience any sense of relation to the greater powers of the world, unable to undergo any epiphany, and after her frustration in love spends the seventh canto in bitter solitude invoking a God of righteous revenge who is but a projection of her own hatred. In a brilliant depiction of the inner torments that divide her, Swinburne describes how she spent 'all that year in Brittany forlorn',

> More sick at heart with wrath than fear of scorn
> And less in love with love than grief, and less
> With grief than pride of spirit and bitterness,
> Till all the sweet life of her blood was changed
> And all her soul from all her past estranged
> And all her will with all itself at strife
> And all her mind at war with all her life (104)

The verse slips queasily from one apparent cause to another, enacting her own bitterness, before turning into a sequence of parallel statements that stress how she has become an embodiment of the principle of division itself. Like Milton's Satan, Iseult of Brittany exhibits a progressive decline, so that when Tristram is dying, her replies come 'Soft as hate speaks within itself apart' (142). Her victory over the lovers is a pyrrhic one. When she speaks the fatal lie that the approaching ship has a black sail, Swinburne refers only to 'she that saw': she has lost even her name, and vanishes from the poem.

But there is another tragic element in *Tristram* that attaches not so much to a character as to the human condition itself, an element which Swinburne describes with the phrase 'our wound of living' (11). Without this wound, there would be nothing for Love to heal. Swinburne knew all about this quality of suffering in human experience, having lost his favourite sister Edith, who died aged 22 in 1863, and losing Mary Gordon to another man less than two years later.[21] Tristram is named after sorrow, and early in manhood is wounded in battle. Iseult helps to heal him with 'holy remedies / Made by her mother's magic' (18) not realizing at first that he has wounded her family by killing her uncle. Fear of some future trouble prompts her mother to make the potion which Tristram and Iseult mistakenly drink. Immediately after this Swinburne says they were 'Wounded, and each mouth trembled for a word' (38). The life of Iseult of Brittany is so 'wounded' it needs no commentary to point this out. That human life should be so wedded to suffering seems the tragedy, though this is at least balanced by the healing force of love – 'For life is born of love to wail and cry, / And love is born of life to heal his woes' (31).

## XI

The beginning and the end of *Tristram* confront us with two cosmic forces, Love and Fate, and various meanings have been ascribed to these words by critics. McSweeney felt that they were 'two names for the same process and that they do not stand for supernatural or transcendent forces'.[22] It is not easy to square this with the effect of some of Swinburne's language. By contrast, Harrison finds in *Tristram* 'a coherent and systematic monistic philosophy';[23] for him Fate is 'analogous to the world's presiding monistic life-force, Hertha' and 'a far more benevolent deity than man's God or than men can understand'.[24] But this is not all, for the attempt to construct a coherent cosmology from *Tristram* must embrace not only Love and Fate but also Chance – the 'chance' that, with 'sorcerous art', is responsible for what happens (150). It must also find a place for a God who appears under various guises ('incognisable', Old Testament jealous, and New Testament Christian), as well as Christ, Swinburne's own god of the Sun, and heaven and hell. It is not easy to see how these can be reconciled given the special difficulties of Swinburne's language, the interaction between his own sensibility and the medieval legend, his own ambivalences, and the way that philosophical accuracy and a stable metaphysic are at moments (especially canto 5) sacrificed to the desire to shock Victorian readers who have orthodox notions of 'sin'. It is a task of interpretation that will call for much patience and some ingenuity.

Does the lack of such coherence damage the poem? I do not think so. A century of exegesis has found much to argue over in other English epics (*Paradise Lost* springs to mind). We have grown used to celebrating poems that enthral us with their own struggles, not their delivery of 'answers'. *Tristram of Lyonesse* offers a similar spectacle.

## XII

I would like to conclude, not with an abstract argument about *Tristram of Lyonesse*, but with a reminder of its deep roots in Swinburne's life and sensibility. The success of the poem springs from the way the subject matter clearly magnetized his powers, even though composition was discontinuous over a period of thirteen years. *Tristram of Lyonesse* is the creation of a highly motivated poet, and the reasons for this are worth reviewing.

On a literary level, it is Swinburne's riposte to the handling of the story by Tennyson and Arnold. Swinburne felt the former had 'degraded and debased' it (*Letters*, 4:260), and that in Tennyson's version 'the story is rather a case for the divorce-court than for poetry' (*Works*, 16:405). He had as an undergraduate tried the legend in the Morris-like tercets of 'Queen Yseult', and knew that, as with *Poems and Ballads* (1866), here was another chance to shock contemporary readers.

But more importantly, he genuinely loved his material and its resonance with his own life and experience. Gosse rightly called Tristram and Iseult 'the life-long companions of his imagination' (*Works*, 19:54), and Edward Thomas said of *Tristram* and *The Tale of Balen* that 'he interwove with them the richest of his own spirit stuff'.[25] Swinburne called it 'the loveliest of medieval legends' (*Letters*, 4:260) and said that 'the story was my delight (as far as a child could understand it) before I was ten years old' (*Letters*, 3:332). Intending it to be, in Gosse's words, 'the very topstone of his poetical monument' (*Works*, 19:239), Swinburne was able to infuse the poetry with some of his most vivid experiences. The sixth canto's homage to 'The mighty moorlands and the sea-walls grey,/ The brown bright waters of green fells that sing' (93) is testimony to his childhood holidays of late summer spent at Capheaton in Northumberland, and later visits to the Trevelyans and William Bell Scott. Writing to Scott after the publication of *Tristram*, Swinburne said, 'you will admit the truthfulness – as far as it goes – of my description of Bamborough Castle, and its surroundings', and reminded him of 'the lovely view of the three blue herons on the ledge of a sea-rock' (*Letters*, 4:282) as they sailed to Grace Darling's lighthouse. Thus in the sixth canto we find:

> Blue as the clear north heaven, clothed warm with light,
> Stood neck to bended neck and wing to wing
> With heads fast hidden under, close as cling
> Flowers on one flowering almond-branch in spring,
> Three herons deep asleep against the sun (95)

In the same letter Swinburne refers to his memories of visits to North Cornwall, where he spent three months with John William Inchbold in 1864, and West Cornwall, with Jowett, in January 1874, and his attempt to describe the beauties of Tintagel, Kynance Cove, and the serpentine rocks of the Lizard. Part of canto 8, from 'Yet, sailing where the shoreward ripple curled' (118) to

'And leave it to be kissed and kindled of the sun' (121), was published under the title 'Kynance Cove' in the 1887 volume of *Selections.* Just after his return from West Cornwall, Swinburne wrote to Powell that the visit had 'left me in love for life with Kynance Cove where . . . I could live and die' (*Letters*, 2:266). It is worth quoting his lines on the visual impact of the rocks as they are briefly enamelled by sea-water into bright colour and then dull as they dry:

> And whensoever a strong wave, high in hope,
> Sweeps up some smooth slant breadth of stone aslope,
> That glowed with duskier fire of hues less bright . . .
> All its quenched flames and darkling hues divine
> Leap into lustrous life and laugh and shine
> And darken into swift and dim decline
> For one brief breath's space till the next wave run
> Right up, and ripple down again, undone (121)

These lines prove that, contrary to the view of his detractors, Swinburne did notice the detail of things. The sheet lightning mentioned in canto 2 may similarly draw on a memory of a channel crossing Swinburne made in 1855. As Oliver Elton observed, 'the whole story moves to the sound of mighty waters'.[26] This legend, with its various settings and journeys, allowed Swinburne plenty of scope to express his passion for the sea.

## XIII

But there is one further avenue of inspiration to be considered. *Tristram* repeatedly invokes the same ideal of Romantic love that Swinburne had mourned for in 'The Triumph of Time'. This goes beyond the mere fact that Tristram's wish to look upon the face of Iseult before he dies is a variation on the story of Rudel, who is alluded to in 'The Triumph of Time'. Compare the latter's 'Twain halves of a perfect heart, made fast / Soul to soul while the years fell past' (*Poems*, 1:35) with the lines 'And each one twain, incorporate sun with sun, / Star with star molten, soul with soul imbued' (33). The ideal is the same. The experience of identification which causes Catherine in *Wuthering Heights* to exclaim, 'Nelly, I am Heathcliff', impels Iseult to say 'I am he indeed, thou knowest, and he is I' (81). Not only does *Tristram* contain many phrases startlingly akin to the earlier lyric ('Though thy love save and my love save not me', (78), to name but one), it also re-states the same dream of Romantic union, and does so without irony. If it is true that 'Let come what will, there is one thing worth, / To have had fair love in the life upon earth' (I. 38), then whatever their destiny Tristram and Iseult at least are not denied such love. For this reason, *Tristram of Lyonesse* is not so tragic a telling of the story as other versions.

But pressing the connection further, it is possible to feel that, to some degree, his celebration of their love offered Swinburne a balm for what he called the 'reverse experience which left my young manhood a barren stock' (*Letters*, 3:51) – the fact that, unlike Gosse, he had been unable to win and keep the woman he loved. At least one critic has responded to the poem by saying 'Swinburne seems to be in love with Iseult, to give her the amorous adoration which had small outlet in the books since *Chastelard* and *Poems and Ballads*' and that 'he loves her before Tristram'.[27] For once in his poetry love is fulfilled and consummated, at least for a time. The fullness of *Tristram of Lyonesse* testifies to Swinburne's immersion in his theme, in song, if not in life, reversing the reverse experience.

## Notes

1. See my 'Swinburne in Miniature', *Victorian Poetry* 23 (1985), 3, 249–65.
2. Kerry McSweeney, *Tennyson and Swinburne as Romantic Naturalists* (1981), 165.
3. Ch'u Ta-Kao (trans.), *Tao Te Ching* (1972), 37.
4. Pauline Fletcher, *Gardens and Grim Ravines* (1983), 219.
5. David G. Riede, *Swinburne: A Study of Romantic Mythmaking* (Charlottesville, Virginia, 1978), 190.
6. Nicholas Tredell, 'Tristram of Lyonesse: Dangerous Voyage', *Victorian Poetry*, 20 (1982) 2, 97.
7. McSweeney, 216 n.17.
8. Anthony H. Harrison, *Swinburne's Medievalism* (1988), 106.
9. Tredell, 107.
10. Harrison, 131.
11. Harrison, 123.
12. Harrison, 112.
13. See my 'Swinburne Without Tears: A Guide to the Later Poetry', *Victorian Poetry*, 26 (1988), 4, 413–30.
14. Francis J. Sypher, 'Swinburne and Wagner', *Victorian Poetry*, 9 (1971), 1–2, 179.
15. Margot K. Louis, *Swinburne and His Gods* (1990), 81.
16. Riede, 168.
17. McSweeney, 175.
18. Richard D. McGhee, *Marriage, Duty, and Desire in Victorian Poetry and Drama* (Kansas, 1980), 203.
19. Harrison, 127.
20. Philipa Julian (ed.), *The Symbolists* (Oxford, 1973), pl. 24.
21. Swinburne's own 'wound of living' may also have included being brain-damaged at birth. See William B. Ober, 'Swinburne's Masochism: Neuropathology and Psychopathology', *Boswell's Clap and Other Essays* (1979, repr. 1988).
22. McSweeney, 166.
23. Harrison, 115.
24. Harrison, 110.
25. Edward Thomas, *Algernon Charles Swinburne* (1912), 211.
26. Oliver Elton, *A Survey of English Literature, 1830–1880* (1930), 71.
27. Thomas, 212.

# 6 The morality of *Poems and Ballads:* Swinburne and Ruskin

Judith Stoddart

In December 1865 Algernon Charles Swinburne received, 'with the old Lecturer's earnest regards', a presentation copy of *The Ethics of the Dust*. Nothing remains of this transaction but a record in a Sotheby sale catalogue;[1] there is no letter of acknowledgement, no indication of Swinburne's reaction to the work. The demure schoolgirls in *Ethics* have little in common with the cruel, sensuous women of the volume Swinburne was preparing for publication. His title, *Poems and Ballads*, with its emphasis on art's formal integrity, challenges Ruskin's reading of morality into matter. Given the distance between them, it is perhaps not surprising that Swinburne's response to the gift remains unrecorded. Perhaps he felt there was nothing to be said.

But Ruskin's reactions to the reciprocal gift of Swinburne's volume are recorded, in a much quoted letter of 9 September 1866. 'I did not like to thank you for the Poems before I had read them', he wrote to Swinburne of his presentation copy of *Poems and Ballads*,

> their power is so great, and their influence so depressing, that I can read but very little at a time. . . . There is assuredly something wrong with you – awful in proportion to the great power it affects and renders (nationally) at present useless. . . . So it was with Turner, so with Byron. It seems to be the peculiar judgment-curse of modern days that all their greatest men shall be plague-struck. . . . I cannot help you, nor understand you . . . But I shall rejoice in hearing that you are at work, and shall hope some day to see a change in the method and spirit of what you do. (*Letters*, 1:182)

Familiar terms of Ruskin's social criticism punctuate the response: 'depressing', 'useless', 'judgment curse', 'plauge-struck.' Swinburne's poetry is an expression of a fallen age, of a self-invested, unruly mentality for which Ruskin had prescribed in *Ethics* a regimen of 'home virtues', discipline and order. Swinburne could hardly have been surprised by Ruskin's judgement: as John Dixon Hunt explains, it was precisely 'in the face of a Victorian like Ruskin's sense of impropriety' that the poet had aimed his amoral verse.[2]

Or so the critical story goes. But was the relation between Ruskin and Swinburne really a simple tale of generational gaps and differences? There is little evidence that Swinburne read it that way. *Poems and Ballads* may, indeed, have represented a rejection of high Victorian values, but not necessarily of Ruskin. Swinburne submitted his manuscript more than once to the sage's inspection, and his letters indicate a solicitous regard for Ruskin's good opinion. When, over dinner, Ruskin admired one of the poems in the volume, Swinburne felt 'so much pleasure', as he told the elder critic, that 'I was determined to send it when I could,' and wrote out 'Before the Mirror' the next morning, despite the fact that it gave him 'far more labour to recollect and transcribe than it did originally to compose' (11 August, 1865; *Letters* 1:130). When urged by friends to suppress parts of *Chastelard* in 1865, it was to Ruskin whom Swinburne looked to settle 'the verdict of the world of readers and critics'. 'It was impossible', he told Lady Trevelyan, 'to have a fairer judge', and he praised the 'frankness with which [Ruskin] accepted' the verses (10 Dec. 1865; *Letters*, 1:141).

Lionel Stevenson sees in such gestures Swinburne's need for an acceptable 'father figure,' and certainly Ruskin's intervention with the Admiral over *Poems and Ballads* suggests he was prepared to play the role.[3] Yet the apostle of aestheticism could surely have found a more attractive model of authority. Ruskin had, after all, firmly declared his social commitments as early as 1860 with *Unto this last*. If the central section of Swinburne's critical essay *William Blake* – which traditionally has been read as the first English manifesto of 'art for art's sake' – was the poet's declaration of independence from Ruskin's commitments in 1862,[4] why did he continue to solicit the sage's support throughout the decade? In 1863 Swinburne had complained to W. M. Rossetti of Ruskin's confusion of 'philanthropic morality' with aesthetic value when reading an early manuscript of *Poems and Ballads* (8 August, *Letters* 1:186). The following summer, he sent Ruskin the manuscript again for approval. Was Swinburne simply playing the prodigal artist, hoping to be embraced by his father surrogate in spite of a few lusty and blasphemous verses? Or did he sense an underlying aesthetic affinity?

The often ambivalent relation between Ruskin and Swinburne conceals, as I will argue, a commonality of artistic purpose ignored by modern critics. The poet not only admired Ruskin: he gave poetic expression to an idea of art strikingly similar to Ruskin's moral aesthetic. In turn, the elder critic felt a sympathy with Swinburne which he rarely found with contemporary writers. The attraction between the Victorian sage and the young aesthete entails a revision of our picture of both figures. It also entails a rethinking of aesthetic genealogies in the period. In making *Poems and Ballads* stand for the transition in art 'from the mastication of social problems and moral and theological dilemmas to a more exotic diet',[5] critics have relied on a clear distinction between art and society alien to the Victorians. Both Ruskin's moralism and

Swinburne's advocacy of 'art for art's sake' depend on a fully contextualized theory of art. Both also rely on the Romantic ideal of art as fundamentally asocial, the product of inspired imagination. In balancing these competing claims, the two writers looked to each other for support and criticism. For Ruskin, Swinburne represented the next generation of Romanticism, the continuer of a line running from Byron to Turner that posed an alternative to the utilitarian aesthetic of Carlyle. For Swinburne, Ruskin was the proponent of an art unbridled by the Evangelical fervour of the age.

According to Jerome Buckley, the young author of *Poems and Ballads* was more accepting of his inheritance than many of his contemporaries and later critics might admit. Ruskin had 'full well realized' from the outset that Swinburne's was not a wholesale rebellion. Though in his verses Swinburne had 'self-consciously flouted an orthodox moral code', at heart he never really had repudiated the 'morality of art'.[6] Buckley explains Ruskin's tolerance by detoxifying Swinburne, by making him assimilable to traditional versions of a high Victorian aesthetic.

Ruskin rejected such a reading of Swinburne's verse. A passage omitted from a letter published in the Library Edition of Ruskin's works shows him unwilling to downplay Swinburne's transgressiveness. Ready to temper accounts of the poet's private behaviour, Ruskin at the same time insists on the integrity of the public voice of rebellion in *Poems and Ballads.* Moreover, he endorses Swinburne's attack on conventional Victorian morality. Critics missed the point when condemning the outspoken author of the volume, Ruskin told his correspondent. It was among 'men who talk with extreme propriety, whom the world wholly admires' that one should look for 'examples of vicious life'.[7] The sentiment was echoed in Ruskin's own publication of 1866, *The Crown of Wild Olive.*[8]

Expected by his friends to denounce Swinburne's 'amoral' verses, Ruskin instead declared his sympathy. 'I dare not be with him', Ruskin confessed, 'he would take me to the Devil along with him in despondency, though not in colour of thought. Even as it is I agree with much that he says'.[9] While one critic dismissed the volume as little more than 'rank blasphemy', (*Hyder*, 33) Ruskin expressed admiration for one of the most blatantly anti-Christian poems in the volume. 'I've got the original MS of the Hymn to Proserpine', he wrote to a friend of the poet, 'and wouldn't part with it for much more than leaf gold' (16 September 1866; *Letters* 1:184). Ruskin's attachment to this song of the 'last Pagan'[10] anticipates his advocacy of pagan mythology in *The Queen of the Air* (1869). But it also looks back to an important critical statement of 1860, when Ruskin, like Swinburne after him, fought to deliver art from a faith he no longer accepted.

The first volume of *Modern Painters* had been grounded in an unashamedly Christian aesthetic, culminating in the image of the 'almost human . . . almost spiritual . . . almost divine' sky, whose 'appeal to what is immortal in us is as distinct as its ministry of chastisement or of blessing to what is mortal is essential' (*Ruskin* 3:344). By the publication of volume 5 in 1860, the centre of value had radically shifted. No longer was art to 'look . . . pleasantly up to the sky' for inspiration, but great art was to 'stoop to the horror' of earth. 'All great and beautiful work', Ruskin declared, 'has come of first gazing without shrinking into darkness' (*Ruskin* 7:271). In the early volumes he had made Divine inspiration the index of artistic ability. Now he argued that only when 'the human spirit . . . by *its* courage and faith' (my emphasis) outfaced the darkness did it rise 'into conceptions of victorious and consummated beauty'. For Christianity, glorifying an ideal, spiritual state at the expense of man's animal nature, emasculated art. 'Great art confesses and worships' both animal and spiritual. 'Man being . . . the crowning and ruling work of God', he explained, 'it will follow that all his best art must have something to tell about himself, as the soul of things, and ruler of creation' (*Ruskin*, 7:264). It was now pagan art, not the work of the Christian Florentine or Venetian religious painters, that Ruskin argued most fully embodied the human condition.

The speaker in Swinburne's 'Hymn to Proserpine' stands at this aesthetic transition between the early and later volumes of *Modern Painters*. After the proclamation in Rome of Christianity, he, like Ruskin, judges the images produced by the new faith and by the classical vision. And like Ruskin, he finds that only the system celebrating humanity literally rises to 'conceptions . . . of consummated beauty'. Christianity celebrates a goddess 'pale and a maiden and sister to sorrow', 'weeping' and 'rejected'. But the unbridled pagan mind envisions a goddess with 'deep hair heavily laden with odour and colour of flowers', who, 'Clothed round with the world's desire as with raiment', 'Bent down unto us that besought her'. The speaker holds firm to this old, fertile faith which, as Ruskin had argued, 'confesses and worships' the whole of human nature. 'For me,' the speaker claims, 'their new device is barren, the days are bare'. In a posture reminiscent of Ruskin's art 'gazing without shrinking into darkness', he refuses to bend to a future hope, but 'standing, look[s] to the end'.[11]

As in *Modern Painters*, 'look' here has a special significance. Christianity, with its heavenward gaze, denies the beauty of material existence: 'Thou hast conquered, O Pale Galilean; the world has grown grey from thy breath.' But the last pagan, staring defiantly earthward, sees the beauty around him, and challenges the new god with his celebration of sensual images.

> Wilt thou yet take all, Galilean? but these thou shalt
>     not take,
> The laurel, the palms and the paean, the breasts of the
>     nymphs in the brake;
> Breasts more soft than a dove's, that tremble with
>     tenderer breath;
> And all the wings of the Loves, and all the joy before

death;
All the feet of the hours that sound as a single lyre,
Dropped and deep in the flowers, with strings that
flicker like fire.
More than these wilt thou give, things fairer than all
these things?
Nay, for a little we live, and life hath mutable wings.
A little while and we die; shall life not thrive as it
may?
For no man under the sky lives twice, outliving his day.
(*Poems* 1:68–69)

If the battle here is read in Ruskinian terms of an integrated, humanist art versus an emasculated, spiritual ideal, then the implications of 'Hymn to Proserpine' are quite different from those generally accepted. Ifor Evans, for example, sees the poem as a Baudelairean triumph of the painfully beautiful over Christian values of good and evil, a statement of a 'philosophy of aestheticism flamboyantly amoral'.[12] While this may at first seem a more apt description of other poems in the volume – of, for instance, 'Dolores', where the 'lilies and languors of virtue' are changed 'For the raptures and roses of vice' – it fails to account for the contrast between the images of beauty celebrated in that hymn to 'Our Lady of Pain' and those validated here.

The 'painfully beautiful' Dolores, though 'splendid', is as soulless and 'sterile' as the rejected Madonna in 'Hymn to Proserpine'. She, too, is 'pallid' and 'barren', frustrating her worshipper, while Proserpine fulfils him. As David Riede points out, the extreme sensualism in Swinburne's volume proves as fruitless and nihilistic as the hollow spiritualism it opposes. It is not 'presented as an alternative to Victorian prudery and complacency . . . but as a ghastly parody of it'.[13] The Gothic exaggerations of 'Dolores', ringing sensual changes on religious language and images, seem to play on Ruskin's terms of attack on Gothic revival architecture in *The Crown of Wild Olive*. Conceived as an expression of the 'great doctrine' of 'the remission of sins', Gothic architecture,

> too often, in certain phases of Christianity . . . [glorified] sin and sickness . . . as if, the more you had to be healed of, the more divine was the healing. The practical result of this doctrine, in art, is a continual contemplation of sin and disease . . . thus we have an architecture conceived in a mingled sentiment of melancholy and aspiration, partly severe, partly luxuriant, which will bend itself to every one of our needs, and every one of our fancies . . . (*Ruskin*, 18:446)

What Swinburne attacks in *Poems and Ballads* is a Christian morality which on the one hand celebrates pain and suffering, and on the other denies the integrity of sensual experience. As Riede argues, his target is 'the ethical position which . . . had dictated Western morality . . . based on a Socratic distinction between . . . soul and body'.[14] By denying the immortality of the soul in 'Hymn to Proserpine' ('Let my soul . . . find place, and forget what is done and undone' the speaker prays to the goddess of death) Swinburne insists on its identification with the mortal body, and images an art which celebrates their union in man. The speaker hymns, not an aesthetic divorced from morality, but an alternative moral aesthetic, one which naturally embraces both sides of human nature.[15]

This is precisely the distinction Swinburne draws in *Notes on Poems and Reviews* (1866), his response to those critics who implied that poems such as 'Dolores' could be made to stand for the philosophy of the volume. 'Where free speech and fair play are interdicted', he argues, 'foul hints and evil suggestions are hatched into fetid life' (*Works* 16:370). Literature 'worthy of men must be large, liberal, sincere', capable of expressing 'the full life of man and the whole nature of things'. His vision of an ideal 'virile' art (*Works*, 16:373) is not so different from Ruskin's ideal in volume 5 of *Modern Painters* of work which is 'universal and manly', encompassing the 'due power of every animal passion' (*Ruskin*, 7:296–7). Swinburne, like Ruskin, advocates an art celebrating 'man as the soul of things'.[16]

It might be objected that by insinuating Ruskinian polemic into his poetry, this parallel reading has confused the very distinction Swinburne fought to maintain in the 1860s. To see the 'Hymn to Proserpine' as proposing a positive moral theory of art seems to be committing what, as Swinburne reminds the reader of *William Blake*, Baudelaire called 'l'heresie de l'enseignement'; to read it, in other words, as a public statement, not as a self-contained aesthetic one. It is, however, Swinburne himself who in his essay on Baudelaire (written, like the 'Hymn to Proserpine', in 1862) provides an example of polemical reading. *Les Fleurs du mal* has 'nothing to do with didactic matter at all', he declares (*Works* 13:417). It is not a sermon or textbook but 'a piece of beautiful drawing' (*Works* 13:422). Yet even beautiful drawings, Ruskin had argued, have social contexts; and so here, Swinburne insists that each poem has 'a distinct and vivid background of morality to it'. 'There is not one of these poems', he claims, 'that could have been written in a time when it was not the fashion to dig for moral motives and conscious reasons' (*Works* 13:423).

Baudelaire himself rejected this critical caveat.[17] Swinburne never wholly did. This is, as Jerome McGann points out, the key difference between the authors of *Les Fleurs du mal* and of *Poems and Ballads*: Swinburne had tried to launch a public performance as Baudelaire had not (*McGann*, 205). *Notes on Poems and Reviews* deliberately dramatizes that performance, enacting for the reader the polemic between his poetry's internal form and external context. The essay, like that on Baudelaire, serves as a model of contextual reading, a model at the very centre of the vision of 'liberal, virile' art with which the essay ends. For when, according to Swinburne, 'all higher forms of the various arts are included within the limits of a stronger race' the exchange between poetry and society will be spontaneous, 'and no one will then need to assert . . . the simple laws of his art which no one will then be permitted to impugn' (*Works* 16:373).

This mutual understanding between art and society sounds surprisingly like Ruskin's own advocacy of a contextualized art, and Swinburne grows more Ruskinian as he gathers momentum. When the two mature together, Swinburne says, 'all accepted work will be noble and chaste . . . pure by instinct and fruitful by nature, no clipped and forced growth of unhealthy heat and unnatural air' (*Works* 16:373). Reflections like these determined Ruskin to work at transforming social structures.[18] Swinburne, on the other hand, vigorously denied the artist's responsibility to redeem the age and remould society (*Works* 13:417). Yet in his own attempts at a polemic in *Poems and Ballads* and *Notes on Poems and Reviews* he attempts at least to remould the public view of art. Declaring that the artist must be free from didacticism, he yet fashions a forceful lesson in critical reading. It is the method of the author of *Modern Painters*, who 'transfer[s] to his readers through description a new kind of relationship with the work of art.'[19]

The distinction between overt instruction and an attempt to provide by example a new way of seeing is made clear in Swinburne's essay on D. G. Rossetti's poem 'Jenny'. With a sympathetic prostitute as its subject, the poem could hardly be mistaken for a moral lesson. And yet, Swinburne argues, its mode of portraying her teaches the reader more about human nature than a sermon or actual account. The poem 'cleaves to absolute fact and reality closer than any common preacher or realist could do; no side of the study is thrown out or thrown back into false light or furtive shadow' (*Works* 15:34). In his defence of Rossetti, Swinburne advocates a Ruskinian realism highlighting every detail of a scene. Advising the poet on an early draft of 'Jenny', he had encouraged him in this case – as Ruskin was to do more generally – to reject symbolism and to hold to the 'vital, tangible, direct loveliness' and 'beautifully actual flesh and blood' of his descriptions (7 December 1869; *Letters* 2:64). Swinburne insisted on this point repeatedly in his letter, and it becomes apparent in his essay what he felt was at stake. Rossetti's poetic realism is used to demonstrate the superiority of the artist's way of seeing 'the outward and immediate matter of the day' (*Works* 15:37): 'the man whose thought is thus gloriously done into words is as other man are, only with a better brain and heart than the common, with more of mind and compassion, with better eye to see' (*Works* 15:35). The artist here is held up not as a moralizer, but as a seer who re-educates by example society's vision. 'To see clearly', Ruskin had argued in *Modern Painters*, 'is poetry, prophecy, and religion – all in one' (*Ruskin* 5:333).

This understanding of the artist's role permeates Swinburne's study of William Blake. If, Swinburne says, 'certain popular theories of the just aims of life, duties of an earnest-minded man, and meritorious nature of practical deeds and material services only, are absolutely correct – in that case the work of [Blake's] life is certainly a sample of deplorable waste and failure' (*Works* 6:132). In the lengthy theoretical centre of the book he insists that art can strike no compromises with conventional notions of social worth. Art, he argues, 'will help in nothing, of her own knowledge or freewill: upon terms of service you will get worse than nothing out of her' (*Works* 6:137). Most critics stop at this negation of the artist's role in society, using it to argue that Swinburne champions an 'exclusive view of the aesthetic, as something discontinuous with the rest of life . . . and concerned only with aesthetic effect.'[20] A few pages later, however, Swinburne does fill the gap left here between art and life. The theoretical exposition, he explains, was essential to understanding Blake's 'labours and purposes', to avoiding the dismissal of his 'eager incursions into grounds of faith or principle' as well-intentioned but mad attempts at a practical system. His work represents an aim altogether higher and more sweeping than such a reading: 'his design being merely to readjust all questions of such a kind by the light of art and law of imagination – to reduce all outlying provinces, and bring them under government of his own central empire – the 'fourfold spiritual city' of his vision' (*Works* 6:140).

To reinforce this picture of Blake's work, Swinburne produces the first critical analysis of the Prophetic Books, an analysis to which the last and longest section of the study is devoted. The final picture of Blake is not that of a proto-aesthete, as some have seen it, but of a visionary. 'No artist of equal power', Swinburne claims, 'had ever a keener and deeper regard for the meaning and teaching – what one may call the moral – of art' (*Works* 6:57). It is a moral embodied not in a set of doctrines, but in a way of seeing. The role Swinburne builds for the artist in this essay looks very like the one Ruskin sketched out in *The Stones of Venice*. 'It is not his business either to think, to judge, to argue, or to know', Ruskin had explained. 'They are for other men and other work . . . the work of his life is to be two-fold only; to see, to feel' (*Ruskin* 11:49).

Ruskin's sympathy with Swinburne's interpretation of the 'morality' of art comes through in one of his most frequently quoted but little considered remarks on the poet. In the first wave of public outcry against the frankness of *Poems and Ballads*, J. M. Ludlow, an eminent social reformer and teacher at the Working Men's College in London, tried to persuade Ruskin to use his influence with Swinburne to move his verse in a more productive direction. 'I should no more think of advising or criticising him,' Ruskin retorted, 'than of venturing to do it to Turner if he were alive again' (*Ruskin* 36:xlix). For Ruskin to compare anyone to Turner is worth noting. But the remark is particularly significant given both its date and its recipient.

By 1866 Ruskin had moved well beyond his beginnings as exclusively a critic of art. Meeting harsh reviews of his political treatises, he was anxious to prove his authority in public matters. And yet here, presented with a chance to demonstrate the relation between his judgement on art and on society – the relation understood, it seems from Ludlow's request, by those who took his social criticism seriously – he categorically dissociates the two and answers, not as the public-minded author of *The Crown of Wild Olive*, but in the recognizable voice of the art critic of *Modern Painters*. Ruskin, like Swinburne, refuses to make the artist a servant even to a cause he supports. His reply to Ludlow stresses, like Swinburne's essay on Blake, the integrity of the artist's vision. In a letter written three days after his response to Ludlow, Ruskin again emphasizes the difference between Swinburne's art and any of his own more apparently upright social writings. 'As for Swinburne not being my superior', he tells his correspondent, '. . . in power of imagination and understanding [he] simply sweeps me away before him as a torrent does a pebble. I'm *righter* than he is – so are the lambs and the swallows, but they're not his match' (*Ruskin* 36:xlix, original emphasis).

Ruskin's insistence on Swinburne's artistic integrity in this instance is often overlooked. Ruskin has been made to stand for the Carlylean position that 'the noble life is better than the production of noble art', an idea with which Swinburne, it is argued, tried to dispose in his study of Blake.[21] As Robert Hewison has pointed out, it was Ruskin's refusal to accept this principle that distinguished his artist/hero from Carlyle's.[22] For Ruskin, a great artist was always great by election, not by good works. 'Greatness in art', he wrote in *Modern Painters*, . . . is not a teachable nor gainable thing, but *the expression of a mind of a God-made great man*; . . . teach, or preach, or labour as you will, everlasting difference is set between one man's capacity and another's' (*Ruskin* 5:189; Ruskin's emphases).

Even after abandoning many of the early Evangelical tenets of his art criticism, Ruskin held to this one, as is evident in his letter to Swinburne on *Poems and Ballads*. 'I would as soon think of finding fault with you', he told the poet, 'as with a thunder-cloud or a nightshade blossom. All I can say of you, or them – is that God made you, and that you are very wonderful and beautiful' (*Letters* 1:182). Publicly to challenge the direction of Swinburne's art would be to deny this instinctive, God-given authority of the artist's vision which Ruskin had worked to establish in *Modern Painters*. 'All the great men,' he had claimed,

> see what they paint before they paint it . . . the whole scene, character, or incident passing before them as in second sight, whether they will or no . . . they not daring, under the might of its presence to alter one jot or tittle of it as they write it down . . . it being to them in its own kind and degree always a true vision or Apocalypse. (*Ruskin* 5:114)

The artist is, according to Ruskin, literally a 'seer', and the instinctive truth of his imagination ensures his place as a primary teacher in society. Binding the artist's vision to a particular moral ideology, in an age when moral systems were under attack, would jeopardize that role.

This argument also ensured that art remained outside the judgement of contemporary systems Ruskin could not accept. The economists' standard of utility, for example, was irrelevant when a work of art was seen not as a material object but as a prophecy. Nor could art be evaluated as a commodity. 'What you can manufacture or communicate,' Ruskin stated, 'you can lower the price of, but this mental supremacy is incommunicable; you will never multiply its quantity, nor lower its price' (*Ruskin* 5:189). The artist's instinct set him apart from conventional measures of value, an argument Swinburne was quick to seize on in his effort to release art from 'the creeds that refuse and restrain'.

Like Ruskin, Swinburne fought against the intrusion of scientific method into aesthetic judgement. Neither science nor art, he argued in *William Blake* 'need wish to become valuable or respectable to the other: each must remain, on its own ground and to its own followers, a thing of value and deserving respect' (*Works* 6:144). There could be no compromise between 'the imagination which apprehends the spirit of a thing and the understanding which dissects the body of a fact' (*Works* 6:143). To ask the artist to follow laws alien to his imagination would be to ask him to produce something other than art, for all great artists' work was born of 'an instinct', an 'evident and native impulse' (*Works* 15:4–5). For Swinburne, as for Ruskin, the artist must follow this inner vision. In the matter of art, Swinburne claimed,

> proscription and prescription are alike unavailing; it is equally futile to bid an artist forego the natural bent of his genius or to bid him assume the natural office of another . . . if ever he attempt to force his genius into unnatural service, constrain it to some alien duty, the most praiseworthy purpose imaginable will not suffice to put life or worth into the work so done. Art knows nothing of choice between the two kinds of preference of the one to the other; she asks only that the artist shall 'follow his star' . . . (*Works* 13:245–46)

The artist's task, in other words, is to be true to his art, not to be acceptable to his society.

In this Romantic view of art, the responsibility of translating the writer's special vision falls not on him, but on his audience. The artist may be an exemplary seer, Ruskin stressed in *The Queen of the Air*, but it is the public who must learn to interpret and apply his prophecies. All 'pieces of [great] art', he explains in an echo of Swinburne's *Blake*, 'are didactic in the purest way, indirectly and occultly, so that, first, you shall only be bettered by them if you are already hard at work on bettering yourself, and when you *are* bettered by them it shall be . . . by a gift of unexpected truth, which you shall only find by slow mining for it' (*Ruskin* 19:308). Writing to Swinburne's father about the reception of *Poems and Ballads*, he emphasized the audience's responsibility to discern the volume's value. The problem, he assured him, was not with his son's vision but with society's. 'The common world', Ruskin complained, 'cannot distinguish between Correggio's Antiope, and a Parisian street lithograph . . . The real guilt is on the part of those who have degraded themselves to this error'. A discriminating reader would, he suggested, see only the purity of the volume: 'the more I read it – the nobler I think it is. It *is* diseased – no question – but – as the blight is . . . on the moss-rose . . . and does not touch . . . however terrible – the nature of the flower' (18 September 1866; *Letters* 1:165). If you are Ruskin, you see the rose; the common world sees superficial imperfections. There is no suggestion here that the poet himself bears responsibility for the disparity in the readings, that he should clean up his verse for the reader. If the public could not get beyond the surface, Ruskin wrote to a friend, 'don't blame [Swinburne], but ask yourself what *national* fault it is' which obscured the purity of his work.[23]

Obscurity of some kinds was even good for the reader. The truth of a work, Ruskin claimed, was often 'withheld on purpose, and close-locked, that you may not get it till you have forged the key of it in a furnace of your own heating' (*Ruskin* 19:308). This belief in the benefit of meaning which had to be worked or 'slow-mined' for would have led Ruskin to appreciate the obscurity of the texts on which many of the poems in Swinburne's volume were based.[24] Ruskin was himself fond of using cryptic titles and references in his works. He stressed Swinburne's learnedness in a letter to a correspondent who had challenged the poet's abilities: 'he is simply one of the mightiest scholars of his age in Europe – knows Greek, Latin, and French as well as he knows English . . . knows nearly all the best literature of the four languages as well as I know – well – better than I know anything' [*Ruskin* 36:xlix]. His view was shared by W. M. Rossetti. In his language, allusions and technical showmanship, Rossetti remarked, Swinburne made few allowances for a general audience. He was, in short, a 'poet for poetic students':

> His writings exercise a great fascination over qualified readers, and excite a very real enthusiasm in them; but these readers are not of that wide, popular, indiscriminate class who come to a poet to be moved by the subject matter, the affectingly told story, the sympathetic interpreting words which in giving voice to the poet's own emotion or perception, find utterance also for those of the universal and inarticulate order . . . (*Hyder*, 71–72)

Ruskin, too, complained of those readers who expected to find their own thoughts confirmed by great writers. To read rightly meant to 'enter into' the ideas of great writers, 'not to find your own expressed by them' (*Ruskin* 18:63). The poet does not speak to or for the masses, but to the serious seeker of knowledge who learns to decipher and understand the language of art.

There seems to be an uncomfortable tension between this notion of an aristocracy of art and Swinburne's and Ruskin's ideal of a polemical art grounded firmly in its social context, aspiring to spontaneous exchange with its audience. In fact, it is a tension which persists in both writers' works and which neither managed to resolve. Five years after *Poems and Ballads* was published, Ruskin began his monthly 'Letters to the Workmen and Labourers', *Fors Clavigera* (1871–84), a paradigm of this ambivalence in its declared intention of social involvement on the one hand, and its Latin title and preoccupation with fine art and artists on the other.[25] It is not so surprising, then, that while he particularly prized the 'Hymn to Proserpine' – the poem advocating an engaged, encompassing art – he also greatly admired 'Before the Mirror', one of the most enigmatic, unengaged pieces in *Poems and Ballads.* Its speaker refuses to turn the image of the girl before the mirror into narrative, refuses to envelop it in emotion: in W. M. Rossetti's words, refuses to give the 'popular class' the 'affectingly told story' or moving subject matter. For the educated reader, however, there would have been an unavoidable subtext to help decipher the poem's meaning: the story of Narcissus, unsuccessfully trying to approach his beautiful reflection until in frustration he kills himself, and his blood is changed into a flower.[26]

To 'follow one's star' is shown in this poem to have beautiful but disastrous consequences – a story not so different from the one told in a familiar Victorian poem exploring the contrast between a privileged and a socially engaged art, the celebration of beauty and of humanity: Tennyson's 'Palace of Art'.[27] To see Swinburne's *Poems and Ballads* as involved in that question as the work of two of his major contemporaries is to understand, for example, the connection between it and Swinburne's next volume, *Songs before Sunrise*, his celebration of the revolutions in Italy. It represents not so much a 'turning away from the subject matter of *Poems and Ballads*', as Philip Henderson would have it, (*Henderson*, 134) as an exploration of one of its underlying themes: the connection between art and society, the realization of an aesthetic celebrating 'man as the soul of things'.

This reading of Swinburne concludes, then, with the poet of *Poems and Ballads* at the heart of the Victorian – and Romantic – dilemma between public and private poetry, not at the head of a new aesthetic movement. Wherever he eventually may have sided – I agree with McGann when he says that *Poems and Ballads*, Second Series, remained 'innocent of the world as the earlier had not' (*McGann*, 206) – it is necessary to re-examine the early roots of Swinburne's art. Ruskin's appreciation of the young poet suggests recognition of a kindred spirit. To ignore such a reception – or to relegate it to a passing citation – is to ignore the resonances of Swinburne's verse for an influential reader, and thus to overlook the assumptions and ideals of art which the two men shared. It was an aesthetic relation which Swinburne himself knew had to be confronted. 'Any artist worthy of his rank,' he admitted to Ruskin, 'must be . . . of course desirous to meet you . . . to let you see his immediate work . . . to have it out with you face to face' (11 August 1865; *Letters* 1:130).

## Notes

1. *Sale Catalogues of Libraries of Eminent Persons, vol. 6, Poets and Men of Letters*, ed. John Woolford (1972), 314. The volume of *Ethics* was purchased by J. H. Whitehouse and is now a part of the collection at the Ruskin Galleries, Bembridge School, Isle of Wight.
2. John Dixon Hunt, *The Pre-Raphaelite Imagination, 1848–1900* (1968), 233.
3. Lionel Stevenson, *The Pre-Raphaelite Poets* (Chapel Hill, North Carolina, 1972), 226. For Ruskin's letter of 18 September 1866 to the poet's father see *Letters* 1.185–6.
4. Robert L. Peters, *The Crowns of Apollo: A Study in Victorian Criticism and Aesthetics* (Detroit, 1965), 65.
5. Kerry McSweeney, *Tennyson and Swinburne as Romantic Naturalists* (Toronto, 1981), 125.
6. Jerome Buckley, *The Victorian Temper: A Study in Literary Culture* (Cambridge, Mass. 1951), 173.
7. Letter to W. H. Harrison, 17 September 1866; unpublished passages quoted from the Ruskin transcripts with the permission of the Bodleian Library Oxford (Ms Eng. misc. c.249, f.213). Reprinted in part in *The Works of John Ruskin*, ed. E. T. Cook and Alexander Wedderburn, 39 vols. (1903–12), 36: xlix. hereafter indicated in the text as *Ruskin*.
8. See, for example, his attack on the middle-class citizens assembled for the dedication of the Bradford Exchange in 'Traffic' (1864; repr. in *The Crown of Wild Olive*). William Buckler has noted this connection between the social message of *Poems and Ballads* and *The Crown of Wild Olive*, for both works strike out at 'the illusion of a monolithic cultural coherence that church, state, and a conservative press might like to sustain' (*The Victorian Imagination: Essays in Aesthetic Exploration* (New York, 1980) 256–7. John Morley complained of the tone of Swinburne's 'vindictive and scornful' look at modern society; his talk 'of snakes and fire, of blood and wine and brine, of perfumes and poisons and ashes, grows sickly and oppressive on the senses' (*Saturday Review* 4 August 1866; *Hyder*. 29, 25). It is interesting to compare the language of Ruskin's 1866 preface to *The Crown of Wild Olive*. As he develops his metaphor of a corrupt society, his phrases seem not so very far from the 'things monstrous and fruitless' in Swinburne's verse: the 'black slime' of a river 'defi*[ed]*' with 'putrid clothes' lies 'circled and coiled under festering scum', in places 'chastis *[ed]* to purity' by the 'trembling and pure . . . body' of the current.
9. Letter quoted above (Bod. Ms Eng. misc. c.249, f.213). Ruskin may have been reacting to Swinburne's forceful letter to him earlier that year, in which he had defended life without faith (*Letters* 1:159–60). The argument of the letter is echoed in Ruskin's preface to *The Crown of Wild Olive*, where he explores whether, 'all the peace and power and joy you can ever win, must be won now, and all fruit of victory gathered here, or never.' In a letter to Swinburne, Ruskin admitted that while he might question the poet's purpose in publishing the volume, he could all too easily identify with the sentiments expressed in it. 'For the matter of it', he wrote, 'I consent too much – I regret much – I blame, or reject nothing' (9 September 1866; *Letters* 1:182).
10. The name Swinburne used to refer to his poem in a letter to Lady Trevelyan, 10 December 1865; *Letters* 1:141.
11. This echo between the two writers' thoughts is repeated in an unexpected concurrence of views on Carlyle's *Frederick the Great*. No fan of Carlyle's works,

Swinburne nevertheless admired his portrait of the ruler as a man of 'clear, cold purity of pluck, looking neither upward nor around for any help or comfort' (15 March 1865; *Letters* 1:115–16). Ruskin wrote to Carlyle that he had convincingly 'shown the power of living without faith – in charity and utility'; Frederick's confession of the 'impossibilities of believing anything is to me the most precious passage of the whole book' (c. 25 September 1870; repr. in *The Correspondence of Thomas Carlyle and John Ruskin*, ed. George Allen Cate (Stanford, 1982), 153).

12. B. Ifor Evans, *English Poetry in the Later Nineteenth Century* (2nd ed. 1966), 49.
13. David G. Riede, *Swinburne: A Study of Romantic Mythmaking* (Charlottesville, Virginia, 1978), 59.
14. Riede, 59.
15. Such a reading would make the poem fit into Julian Baird's moral context for the volume. Using Swinburne's essay on Blake to situate Swinburne's views of Theism and Pantheism, Baird argues that the theme of *Poems and Ballads* is that ' "all deities reside in the human breast" '; that except humanity there is no divine thing or person (*Works* 16: 269n; quoted by Baird in 'Swinburne, Sade, and Blake: The Pleasure-Pain Paradox', *Victorian Poetry* 9 (1971), 53).
16. For a revealing look at the implications of this shared emphasis on a 'manly' art, see Richard Dellamora, *Masculine Desire: The Sexual Politics of Victorian Aestheticism* (Chapel Hill, North Carolina, 1990), chapter 4 ('Poetic Perversities of A. C. Swinburne') and 123ff.
17. 'Permettez-moi . . . de vous dire que vous avez poussé un peu loin ma défense', Baudelaire wrote to his young reviewer. 'Je ne suis pas si *moraliste* que vous feignez obligeamment de le croire' (10 October 1863; Baudelaire's emphasis; *Letters* 1:88).
18. Ruskin had complained in *The Seven Lamps of Architecture* (1849) of the effect of 'cramped' social conditions and 'minute misanthropy' on national architecture. The art of modern England could be recognized by its 'formalised deformity . . . shrivelled precision . . . starved accuracy' (*Ruskin* 8:136). The work of a healthy, expansive society would, by contrast, be 'kingly', 'pure' and 'serene'.
19. Elizabeth Helsinger, *Ruskin and the Art of the Beholder* (Cambridge, Mass, 1982), 16.
20. R. V. Johnson, *Aestheticism* (1969), 61.
21. Peters, 65.
22. Robert Hewison, *John Ruskin: The Argument of the Eye* (1976), 144.
23. 17 September 1866; Bod. MS Eng. misc. c.249, f.213.
24. Even in the nineteenth century, several of the myths and figures were recognizable only with the aid of Lemprière's Classical Dictionary. See John Morley's reaction (*Hyder*, 23).
25. Contemporary readers were also uneasy with this combination. 'We could understand Mr. Ruskin's "serial" much better', wrote one reviewer, 'if we were at liberty, as we are not, to regard it as a semi-ironical Platonic monologue addressed to educated men. As such, it would have much merit, but the working classes will be able to make nothing of it . . . The illustrations, which delight the cultivated eye, will be as much *caviare* to them as the text.' (*The Guardian*, 16 August 1871, 995).
26. The girl in 'Before the Mirror' is repeatedly described as – and sees herself in the reflection as – a rose. An expectation of death is created in the second stanza ('Late rose whose life is brief'), and the poem ends in a metaphorical drowning in

a stream, evoking the stream into which Narcissus, in some versions of the myth, threw himself.

27. Leonard M. Findlay singles out this poem of Tennyson's as expressing the Poet Laureate's irreconcilable difference with Swinburne's practice. He speculates that the 'aestheticism of *Poems and Ballads* . . . must have been galling to a man who had conquered his own strong attraction to such a philosophy of art only after a hard struggle' ('Swinburne and Tennyson'. *Victorian Poetry*, 9 (1971), 224). Findlay's narrative of rivalry between the poets seems too neatly constructed. Although he produces an interesting reading of Tennyson's 'Lucretius', he is so firmly locked into the categories of aesthete and moralist that he never considers what the poetic echoes between the two writers have to say about Swinburne's practice. W. David Shaw's version of the Laureate in *Tennyson's Style* (Ithaca, 1976) would make a strong beginning to a very different story of relationship. His view of Tennyson's visionary artist and his Swinburneian 'subversive speculations' (316) suggests a continuing development of Romantic concerns through the end of the nineteenth century. In this more integrated model of Victorian poetics, Swinburne would be read less as a poet whose verse breaks out of conventional models, than as one who revives a Romantic agenda in altered circumstances. In his prose writings he was in fact dedicated to reinterpreting the earlier poets for his Victorian audience, an enterprise applauded by Ruskin (see Swinburne's letter of 22 March 1866; *Letters* 1:161).

# 7 The politics of Sado-Masochism: Swinburne and George Eliot

Dorothea Barrett

On the face of it, George Eliot and Algernon Charles Swinburne would seem to represent opposite extremes of the Victorian spectrum. She has been called 'the moralist of the Victorian revolution', 'Pallas with prejudices and a corset', the exponent of an ethos of duty and renunciation. He has been called 'the Red Flag incarnate', 'the libidinous laureate of a pack of satyrs', the exponent of a 'prurient poetics'. She was a female novelist of the first generation of Victorians, from a lower-middle-class background, and has been seen as the epitome of the mid-Victorian belief in art for moral instruction. He was a male poet of the second generation of Victorians, from an aristocratic family, and an enthusiast of aestheticism, one of the movements which, according to Oliver Elton, was instrumental in the posthumous decline of George Eliot's literary reputation.

Donald Thomas, in his biography of Swinburne, describes George Eliot's 'moral intensity' as 'almost the opposite of Swinburne's aestheticism'.[1] Swinburne himself referred to George Eliot as 'an Amazon thrown sprawling over the crupper of her spavined and spur-galled Pegasus' (*Works*, 14:12). Edmund Gosse found Swinburne obsessed by the idea that 'George Eliot was hounding on her myrmidons to his destruction.'[2]

Yet these two very disparate contemporaries had a great deal in common. Although of different generations, their careers were roughly coextensive in that Swinburne's first published work appeared in 1861, only five years after George Eliot's, and his best poetry had been written by the time of her death in 1880. They were the two most learned writers of their period, and each has been criticized for putting too much learning and too little poetic inspiration into the production of literature. Both were influenced by the Pre-Raphaelites in the early 1860s, and George Eliot's *Romola* (1863) is as self-consciously Pre-Raphaelite as Swinburne's poetry before 1865. They had several friends in common, among them Monckton Milnes, although the face he presented at

George Eliot's Sunday salons at the Priory must have been very different from that he showed the admirer of de Sade. Mathilde Blind, George Eliot's first biographer, was unrequitedly in love with Swinburne. Both George Eliot and Swinburne were interested in and sympathetic to the struggles of the Jews, a subject that found little sympathy among other major Victorian literati. Swinburne's poem 'On the Persecution of the Jews', published in 1882, followed George Eliot's *Daniel Deronda* (1876) and *The Impressions of Theophrastus Such* (1880), both of which dealt sympathetically with Judaism. Swinburne and George Eliot were both admirers of Mazzini. Each passed from a youth of rebellions against political, religious, and moral convention, to avowed conservatism in later life. The second half of each of their lives was passed in the care of a loving and reverent male protector (G. H. Lewes called George Eliot 'Madonna'; Watts-Dunton referred to Swinburne as 'The Bard'). Both George Eliot and Swinburne enjoyed their highest acclaim in their own lifetimes; both literary reputations suffered drastic posthumous decline. Both names, on everyone's lips in the 1860s and 70s, were rarely mentioned by the 1920s and 30s.

However, the affinity on which I wish to focus here is none of these. The most striking similarity between Swinburne and George Eliot lies in their treatments of sexuality, and in the intimate connection between the political and sexual in their work.

It is a commonplace observation that Swinburne's poetry is riddled with lesbianism, sado-masochism, incest, and death-wish. It is also commonplace to link the breaking of sexual taboos with cultural, religious, and political iconoclasm. This, of course, is problematic, and in Swinburne studies the problems become most obvious when the sexual deviations one has been assiduously relating to revolutionary verve prove to be, in Swinburne's case, autonomous and demonstrably stronger than any political belief. The most discouraging example is his enthusiasm, in 1876, for the Turkish leader Sadick Bey, whose career of violence and rape in Bulgaria so impressed Swinburne that it completely eclipsed his prior sympathy for the persecuted race. However, it is essential to distinguish between judging a poet's personal proclivities (which are none of our business) and exploring how these are used and transmuted in the process of textual production. Many critics have ignored the more disturbing elements of Swinburne's poetry because of an aversion to the biographical correlatives, preferring, rather, to emphasize his formal excellence. This, I think, is a great disservice to Swinburne studies, since, for all his worship of art for art's sake, Swinburne is most memorable not for the excellences of his form but rather for the disturbances of his content. This too he shares with George Eliot, who is outranked in terms of structural unity not only by arguably disturbing writers such as Jane Austen and Henry James but also, as Raymond Williams has pointed out, by Trollope. Lionel Stevenson has succinctly elucidated the contribution that Swinburne's sexual preoccupations made to his poetic effectiveness:

> His fixation upon passionate and often perverse sex challenged the prudish taboos of his era; his assertion that physical love is a compound of ecstasy and agony contradicted the sentimental stereotype of domestic affection; his fatalistic insistence upon the prevalence of cruelty, both in individual behaviour and in the human predicament, negated alike the smug belief in a benevolent deity and the Rousseauistic faith in man's innate goodness.[3]

I have suggested elsewhere that very similar claims can be made for George Eliot.[4] Her critical canon has been characterized by a tendency to see her as earnestly didactic, and her novels as texts that answer rather than raise questions. This trend was encouraged by Marian Lewes herself, and the persona she presented at her Sunday salons in the 70s, though exacting almost worshipful devotion at the time, was clearly instrumental in the posthumous decline of her literary reputation. The commentary of F. W. H. Myers, Charles Bray, and John Walter Cross shortly after her death emphasized the sybilline, selfless, and sexless image her own anxiety for vindication had created. Their comments echo through the generations of subsequent criticism, quoted and requoted by conservative critics eager to claim her and by radical and feminist critics only too willing to abandon her to a conservative and patriarchal tradition. The result has been the formation of critical cataracts, obscuring what was perfectly apparent to her contemporaries: that in George Eliot we confront a strongly erotic and subversive imagination. The subversiveness is most fully apparent in the erotic elements of her work, and both are submerged, but only just, beneath the surface of her texts. Neither the existence of such elements nor their submersion is surprising when we reflect that those texts were the means by which Marian Lewes – the plain and provincial lower-middle-class spinster who lived openly with a married man – became George Eliot, a leading novelist, moralist, and intellectual of her time.

Swinburne, by contrast, had little motivation to conceal, either consciously or otherwise, his political and sexual identity. Lionel Stevenson claims that Shelley, Byron, and Swinburne, the only major poets produced by England's aristocracy, were unparalleled in

> their defiance of accepted political opinions and moral restraints . . . social prestige protected the occasional deviant nobleman from the sort of anxiety about financial resources or public opinion which may handicap less privileged persons in departing from convention. Artistocratic origin guaranteed freedom to be as eccentric as one pleased . . .[5]

Stevenson's point is undeniable, but why use that tone of condescension? He implies that, because their open expression was a privilege of aristocracy, the revolutionary elements of Shelley, Byron, and Swinburne can be dismissed as the rantings of over-indulged children. We should rather regret that 'anxiety about financial resources or public opinion' silenced or muted the radical impulses of their less privileged literary peers. In the case of George Eliot, rebellion, eroticism, and rage were not silenced, but they were certainly forced underground to erupt spasmodically through a narrative surface of conventional appearance.

The distortion of our image of Geroge Eliot has led critics of all political colours to listen too credulously to the 'wise woman' narrator, and to assume that her presence is pervasive and in full control of the texts. I suggest that in each of the major novels, the 'wise woman' is just one facet of a fluctuating and self-divided narratorial presence. Other facets reveal other identities, far from the earnestly didactic, and it is in these that we can detect the affinities between Swinburne and George Eliot.

William Myers has remarked elements of sadism and masochism in the characterization of Dinah, in *Adam Bede*,[6] David Smith has argued that Maggie Tulliver, in *The Mill on the Floss*, has an incestuous love for her brother Tom;[7] and Dierdre David has noted that Gwendolen, in *Daniel Deronda*, seems to love her mother 'lover-wise'.[8] Alexander Welsh has remarked that the George Eliot canon is full of tales of love and murder, often involving a woman with a knife wanting to stab her lover or husband: Tina in 'Mr Gilfil's Love Story'; Laure in *Middlemarch*; Gwendolen in *Daniel Deronda*.[9] In both her male and her female characters, the sexual is closely linked to the violent: Janet Dempster is beaten by her husband: Hetty Sorrel kills the child that is evidence of her sexual knowledge; Lydgate is in danger of strangling Rosamond. When taken together, these elements constitute not occasional aberrations in an otherwise earnestly didactic canon but a pervasive counter-discourse, a discourse of the body running concurrently and often at cross-purposes with the discourse of intellect and moral philosophy. The result of this is not collapse of meaning, loss of purpose and integrity, but a constant binding together, breaking in conflict, and recombining, a pervasive dialectical engagement of heart and head, body and mind, reality and possibility.

This entwining of the two meanings of the word 'passion', this proximity of love and violence, is one reason why George Eliot repeatedly insists upon the need, in both men and women, for vocation, not merely occupation, for a task engrossing enough to preclude all thoughts of self and the pain to which that self is constantly subjected. The reflexivity of 'Armgart', which Gillian Beer has discussed at length, illuminates George Eliot's view of the relation between vocation, love, and murder:

> She often wonders what her life had been
> Without that voice for channel to her soul.
> She says, it must have leapt through all her limbs –
> Made her a Maenad – made her snatch a brand
> And fire some forest, that her rage might mount
> In crashing roaring flames through half a land,
> Leaving her still and patient for a while.

'Poor wretch!' she says, of any murderess –
'The world was cruel, and she could not sing:
I carry my revenges in my throat;
I love in singing and am loved again.'[10]

In *Felix Holt*, we are told of 'that higher consciousness which is known to bring higher pains', and in all George Eliot's novels, pleasure occurs in inverse proportion to consciousness: the lower the consciousness the more capable it is of experiencing pleasure. This explains why, in George Eliot's fiction, all seductions and murders take place in a semi-conscious haze. One might accept this and yet maintain that George Eliot stands firmly on the side of higher consciousness and higher pains, and that is clearly the ideal to which Marian Lewes aspired, but the implied author behind the novels is torn between the two. The discourse of language and desire can be traced throughout the canon; it is ambivalent, disturbed, self-questioning. Time and time again the reader is confronted with the volcanic power of thwarted desire which inevitably erupts in a painful catharsis. The association of love and murder in this way anticipates what Freud was to approach at the end of his career: the notion that Eros and Thanatos are identical.

Having located the elements of violent and deviant sexuality in both George Eliot and Swinburne, the question arises, Why are they there? What purpose do they serve? Are they simply, in Swinburne's case, as several critics have suggested, a display of personal proclivities best kept under cover? In George Eliot's case, are they merely the splenetic outbursts of a self she spent her life trying to restrain, a self quite other than the achieved self who was the great artist and thinker? Needless to say, I think not. For Swinburne sado-masochism provided a network of rich metaphoric complexity with which to describe the world. In *Lesbia Brandon* he uses it as a metaphor for the writing and reading of poetry; in *Songs Before Sunrise* as a metaphor for the revolutionary's relation to his country; in 'On the Russian Persecution of the Jews' as a metaphor for humanity's relation to God. Perhaps 'metaphor' is not the appropriate word here, because when Swinburne uses images of flogging to describe the sensations caused by the writing and reading of poetry he is not simply comparing two disparate entities that share one similar attribute: he is locating a root form from which all human interaction is generated. And in these contexts it is recognizable to people of the most home-spun sexual preferences. Swinburne's discussion of sado-masochism in its broadest context allows us to confront the mutability and proximity of pleasure and pain not only in our personal but also in our political and religious lives.

We can see this in the poem 'On the Russian Persecution of the Jews':

O son of man, by lying tongues adored,
  By slaughterous hands of slaves with feet red-shod
  In carnage deep as ever Christian trod

Profaned with prayer and sacrifice abhorred
And incense from the trembling tyrant's horde,
  Brute worshippers or wielders of the rod,
  Most murderous even of all that call thee God,
Most treacherous even that ever called thee Lord;
Face loved of little children long ago,
  Head hated of the priests and rulers then,
    If thou see this, or hear these hounds of thine
    Run ravening as the Gadarean swine,
Say, was not this thy Passion, to foreknow
  In death's worst hour the works of Christian men?

(*Poems*, 5: 245)

There is nothing deviant or objectionable in this poem, and yet it contains the same juxtapositions of passion and pain that were found objectionable in *Poems and Ballads* of 1866. In a religious context these things are not deviant. The sado-masochistic elements of the Judaeo-Christian tradition, which Nietzsche described as slave-mentality, and which is most evident in Medieval religious painting and the lives of the saints, are encapsulated in the use of that word 'passion' for the sufferings of Christ. In this poem, Swinburne anticipates Graham Greene's image of the punch-drunk Christ at the end of *The Heart of the Matter*, which even mid-twentieth-century agnostic critics found disturbing and blasphemous. Beneath the poignant indictment of persecution is a disturbing portrait of man's need to profane and humiliate what he worships.

In *Adam Bede*, George Eliot explores religious fervour as a mask over and transmutation of desires that cannot consciously be recognized or admitted. Hetty and Dinah have been seen by critics as representatives of egoism and altruism, a reproduction of the conventional harlot/madonna dichotomy. I suggest that both are ambivalently treated and that through them women's vocational and sexual needs are dialectically explored. What the narrator tells us elevates Dinah and condemns Hetty, but what we are shown tends to question Dinah and vindicate Hetty. The novel can be read as a battle between the rebel and the reactionary within George Eliot.

William Myers has pointed out that when, in the chapter entitled 'Two Bed-Chambers', Dinah imagines Hetty's future travails, the gory physical details suggest that Dinah is having sadistic fantasies about her rival for Adam's love. In light of this, Dinah's meditations in her bed-chamber can be seen as sexual fantasies about Adam, with whom she has had her deeply disturbing first contact that day.

> She closed her eyes, that she might feel more intensely the presence of a Love and Sympathy deeper and more tender than was breathed from the earth and sky. That was often Dinah's mode of praying in solitude. Simply to close her eyes, and to feel herself enclosed by the Divine Presence; then gradually her fears, her yearning anxieties for others, melted away like ice-crystals in a warm ocean.[11]

The succession of verbs in this passage describes the systole and diastole of female sexual response. The interchangeability of sexual and religious feeling has been explicitly discussed in the context of Seth's love for Dinah: 'Love of this sort is hardly distinguishable from religious feeling. What deep and worthy love is so?'[12] And the passage bears a striking resemblance to one of Marian Evans's early letters.

> I endeavoured to pray for the beloved object to whom I have alluded, I must still a little while say *beloved*, last night and felt soothingly melted in thinking that if mine really be prayers my acquaintance with him has probably caused the *first* to be offered up specially in his behalf.[13]
>
> (Marian Evans's emphasis)

In this reading, 'Two Bed-Chambers' is not a contrast of vain harlot and soulful madonna but, as its title suggests, of two differing forms of sexual yearning, one transmuted into desire for social mobility, and the other into religious ecstasy.

For Swinburne, as for George Eliot, the religious and the literary are closely related. Though both were avowedly agnostic in their early years, the attitudes of both towards religion became more ambiguous as they grew older. Both were brought up steeped in religious imagery, and that imagery pervades both bodies of work.[14] For George Eliot the connections between religious and literary vocation were direct: she saw herself as a moral guide in a newly secular world, and there is a reflexivity in all her discussions of religious vocation, which becomes most explicit when Dinah says 'The Word was given to me abundantly'. Dinah's conflict towards the end of the novel is the choice between Eros and Logos, love and the Word. As Kathleen Blake has remarked, George Eliot and Elizabeth Barrett Browning were the two female writers of their time who came closest to finding both erotic and vocational fulfilment in their own lives, yet they are the most obsessed with the irreconcilability of the two for women.[15] There is, of course, no such opposition in Swinburne: the problem was then and is still in large part a woman's problem. Yet Swinburne's work reflects the same tortured relation betwen language and desire. Poetic experience, like sexual experience, is for him a compound of pleasure and pain, and this not because of any societal impediment to the consummation of one or the other: for him pleasure and pain are *intrinsic* to sexual and poetic experience, are indeed essential to them, since pleasure is perceived only in contrast to pain. Swinburne's is a relative world in which all opposites are embraced because perception is impossible without difference. In his novel, *Lesbia Brandon*, the affinity between the wounding of poetry and the wounding of love is underlined in the scene where Margaret, having painfully parted from her lover, sings to her children and talks about the pain of words in song:

> Things in verse hurt one, don't they? hit and sting like a cut. They wouldn't hurt us

> if we had no blood, and no nerves. Verse hurts horribly: people have died of verse-making, and thought their mistresses killed them – or their reviewers. You have the nerve of poetry – the soft place it hits on, and stings. . . It's odd that words should change so just by being put into rhyme. They get teeth and bite; they take fire and burn. I wonder who first thought of tying words up and twisting them back to make verses, and hurt and delight all people in the world for ever. For one can't do without it now: we like it far too much, I suspect, you and I. It was an odd device: one can't see why this ringing and rhyming of words should make all the difference in them: one can't tell where the pain or the pleasure ends or begins.
>
> (*Hughes*, 148)

This passage treats not only of the pain of poetic language but also of its autonomy, its ability to surprise and to take on a life of its own. Swinburne clearly delights in this autonomy, is more than willing to relinquish conscious control over his texts in exchange for the uncertainties of the subconscious and the surprises of a battle with language in which language, more often than not, gains the upper hand. This in itself is by implication radical – an embracing of uncertainty and struggle rather than hierarchy and control – but in Swinburne it is clearly perceived as a personal and enclosed experience between poet, or reader, and text. It is therefore depoliticized, becomes part of Swinburne's aestheticism, as the lover of art for art's sake takes a Barthesian delight in the multi-referentiality of language that defies the limits of interpretation. George Eliot's attitude is both more ambivalent and more overtly political. She is more ambivalent in that the 'wise woman' narrator is the clear expression of an impulse towards ascendancy and control over the other discourses in a given text and yet other narratorial avatars of George Eliot seem as willing to give up, or admit the tenuousness of, control as is Swinburne. She is more overtly political in that she discusses not only literary but all kinds of discourse, written and spoken, and she sees discourse in general as a struggle for power.

The clearest example of this is *Felix Holt*. The novel is self-divided to the point of collapse. On one side is Felix, the spurious radical, a model of benign control in both the political and sexual spheres, who stands as a warning to men and the ruling class of how to retain their power and is a product of the conscious conservative in George Eliot; on the other is Mrs Transome, the spurious Tory, whose conservatism conceals the real threat she poses to patriarchy, and who is a mocking self-portrait of George Eliot's self-hating egoism and superficial conservatism. Mrs Transome successfully subverts this otherwise conservative and patriarchal novel by being its most memorable character, and, through her fear of exposure to the utterances of others and her desire for release in her own confession, she plays out her author's ambivalent relation, as woman and writer, to language.

In *Felix Holt* spoken language is seen as the central weapon of power-struggle: Rufus Lyon attempts to gain ascendancy over Augustus Debarry through debate; fear of a conflict of words leads Debarry's curate to run away; and Johnson, Felix, and the trade union man all attempt to win the workers over by means of oratory. In *The Mill on the Floss* Latin is seen as the central tool of male ruling-class power: when Stelling tells Tom that he lacks the equipment necessary to be a man, he is referring to Latin. Although this political dimension to language is missing from Swinburne's work, he was certainly aware of it, as was clear in his defence of *Poems and Ballads*. Donald Thomas tells us that:

> Swinburne inquired, if the loves of Sappho were so shameless and abominable, how was it that her surviving poems were on the syllabuses of England's great schools, where sternly moral pedagogues enforced the learning of them with the aid of the birch and other disciplinary sanctions? Was there not, somewhere, a strong and nauseating whiff of hypocrisy in all this simulated outrage over 'Anactoria' and her sisters?
>
> In this, at least, he raised a question calculated to embarrass Victorian educators and critics. A modern novel which dealt explicitly with straightforward copulation between husband and wife would have led to a successful prosecution . . . On the other hand, Sophocles' *Oedipus Tyrannos*, whose hero murdered his father and then fathered children himself on his own mother, was published by the Clarendon Press in Greek 'For the Use of Schools'. . . Swinburne had trespassed by crossing, as it were, the language frontier and making such material available to those who had not the accredited passport of a classical education.[16]

Thomas's point is an interesting one as regards the idea of a language frontier, separating classes, and of course the sexes in that ruling class women were not generally educated in Latin and Greek. George Eliot, being a classics autodidact, had access to classical literature, and therefore she was mentally a man in a very different sense from that generally attributed to her. In Swinburne's defence of *Poems and Ballads* we again glimpse the political potential of his eroticism, both in terms of class and of gender politics. Like George Eliot, he was more successful in his dealings with gender than with class. His revolutionary interest, like those of Shelley and Byron, were focused on the exotic oppressed abroad rather than the prosaic British poor. Nevertheless, in *Songs Before Sunrise*, he again managed to put his sado-masochistic imagery to interesting and original political use. 'Non Dolet' is perhaps the briefest and clearest example:

> It does not hurt. She looked along the knife
> Smiling, and watched the thick drops mix and run
> Down the sheer blade; not that which had been done
> Could hurt the sweet sense of the Roman wife,
> But that which was to do yet ere the strife
> Could end for each for ever, and the sun:
> Nor was the palm nor was the peace yet won
> While pain had power upon her husband's life.
>
> It does not hurt, Italia. Thou art more
> Than bride to bridegroom; how shalt thou not take

The gift love's blood has reddened for thy sake?
Was not thy lifeblood given for us before?
And if love's heartblood can avail thy need,
And thou not die, how should it hurt indeed?

(*Poems*, 2: 209)

The poem is an extended metaphor of sado-masochistic love and revolutionary self-sacrifice. Sado-masochism is naturalized in the second stanza by the reference to the spilling of blood in the breaking of hymen, so that Italia's spilling of her husband's blood is seen as natural reciprocity. The breaking of hymen as the type and foreshadowing of the bleeding of childbirth suggests that one's blood is owing to the country of one's birth. The spilling of blood reddens the poem with the symbolic redness of revolution. What Donald Thomas calls Swinburne's 'childish and masochistic obsessions'[17] provide a matrix of rich metaphoric complexity. Many critics maintain that Swinburne's revolutionary poetry was not his best, and certainly there was conflict between his aestheticism and the sustaining of political content, as became most apparent in his reluctance when Mazzini urged him to use his art more steadily for political ends.

The gender-political in Swinburne's poetry, however, is less wholly in conflict with his aestheticism. His preoccupations with powerful images of women, with androgyny, generated startling new ideas of femininity and of the relations between the sexes, without any necessity to conform to a polemical purpose. Perhaps most startling is 'Dolores', in which the repeated invocation 'Our Lady of Pain' completely reworks the idea of the madonna, keeping only her stature and power, but reversing all her other attributes.

George Eliot obeys a similar impulse in her monumental characterizations of her heroines. Gwendolen Harleth is the last of a series of monumental heroines, but she and Mrs Transome are the only ones who are not (on the conscious level) altruistic. In Gwendolen's story we find a reworking of the idea of women being attracted to the 'strong arm'. The strong arm is both an object of desire and an instrument of violence. We have seen it before, when Dinah chooses Adam over Seth and when Maggie chooses Stephen over Philip, and throughout George Eliot seems to suggest that women, in some measure, desire that which entails their own subjection. The idea finds fullest expression in Gwendolen's choice of Grandcourt over Rex. The brilliant formulation of Gwendolen's first reaction to Grandcourt 'He was not ridiculous' begs the question 'What was he?' A man who spends his time 'abstaining from literature' and declaring everything 'a bore' might well seem ridiculous. What keeps Grandcourt from being ridiculous is that he is a sadist. Lush considers that in desiring to marry Gwendolen, Grandcourt is 'fey', is obeying a death-wish. But Gwendolen is also 'fey'. She is playing out on a larger and more literal scale the seduction by power, the ambiguous fascination of the strong arm, that has been worked and reworked throughout the canon.

Gwendolen's relation to Daniel would seem to provide contrast, but on closer inspection the parallels loom large. Gillian Beer has pointed out that Sir Hugo calls Daniel 'a kind of Lovelace'. Given that, the similarity between Gwendolen's name 'Harleth' and the name of Richardson's victim-heroine 'Harlowe' can hardly be coincidence. Throughout the novel, Gwendolen has been seen as a strong, assertive, combative, androgynous figure. These attributes have been seen ambivalently, both as virtues and vices. The knife that Gwendolen dreams of putting under her pillow is one of many instances of her aspiration to the man's role, wishing to penetrate before she is penetrated. However there are also positive images of her androgyny. Her name, as Dierdre David points out, is that of an ancient British moon goddess, the equivalent of Artemis, and her archery conjures images of both Artemis and Rosalind in *As You Like It* (which could have been an ironic title for Gwendolen's part of the novel).[18]

Although Daniel's guidance helps Gwendolen through her crisis, the metamorphosis it effects in her is not all positive. It diminishes her, as marriage diminishes Dinah and Dorothea. The Gwendolen of the opening scene might have been vain, manipulative, deluded, and selfish, but she was also strong, monumental.

In the opening chapter, two male characters (of whom we are to see and hear no more) discuss Gwendolen's mouth:

> 'And her mouth – there never was a prettier mouth, the lips curl back so finely, eh, Mackworth?'
>
> 'Think so? I cannot endure that sort of mouth. It looks so self-complacent, as if it knew its own beauty – the curves are too immovable. I like a mouth that trembles more.'[19]

Up to the last sentence, we might agree with Mackworth. We have already seen complacency in Gwendolen, and it has been presented with ironic disapprobation. But the last sentence changes the lights for us: it is a crude expression of sadism, of the desire, inextricable in Mackworth's case from his sexuality, to subjugate, intimidate, and break the spirit of the object of his desire. Mackworth foreshadows Grandcourt, and throughout the description of their courtship, Gwendolen's smiling mouth is seen fascinating and challenging the lizard-like Grandcourt. But it is only at the end of the novel, in her final interview with Daniel, that we see Gwendolen conquered: 'She looked at Deronda with lips childishly parted'; 'Gwendolen's lip began to tremble. "But will you come back?" she said'. Certainly her complacency has vanished, but so too has her monumentality. Daniel has achieved through gentle rejection what Grandcourt's sadistic embrace attempted but failed to achieve: he has wiped the smile off Gwendolen's face; he has made her mouth tremble.

In these examples, George Eliot is describing what she sees as the sado-masochistic basis of all heterosexual relationships. Since the gratification of sexual desire for women generally means the eclipse or loss of self, Eros and Thanatos are, in her novels, truly identical for women. If this notion can be found in a writer whose work has been generally considered so morally upright as to be prohibitive, surely the critical aversion to its more open expression in the poetry of Swinburne is, as Swinburne himself claimed, hypocritical and unjust. More than one modern male critic has deplored the fact that Swinburne was a masochist rather than a sadist; two male critics have offered the greater expense of practising sadism as a shaky apology for what they clearly perceive as Swinburne's unmanly preference for masochism. Thus while expressing aversion to the whole deviant business, these critics tacitly acknowledge that there is a propriety of sadism and masochism in their own experience of heterosexual relations.

Swinburne and George Eliot are strange bedfellows, but between them, in their very different ways, they tried to erode what Lionel Stevenson calls 'the sentimental stereotype of domestic affection',[20] and the broader sentimentality that spread from the Victorian view of the nuclear family out into ever wider areas of Victorian thought and life. Attitudes to the poor and to imperialism were incalculably affected by it. And when seen from this point of view the concern for the connections between pleasure and pain, loving and violating, embrace and stranglehold are neither narrow nor deviant but of the most central and far-reaching significance.

## Notes

1. Donald Thomas, *Swinburne: The Poet in his World* (1979), 186.
2. Edmund Gosse, 'Swinburne', *Portraits and Sketches* (1912), 16.
3. Lionel Stevenson, *The Pre-Raphaelite Poets* (Chapell Hill, 1972), 209–10.
4. Cf. Dorothea Barrett, *Vocation and Desire: George Eliot's Heroines* (1989).
5. Stevenson, 184–5.
6. William Myers, *The Teaching of George Eliot* (Leicester, 1984), 148.
7. David Smith, 'Incest Patterns in Two Victorian Novels', *Literature and Psychology*, 15 (1965), 135–62.
8. Deirdre David, *Fictions of Resolution in Three Victorian Novels* (1987), 166.
9. Alexander Welsh, *George Eliot and Blackmail* (Cambridge, Mass., 1984) 282–3.
10. George Eliot, *The Works of George Eliot*, 'Cabinet Edition', 20 vols. (1878–80), *Jubal and Other Poems*, 75.
11. *The Works of George Eliot*, *Adam Bede*, 1: 235.
12. *The Works of George Eliot*, *Adam Bede*, 1: 51.
13. Gordon S. Haight, *The George Eliot Letters*, 9 vols. (New Haven, 1954–78), 1: 46–47.
14. See Margot K. Louis, *Swinburne and his Gods* (1990).
15. Kathleen Blake, *Love and the Woman Question in Victorian Literature* (Brighton, 1983), 198.
16. Thomas, 131.
17. Thomas, 149.

18. David, 184.
19. *The Works of George Eliot*, *Daniel Deronda*, 1: 12.
20. Stevenson, 209.

# 8 Swinburne and the 'Nineties

Murray G. H. Pittock

In the age which was to be mythologized by his great successor as that of the Tragic Generation, Swinburne's misfortune was to survive too long. The closely monitored atmosphere of Putney, at odds with the flux of Swinburne's tidal anapaests and the Heracleitan values of a Paterian age, removed him from the very period to which it is often presumed he stood godfather. As Philip Henderson puts it,

> . . . since the *goût de l'horrible* is once more in fashion, then why not such poems as 'The Leper', 'Les Noyades', 'Anactoria' and 'Faustine'? For there, in the mid-nineteenth century, will be found all the elements that were to be taken up and developed by the symbolist and *fin de siècle* writers and painters all over Europe.
> (*Henderson*, 3)

This opinion of Swinburne's influence is by no means unusual. And yet, a search for detail in the accounts of his effect on the 'Nineties reveals a paucity of specific references. Literary influence is a difficult thing to prove, as Harold Orel has said; yet in Swinburne's case it is often simply assumed.[1] Allusion is conventionally made to his role in introducing Baudelaire to English readers, to his place as a middleman in French influence on English literature, and to Swinburneian metrical echoes (not often discussed in detail) in the work of the poets of the Rhymers' Club. It is a legacy more often invoked than defined.[2]

The most detailed work is on Swinburne's relationship to Baudelaire. But even this becomes of limited value when it is considered how over-exposed Baudelaire, Verlaine and Mallarmé are in discussions of the English 'Nineties, in comparison with the great revival in native Jacobean, Caroline and Jacobite writers and values, which in turn gave birth to 'The Myth of the Seventeenth Century', adopted in diverse forms by the Modernists. For Eliot, the great rupture in consciousness was the Dissociation of Sensibility; for Yeats it was the Boyne.[3] Both views stood in close relationship to the revaluing of the seventeenth century in the works of 'Nineties writers, which in turn was foreshadowed by Swinburne.[4]

Swinburne was, of course, a great enthusiast for both the Stuarts and the seventeenth century, particularly its drama. This interest, noteworthy in his criticism and praised by Eliot, I shall deal with in part later. First it is important to establish how a writer whom a recent critic admits makes 'no reference to Decadence'[5] should have come to appear the progenitor of the era he appears to ignore. Yeats's triumphant assumption of the title of King of the Cats on Swinburne's death suggests just how potent a totem the absent and largely silent old poet had become. The acknowledgement of this significance by contemporaries has helped to obscure the need for a more detailed study of its cause.

When R. K. R. Thornton, for example, constructs a composite poem from lines by Dowson, Swinburne and Poe, he is subtly and perhaps subconsciously downgrading the complexities of direct influence in favour of a conflation of relationship.[6] There are lines from these poets (and indeed many others, such as Tennyson) which sound similar, but this is once again the criticism of allusion, not the demonstration of influence (a three-way question here, as Dowson was much drawn to Poe). Similarities are established, but specificities are lacking, only occasionally being found in citations of poetic echo, such as that of Swinburne's sonnet on *Mademoiselle de Maupin*, 'This is the golden book of spirit and sense', a quotation which clearly anticipates Wilde's 'golden book' in *The Picture of Dorian Gray* (*Henderson*, 176).

This essay argues that much clearer and larger-scale links can be drawn between Swinburne and the writers who succeeded him by considering some broader features of his verse and its themes. The artificial, bookish streak in both his metre and verse, early noted and long one of the main grounds for criticism of the poet,[7] reinforces his rebellion against the mores of his age while seeming to undermine it. Far from the fleshly poet being pornographic and popular, he is artificial and refined. Swinburne's verse can appear to be liberating, but it is too internalized to bear out that reality, rendering, as it does, sexuality in terms of a detachment from human life, rather than a great participation in it. Writing so often of the natural world, Swinburne is nevertheless more concerned with artifice in his explication of it than any of his contemporaries, and it is this deep preference for the explicit construct rather than the fruits of serious psychological or physical observation which set him apart from most of his contemporaries, and which appealed to the 'Nineties. If Shelley was an 'ineffectual angel' to the High Victorian period, Swinburne was an effectual demon. 'A poet writing for poets', he is, as Arthur Symons remarked, one of those writers who 'can never really be popular. . . any more than gold without alloy can ever be turned to practical uses. Furthermore, the sea has passed into his blood like a passion and into his verse like a transfiguring element'.[8] The metaphors are revealing: the elemental Swinburne is composed of metal, and the tides of his vision of the world are internalized ones. Swinburne does not write about the sea so much as about the sea in 'his blood'; the anapaestic rhythm of its waves is the 'transfiguring element' which infects his verse. This interiority of landscape is, as I will later argue, a vital part of symbolist poetic value. Swinburne's fleshly nonconformity takes place within artificial paradises. The pathetic fallacy is taken one stage further and subsumed into the mental process itself:

> The sea gives her shells to the shingle,
> The earth gives her streams to the sea;
> They are many, but my gift is single,
> My verses, the firstfruits of me.
> Let the wind take the green and the grey leaf
> Cast forth without fruit upon air;
> Take rose-leaf and vine-leaf and bay-leaf
> Blown loose from the hair.
>
> The night shakes them round me in legions,
> Dawn drives them before her like dreams;
> Time sheds them like snows on strange regions,
> Swept shoreward on infinite streams;
> Leaves pallid and sombre and ruddy,
> Dead fruits of the fugitive years;
> Some stained as with wine and made bloody,
> And some as with tears.
>
> ('Dedication') (*Poems*, 1: 293)

The second stanza makes explicit the fact that the natural processes of the first take place only within the mind: 'The night shakes them', they are 'like dreams', 'fruits of the fugitive years . . . stained . . . with tears'. Cecil Lang writes that Swinburne's 'poems of enduring appeal nearly always endeavour to explore . . . the relationship betwen . . . *natural* experience and the external world' (*Letters*, 1: xix). But they habitually accomplish this only in a sense in which the former usurps the latter:

> No growth of moor or coppice,
> No heather-flower or vine,
> But bloomless buds of poppies,
> Green grapes of Proserpine,
> Pale beds of blowing rushes
> Where no life blooms or blushes
> Save this whereout she crushes
> For dead men deadly wine.
>
> (*Poems*, 1: 170)

Here, natural experience relates itself to the natural world only through an act of artifice: the landscape is inverted, and simultaneously made metaphorical in the 'Green grapes' of Proserpine's oblivion, which places 'all things mortal/ With cold, immortal hands', the spiritual antithesis of the apparently physical regeneration promised by the stanza's central colour of green. The coldness of immortality is the paradox underlying the unnaturalness of this natural world, a poetic device descended from Dante and Milton's Hell, but here confined to a single figure. The power of such inverted landscapes is realized later most fully by Lawrence in 'Bavarian Gentians'; before him, Dowson was the most noted exponent of this Swinburneian theme. The images of the natural world are made symbolic of their opposite through inversion, and this inversion is an anti-creation, a kind of artifice. Just as the 'leaves' of Swinburne's poetry are those of 'rhythm and rhyme', not of nature in Hardy's analysis (again reminding us of Symons, quoted above), so his imagery of inversion is a forerunner of the 'unknown God of unachieved desire' (*Poems*, 3: 66) of the decadents.[9] The fleshly poet is a Pygmalion caressing the eroticism of Proserpine back into the form of a statue, with its 'cold, immortal hands' (*Poems*, 1: 170).

Pater, although his knowledge of French literature far surpassed Swinburne's, was clearly influenced by him, as was early noted by Rossetti and admitted by Pater himself.[10] Symons noted this affinity in a review for the *Athenaeum* twenty years later, by which time it was generally accepted. Foreshadowing the generalities of more recent criticism, an anonymous contribution to the *Academy* at the beginning of 1898 stated that Swinburne was 'the most sedulously imitated of poets' for twenty years after the appearance of *Atalanta in Calydon*.[11] Further details are lacking, but these and similar statements frequently leave us uncertain as to whether the grounds of any similarity are poetic or moral. Yeats himself compares Symons with Swinburne, but only to tell us that *London Nights* 'is a degree franker than Mr. Swinburne's "Poems and Ballads" '.[12] In references to Pater also, Swinburne's moral and stylistic influences are not separated: 'What may be called the fascination of corruption penetrates in every touch', Symons comments on Pater's description and evaluation of Leonardo.[13] The association of Christianity with death, present in 'Hymn to Proserpine', with its rebellious gloss of the dying words of the Emperor Julian, who thought Christianity a religion of charnel-houses, is also echoed in Pater's *Marius*, a book perhaps more influential on writers like Dowson and Johnson than the *Renaissance*. Pater's usual exquisite equivocation neutralizes the Swinburneian legacy on this occasion, however.[14]

Max Nordau's discussion of Swinburne as a 'higher degenerate' is also related to this general perception of his moral spirit as the leading edge of his influence on the writers who followed.[15] Swinburne effectively compromises the moral pretensions of Romanticism by negating the 'otherness' of the external world, and rendering all passions as the property of landscapes belonging only to the imagination. Theodore Wratislaw comments on this interior vision, saying that 'he [Swinburne] creates an artist in sensation'.[16] This *reduction* of the claims of nature to the dimensions of imagination, in itself partially created the altered moral sense which outraged his contemporaries. Chris Snodgrass examines the limits of this Orc-like revolt in his essay on 'Swinburne's Circle of Desire', and suggests its confining nature.[17] Ian Fletcher, the editor of the collection in which Snodgrass's chapter appears, agrees when he writes elsewhere that the poet's 'proposed self-liberation has no goal', and that although Swinburne has the 'cardinal insight . . . that sexuality *is* politics', such identifications tend to a reductive vision of experience: 'all meaning is projected by the mind, and . . . the outer world is not even hostile but indifferent'.[18] Or, indeed, compliant in the mind's own constructs to its purposes, as I wish to suggest.

By piecing together the implications of Swinburne criticism we can thus arrive at four reasons for the acknowledgement of his influence on his successors in the 'Nineties: his 'part in keeping the French master's reputation alive'[19]; his moral atmospheres; his artificial and reductionist readings of experience, internalized away from a concept of high seriousness; and the verbal and stylistic echoes which haunt successors like Dowson, Pater and the ever-fashionable Wilde. In *Lesbia Brandon*, Enid Starkie tells us, 'The characters of the novel live for art . . . the sentiments are those . . . of Oscar Wilde'.[20] In that *Lesbia Brandon* is a novel which discusses the pursuit of an unnatural ideal, it is clearly an unread forerunner of *Dorian Gray*. Yet its plot also contains two common features of Swinburne's work which foreshadow a much broader spectrum of 'Nineties poetic imagery and practice: the sea and the Stuarts.

As elsewhere in Swinburne, the sea in *Lesbia Brandon* is not a natural force so much as an intensifier of human artifice: a metaphor associated with the emotion created through the constructs of an aristocratic milieu with its rigours and beach floggings (*Hughes*, 5–41). The sea is connected (as in Pater and Böcklin among others)[21] with a vision of a *femme fatale*, and also with the great dynasty exiled beyond it (with whom had gone some of Swinburne's own family (*Henderson* 5–6; *Letters*, 3: 10). Denham says:

> I think they were right to put a lot of women in the sea: it's like a woman itself: the right place for sirens to come out of, and sing and kill people.
>
> (*Hughes*, 24)

Lady Warriston, whose Jacobite ancestry is emphasized, sings to enchant the assembled company a song of the Stuarts based on the exile of the Jacobites overseas, and, of course, written by Swinburne himself,

> she seemed to see into the prison and beyond, to speak without fear and with no ignoble regret: as though the spirit of that . . . ruined cause had passed into her and issued again at her lips.
>
> *There's nae mair lands to tyne, my dear*
> (*Hughes*, 73)

The Jacobite exile sings his long farewell. Swinburne, whose family 'had given their blood like water and their lands like dust for the Stuarts' (*Letters*, 3: 10), associates the sea, internalized metaphor for human emotional flux and loss, with both their political and sexual fortunes, frequently united in the person of Mary Stuart, Queen of France and Scots: Chastelard's Dolores, and a more effective White Devil than Vittoria Corombona in Swinburne's work. She is his central type of the fatal woman: and the metaphor of the sea unites the emotional turmoil of attraction to the fatal woman with an illustration of the exiled fortunes of her dynasty, and their links (like the poet's) to France.

Characterized by Cecil Lang as 'a Jacobite gentleman', Swinburne's interest in the queen is recorded as early as a letter to his mother of 15 April 1860 (*Letters* 1. xxxix, 35). It was the glamour of a lost cause which enhanced the nobility and pathos of his own family (and poetic vocation) which captivated him. The figure of Mary provided a mythicized historical correlative to the internal, symbolist landscape of fatal women: the 'Lady of Pain' is a real queen, a Mary of earth not of heaven, both sexually and politically captivating, annihilating the distinction between them. Poems like 'A Jacobite's Farewell' and 'A Jacobite's Exile' emphasize both the glory of exile from life and the Cavalier or Paterian seizing of the moment within life:

> But kiss me till the morn's morrow,
> Then I'll kiss ye nae mair.
>
> (*Poems*, 2: 281)

Curtis Dahl long ago noted the frequency of a 'theme of exile and especially exile to or from France' in Swinburne's work, arising out of a 'pride in his ancestry' who had found in Jacobitism 'a faith worthy of . . . adherence'. The loss of the world aligns itself with the intensest appreciation of that world, as shown in loyalty to the 'Queen for whose house my fathers fought' (*Poems*, 5: 259), herself a dangerous symbol of dominant female sexuality and an increasingly obsessive icon for Victorian art. As Dahl points out:

> In the staid, settled era of Victoria, Jacobitism was merely a lost cause – a hopeless gesture of revolt against middle class political morality.

This revolt 'against the drab, Protestant, Hanoverian present with its strict code of sex and its contempt for art', setting up against it the isolated icons of Swinburne's Mary or Lionel Johnson's Charles, is a noteworthy common feature of the work of Swinburne and his successors: the natural refuge from bourgeois culture was to be had in the arms of its last serious opponents.[22] Johnson's King Charles, Dowson's and Beardsley's St. Germain, for a quarter of a century the court of King James, and Yeats's Red Hanrahan, himself a conflation of two Irish Jacobites,[23] were the native icons to oppose to a new

Puritanism which from Carlyle onward had made Cromwell a hero, and of which there was to be much evidence in the 1890s. Swinburne's attraction to the Stuarts as metaphors of exile and rebellion from life, glorifiers of art and artifice, was to be the forerunner of the British *fin-de-siècle*'s attempt to construct a reactionary poetic around the Stuart cult, one prominent enough to attract figures like Ruskin, and which earned the scorn of parody from its opponents.[24]

In mood, style, and ethic then, Swinburne was the forerunner of a series of inheritors. In particular, his 'hunger for the past' can be seen as symptomatic, if not generative, of a whole late Victorian idea:

> Swinburne here joins the ranks, if he is not, indeed, the leader, of those writers (Arnold, Pater, John Addington Symonds, Oscar Wilde and Arthur Symons among them) who contrasted their hunger for a romanticized past with a desperate Philistine present.[25]

In this sense, perhaps, 'Hymn to Proserpine' is the complement to *Culture and Anarchy*. In a world of social-Darwinian progress, little is more artificial than history, as Ford (apocryphally) and Huxley (satirically) have pointed out. One of the central ways to *épater les bourgeois*, to undermine the values of the ascendant middle class, central to the practice of *fin-de-siècle* writers, came from exalting a past in which the bourgeois did not wield power, especially if it was also one which lent high status to art (Byzantium, the Renaissance, the age of the Stuarts). A recourse to a constructed past simultaneously nourished fantasies of power, loss, and a passive ideology of impractical politics: the artifice of nostalgia posing as the artifice of eternity, a defence of history's constructions against their appropriation by social Darwinism as either heritage artefacts or superseded realities. Baudelaire's attack on the idea of progress is one of the central statements of this addiction to the past, of which Swinburne was a central exemplar.[26]

In the three series of *Poems and Ballads*, well over half the poems deal with past ideas and events, and the *psychological* interpretation of the great stories of western culture found in 'Dolores', 'Laus Veneris' and 'The Garden of Proserpine' among others, greatly reinforces the enclosed nature of the poet's fantasy of the past, and the extent to which its immediacy is internalized. Chris Snodgrass in his essay 'Swinburne's Circle of Desire', cited above, shows how enclosed Swinburne's vision can be. Even 'The Triumph of Time' (a poem that sees history conquering progress rather than vice versa), which seems to set disappointed love in a wider context, strategically detaches itself from that context by mythologizing feelings as soon as they are expressed. The whole relationship becomes a part of the past immediately (most truly Heracleitan), and the imagery in which it is rendered has little to do with the context of experience it seeks to express:

We had stood as the sure stars stand, and moved
  As the moon moves, loving the world; and seen
Grief collapse as a thing disproved,
  Death consume as a thing unclean.
Twain halves of a perfect heart, made fast
Soul to soul while the years fell past;
Had you loved me once, as you have not loved;
  Had the chance been with us that has not been. . .

. . . Where the dead red leaves of the years lie rotten,
  The cold old crimes and the deeds thrown by,
The misconceived and the misbegotten,
  I would find a sin to do ere I die. . .

(*Poems*, 1:35,41)

Sin is the only way to re-authenticate an experience collapsing into abstraction, as Pater saw but did not admit. Here Swinburne foreshadows Symons' later call for 'A strenuous virtue, or a strenuous sin' to prove that 'life was not all vain'.[27] This is how symbolist thought could stamp its mark on 'reality', existentially providing a new destiny for the soul:

Far off it walks, in a bleak blown space,
Full of the sound of the sorrow of years.
I have woven a veil for the weeping face,
Whose lips have drunken the wine of tears. . .

(*Poems*, 1:40)

This mythologizing of the soul it its separateness carries with it a moral inversion, found in 'Laus Veneris' and 'Dolores'. 'My love' and 'mine own soul' become 'more beautiful than God'. But far from love taking God's place on a Brontean throne, Swinburne emphasizes its mutability, an emphasis necessary to support the underlying assumptions of nostalgia: that what is lost makes better history to fall in love with. The sea, an agent of that transience ('Mother of loves that are swift to fade, /Mother of mutable winds and hours') is the natural force which, in its perpetual restlessness under the moon, symbolizes the change brought by Time to history and places ('A Forsaken Garden'; *Tristram of Lyonesse*), to women, and to mental states (the place of peace [death] is an end of 'sound of waters shaken'). Yeats was to use it thus in 'The Wanderings of Oisin', *The Only Jealousy of Emer*, and 'A Prayer for My Daughter' among other works:

Imagining, in excited reverie
That the future years had come
Dancing to a frenzied drum
Out of the murderous innocence of the sea.[28]

The Swinburneian sea dominates all moods: 'The loves and hours of the life of man', 'Or poisonous foam on the tender tongue' (*Poems*, 1:36,37,25,172).

The fatal woman is, as I suggested earlier, also closely associated with the sea. 'Mother of loves' that it is, the sea (from which Aphrodite rose at Cyprus) orchestrates not only mood and history, but love: 'My lips will feast on the foam of thy lips' (*Poems*, 1: 43) as Swinburne tells us. Elsewhere the 'wrecking wave' helps to symbolize the destruction of love's potential in *Tristram of Lyonesse* (*Poems*, 4:12). Iseult is 'more fair than foam or dawn'; her eyes 'shone as the sea's depth swallowing . . . the sky's' (*Poems*, 4: 13–14); and the end of her life and love lies under 'The light and sound and darkness of the sea' (*Poems*, 4: 151). Thus it is that 'the foam of the present . . . sweeps to the surf of the past' (*Poems*, 1:69). The 'flowers of foam' are in 'love's hand to-day'; but tomorrow who can say (*Poems* 1:179)? After all, 'Love deep as the sea as a rose must wither' (*Poems*, 3:24).

Beyond love, the end of Time itself will be seen in the sea's conquest of all things: when the symbol of change takes the mutable world it symbolizes into its poisonous salty province:

> Till the slow sea rise and the sheer cliff crumble,
>   Till terrace and meadow the deep gulfs drink,
> Till the strength of the waves of the high tides humble
>   The fields that lessen, the rocks that shrink.
>
> (*Poems*, 3:25)

This is the apocalyptic finale which in certain moods Swinburne seeks. Meanwhile fatal woman, both symbol and reality, mediates between the worlds of sea and land. 'The lips and the foam and the fangs' of Swinburne's marine vampires prove them destructive Aphrodites indeed (*Poems* 1, 157).

The salivation of the sensual vamp is called 'foam' by Swinburne, to link it strongly with the sea: 'The foam of a serpentine tongue/ The froth of the serpents of pleasure' belongs to 'Our Lady of Pain', who is 'Foam-white, from the foam'. 'The froth of the serpents of pleasure/ More salt than the foam of the sea' (*Poems*, 1: 158) prepares us for Arthur Symons's later use of the sea woman in his much more straightforwardly blasphemous 'Stella Maris'.[29] Swinburne keeps far more to generalities than does Symons: his pains are as abstract as his pleasures, intellectualized into the flux of history, whence the recurrent myth of such as Dolores redeems the generations from progress (here Swinburne agrees with Baudelaire), and condemns them instead to repeat their sins. 'Our Lady of Pain' who redeems 'from virtue' has more sins than the Virgin has sorrows; she is 'immortal', 'fresh from the kisses of death', 'our lady of Torture', beyond Venus, Astarte or Astaroth, 'daughter of Death and Priapus': a figure like Stoker's White Worm or Rider Haggard's Ayesha. In the enclosed world of the symbolist imagination, the transformed and perverse sexuality of the eternal feminine lingers (as in Eliot's *Prufrock*) to promote the changes of history and affection, and also to prevent man from adapting to and learning from them, compelling him to the hideous liberty of sin. Dolores has the double power of perversion and interiority, and is a fitting mother to the Dark Angel of the 1890s:

> When sunlight glows upon the flowers,
> Or ripples down the dancing sea:
> Thou, with thy troop of passionate powers,
> Beleaguerest, bewilderest, me.[30]

To such imagery Swinburne was a fitting parent also (Poems, 1: 154, 156, 158, 163, 167).

As already noted, Swinburne's first Fatal Lady, to whom he devoted reams of verse and three plays of declining merit, was Mary, Queen of Scots. In Swinburne's Jacobite poems, the sea is an agent of change as would be expected: seldom was the sea in fact so politically important as from 1689 to 1759, under the influence of 'Protestant winds'. Swinburne's Mary also shares the Cyprian's marine characteristics. To Chastelard she is:

> Fair fearful Venus made of deadly foam. . .
> Your splendid supple body and mouth on fire. . .
>
> (*Tragedies*, 2: 128)

Of Mary, Swinburne uses the most potent images of power and destruction. 'Man by man/ Your lips will bite them dead', says Chastelard:

> For all Christ's work this Venus is not quelled,
> But reddens at the mouth with blood of men . . .
>
> (*Tragedies*, 2: 142, 153)

Her entrapments in the end entrap her: but Mary, like an Axel, dies for her image of herself: a truly symbolist queen.

Swinburne's vision of the sea's role as that of an echo or symbol of the interior world of imagination and emotion, or the vanished world of history, a watery 'ou-boum', is clearly also found in some of the writers who followed him. In his preface to *London Nights*, Symons, after informing us that, 'The whole visible world, we are told, is but a symbol' (a fantasy like that of Gerard de Nerval for his lobster, who knew 'the secrets of the sea'), uses an important image to defend his poetry against adverse moral comment:

> It is as if you were to say to me, here on these weedy rocks of Rosses Point, where the grey sea passes me continually, flinging a little foam at my feet, that I may write of one rather than another of these waves, which are not more infinite than the moods of men.[31]

Even the smallest changes of mood are 'a ripple on the sea'.[32] *London Nights* was the volume with which, Patricia Clements tells us, 'Symons placed himself in the line of Gautier and Swinburne'.[33] Yeats, as noted above, thought it 'a degree franker than. . . "Poems and Ballads" ': and that 'degree' is perhaps the step Symons takes from the interior vision of abstract sins and histories to the outer world of matter-of-fact, physical sin. Whether or not we accept Symons' self-portrayal as the naughtiest boy in town, his vision claims our attention in a way directly related to physical experience. 'The Nereid of a moment there', of whom Symons asks 'is it seaweed in your hair?' is a prostitute of whom he claims 'My share of your delicious shame'. In another poem the 'secret deep of deeps' is only the scent of White Heliotrope; the girl whose hair, 'streams, a dark and tumbled drift', lies beside Symons in a 'little bedroom papered red' under 'The gas's faint malodorous light'. Those who come 'Out of the night, out of the sea' have to accept second best if they go to bed with Arthur. The 'strenuous sin' is explicitly linked to 'The charm of rouge on fragile cheeks'. Maquillage has replaced mystery. Symons has socialized the elemental metaphors of Swinburne: his is a housetrained iniquity.[34]

Although Sir Desmond Flower tells us that 'Swinburne's legacy to Dowson was one of tone', he suggests that the 'outlook' of his poems 'is quite different'.[35] This is true only in a limited sense. Dowson's vision of a chilly inverted world of erotic consciousness with its 'pale, cold eyes,/Kissed shut by Proserpine' is certainly akin to Swinburne's, as is his attitude to the sea, beside which 'dear dead people with pale hands/ Beckon me to their lands'. He waits for the 'ruining waters' to fall, before 'the great waves conquer in the last vain fight' one who is 'tempest-tost, and driven from pillar to post' on 'life's passionate sea'. Besides this interior emotional landscape, the sea is a fatal woman for Dowson also: he can feel 'thy kisses on my face' and 'thy salt embrace/ When thy fierce caresses blind my eyes and my limbs grow stark and set'. Man, more conventionally, is 'As the helmless ship in a storm' on a sea where there are no 'Fortunate Islands', places of refuge Dowson exposes as fictional. His world, as interior as Swinburne's, is composed of vanished passion and cravings for oblivion:

Ere I go hence into the deathless sleep
That lies beyond the land, where cold and deep,
The stream of Lethe flows thro' endless night,
Let me once more my sweet child-love, behold
Thy pure grey eyes, thy tresses of bright gold-
  Ere I go hence.

Dowson's loves are chilly Perditas, who consume rather than distribute flowers. The 'flung roses' are the diet of these demanding statuettes:

To my last love
Loved all above

At evening
Of autumn
One chrysanthemum
Is all I have to bring.[36]

Wilde's inheritance from Swinburne largely lacks direction. Poems such as 'The Burden of Itys' display a largely superficial level of imitation; it is only when Wilde wholeheartedly enters the interior world of symbol, as in 'The Harlot's House', rather than toying with its accessories, as in 'The Sphinx', that he successfully exemplifies Swinburneian practice. 'The Ballad of Reading Gaol', with its great movement from particular to general, a strength the ballad shares with the fairy story, marks the height of the 'Nineties revival of the form, a revival anticipated by Swinburne's use of balladic form, and evident also in the work of John Davidson, with whom Swinburne was acquainted. Both ballad and fairy story were perhaps popular because symbolists sought to derive from their symbols as wide a range of 'histories against progress' as possible. In such a revival, nostalgia for the past became part of the past itself through the means of its recall through forms so emphatically archaic. The symbolist search was wedded to its object.[37]

Lionel Johnson was the poet who celebrated this marriage tragically, as Yeats was later to celebrate it successfully in his (overheard) invocation in '*Ballad and story, rann and song*' to the Fenian dead to rise from their graves in their nation's cause.[38] Johnson's hieratic style and personality, more in tune with 'Virgil, the melancholy, the majestical' than with Aeschylus or Villon, nevertheless make Swinburne's infuence felt in his verse.[39] Johnson links the vision of the sea as an agent of change with the frozen past of the lost Celtic kingdoms. In 'Ireland', he comments that 'Thy sorrow, and the sorrow of the sea/ Are sisters'; 'Thy children hear the voices of old days/ In music of the sea upon thy shore'. Haunting 'Tirnanoge within the sea' now lies outwith current human ken. Sea-gulls are 'over Maes Garmon side', and 'Ancient delights' are on the 'ancient sea' of Cornwall or Brittany. Johnson comments on his 'solitary griefs' that 'Mine is the sorrow on the sea', the sorrow of death or change. Elsewhere 'Eternal sorrow finds/ Eternal voice' in 'The cry of Irish seas', and the 'Voice of the sorrow, that is on the sea' is a 'Long Irish melancholy of lament'. The Celtic lands are seen as internally exiled beyond change as a

White Land within the West
Upon the breast
Of some divine and windless sea. . .

The process of sea-change has brought them beyond change, mythologized in their exile from reality, like the Stuarts themselves for whom Johnson was also an enthusiast. This sense of mythicization escapes from flux, because, unlike Swinburne, Johnson believed in the ultimate and absolute God:

Ah, how the City of our God is fair:
If, without sea, and starless though it be,
For joy of the majestic beauty there,
Men shall not miss the stars, nor mourn the sea.

Thus occasionally there can be an escape from the sea-symbol of separation and lost time. But not often: and Swinburne's symbol remains powerful in Johnson's work.[40]

The sea and the West are closely associated in our culture with the Celtic lands, and are also linked as images of travel towards death. These elements are fused in Swinburne's only major contribution to the birth of the Celtic Twilight, *Tristram of Lyonesse*, which concerns itself with Brittany, Cornwall, Ireland, Wales and the binding metaphor of the sea, from 'the wild wrath of the Cornish foam' which opens 'The Sailing of the Swallow' to the 'light and sound and darkness of the sea' with which the poem ends (*Poems*, 4: 13, 151). Iseult, 'more fair than foam' is the symbolist heroine: her characteristics, as the characteristics of her love, reduce nature to a metaphor for herself:

And alway through new act and passion new
Shines the divine same body and beauty through,
The body spiritual of fire and light
That is to worldly noon as noon to night . . .

(*Poems, 4: 5*)

She felt 'Through her own soul the sovereign morning melt,/And all the sacred passion of the sun' (Poems,4:27). Iseult is a sexual focus of the sea's flux, promising a deathly changelessness posing as an immortal renewal:

Their heads neared, and their hands were drawn in
one.
And they saw dark, though still the unsunken sun
Far through fine rain shot fire into the south;
And their four lips became one burning mouth.

(*Poems*, 4: 38)

This image is repeated later, its deathliness more explicit:

. . .and her head
Bowed, as to reach the spring that slakes all
drouth,
And their four lips became one silent mouth.

(148)

In some ways Yeats's *Wanderings of Oisin*, another metaphor for Celtic defeat, echoes this poem. To Yeats and his brother the sea at Sligo was a place of magic and transformation; in *The Shadowy Waters* it is as mutable in love and legend as Swinburne could have desired, and *The Only Jealousy of Emer* goes further in its direct echoes of Swinburne's *Tristram*:

*Fand*: And there shall be oblivion
Even to quench Cuchulain's drouth,
Even to still that heart.

*Ghost of Cuch*: Your mouth![41]

*Tristram of Lyonesse* is a tragic poem where elemental passions give way to the forces of experience. Like Iseult, Tristram is at one with passion, the 'Limitless love that lifts the stirring sea':

And all the bright blood in his veins beat time
To the wind's clarion and the water's chime . . .
(*Poems*, 4: 126)

The defeat of their passion in the world that 'by ruth's relenting doom' has commemorated 'their tomb' in Tintagel is a metaphor for the defeat of the Celtic peoples and the loss of the heroic age. The changes of time are once again rendered through the changes of the sea: 'their sleep/ Hath round it like a raiment all the deep', and the sea too will swallow not only the lovers who rendered its passion in their lives, but the generations themselves:

What so sublime sweet sepulchre may be
For all that life leaves mortal, as the sea?

Thus, symbolically, the sea overcomes the (Christian) chapel Mark builds for the lovers: 'the strong sea has swallowed wall and tower', taking back its own for ever (*Poems*, 4: 149–50).

*Tristram of Lyonesse* provides a vision close to that which the Celtic Twilight was to inherit: the decline of the Celtic world as a paradigm for erotic, historical and personal loss, as well as for an overwhelming feeling of isolation. Mythic, isolationist, inverted (the love appears the positive it is not), and highly interior, it is typical of the inward text through which Swinburne spoke to his successors in terms which are 'out of nature' in exactly the Yeatsian sense, and which emphasize alienation even as they seem to rejoice. Among Swinburne's metaphors, the sea shows the perpetual conquest of history by itself: the flux of multiple interior worlds, of love, politics and high passions. Out of it comes the fatal woman, motif of decadent art from Böcklin to Beardsley. Swinburne provides us with a 'Nature' which richly deserves its inverted commas, a hothouse of psychological and historical change: its artificial implications fill the worlds of his successors. Swinburne's view of Nature is that of a Des Esseintes pretending to to be a Wordsworth, or at least a Tennyson. The triumph of that view lies in its related reductive and transforming tendencies which incestuously engender the unstable interior landscapes of the decadent and Modernist writers, as well as being instrumental in creating the hunger for the past these writers displayed.

## Notes

1. Harold Orel, 'Hardy, Kipling and Haggard', *English Literature in Transition*, 25 (1982), 4, 232.
2. Arthur Symons, *Figures of Several Centuries* (1916), 310; Enid Starkie, *From Gautier to Eliot* (1960), 40–57 and passim; R. K. R. Thornton, *The Decadent Dilemma* (1983).
3. Lucy McDiarmid, *Saving Civilization* (Cambridge, 1984), 34 ff.
4. For a more detailed argument on this point see Murray G. H. Pittock, 'Decadence and the English Tradition', unpub. D. Phil. thesis (Oxford, 1986).
5. Thornton, 38.
6. Thornton, 86–7.
7. T. S. Eliot, *Selected Essays* (1932), 327.
8. Symons, 153, 161.
9. cf. Ernest Dowson, *Poems*, with a memoir by Arthur Symons (1926), 15, 25, 43, 45, 57, 131; James Gibson (ed.), *The Complete Poems of Thomas Hardy* (1976), 323.
10. John J. Conlon, *Walter Pater and the French Tradition* (Lewisburg, 1982), 10, 31; *Letters*. 2: 58.
11. Symons, review in *The Athenaeum* (14 December 1889) 813–14; *Academy* liii (1 January 1898). 13–14.
12. John P. Frayne (ed.), *Uncollected Prose of W. B. Yeats* (2 vols., 1970), 1:373.
13. Arthur Symons, *A Study of Walter Pater* (1932), 109.
14. Walter Pater, *Marius the Epicurean* (2 vols., 1909), 2: 99, 192–96, 224.
15. Max Nordau, *Degeneration* (1895), 94.
16. Theodore Wratislaw, *Algernon Charles Swinburne* (1900), 27.
17. Chris Snodgrass, 'Swinburne's Circle of Desire: A Decadent Theme', in *Decadence and the 1890s*, ed. Ian Fletcher (1979), 61–87.
18. Ian Fletcher (ed.), *British Poetry and Prose 1870–1905* (Oxford, 1987), xl, xli.
19. Jean Pierrot, *The Decadent Imagination 1880–1900* (Chicago, 1981), 43.
20. Starkie, 44.
21. cf. Bram Dijkstra, *Idols of Perversity* (Oxford, 1987).
22. Curtis Dahl, 'Swinburne's Loyalty to the House of Stuart', *Studies in Philology*, 46 (1949), 453–69.
23. Mary Helen Thuente, *W. B. Yeats and Irish Folklore* (New Jersey, 1980), 198 ff.
24. cf. *The Royalist*; *The Athenaeum* 1897–1900; 'Richard de Lyrienne', *The Quest of the Gilt-Edged Girl* (1897), 48 ff.
25. Robert L. Peters, 'Swinburne: A Personal Essay and a Polemic', in Richard A. Levine (ed.), *The Victorian Experience: The Poets* (Ohio, 1982), 156.
26. Charles Baudelaire, *Selected Writings on Art and Artists*, trans. P. E. Charret (Harmondsworth, 1972), 120 ff.
27. Arthur Symons, *London Nights* (1897), 106.
28. W. B. Yeats, *Collected Poems* (1950), 212.
29. Symons, *London Nights*, 40.
30. Ian Fletcher (ed.), *Lionel Johnson: Collected Poems* (New York, 1982), 52.

31. Symons, *London Nights*, xiv.
32. Arthur Symons, *The Symbolist Movement in Literature*, ed. Richard Ellmann (New York, 1958), 7, 80.
33. Patricia Clements, *Baudelaire and the English Tradition* (Princeton, 1985), 184.
34. Symons, *London Nights*, 40, 46, 50; *Silhouettes* (1892), 17.
35. Sir Desmond Flower (ed.), *The Poetical Works of Ernest Christopher Dowson* (1934), xxv.
36. Flower, 5, 22, 51, 56, 83, 86, 105, 136, 144, 170.
37. Oscar Wilde, *Poems* (1909), 63, 225, 245, 303.
38. Yeats, *Poems*, 56.
39. Murray G. H. Pittock (ed.), *Lionel Johnson: Selected Letters* (Edinburgh, 1988), 7–8.
40. *Lionel Johnson: Collected Poems*, 15, 17, 20, 60, 73, 93-98, 166, 168.
41. W. B. Yeats, *Collected Plays* (1952) 293. Cf. *Uncollected Prose*, 350; *Collected Poems*, 473 ff. See also A. Norman Jeffares (ed.), *Yeats, Sligo and Ireland: Irish Literary Studies 6* (Gerrard's Cross, 1980), 77.

# 9 Influence, intertextuality and tradition in Swinburne and Eliot

Thaïs E. Morgan

'The domain of culture begins when one HAS "forgotten-what-book".'

(Ezra Pound, *A Guide to Kulchur*)

Though Swinburne has been relegated to the margins of literary history during most of the twentieth century, references to his work occur repeatedly in the writings of the Modernists.[1] Indeed, one might speak of a Modernist canon of 'Swinburne', that is, a consistently preferred and collectively assimilated group of Swinburne texts which circulates throughout the Modernists' letters, criticism, and poetry. Recent studies have discussed the crucial role of such Victorian writers as Matthew Arnold and Walter Pater in the formation of Anglo-American Modernism, with attention to literary influence (the Victorians on the Moderns) and literary appropriation (the Moderns from the Victorians).[2] What I would like to explore in this essay is the intertextual network that links Swinburne's poetics to Modernism. My case in point will be one of T. S. Eliot's best-known books of criticism, *The Sacred Wood* (1920). Methodologically, my inquiry will consist less in tracing the paths of literary or personal influence than in examining the structure of one intertextual site – a site constructed around Swinburne's poetry and literary criticism – in High Modernism.

As Carol Christ and Perry Meisel have shown, both T. S. Eliot and Ezra Pound were concerned to position themselves *qua* Modernists in relation to the 'major' Victorian poets, including Robert Browning, Alfred Tennyson, and Matthew Arnold. Eliot in particular, I would suggest, found the ambiguous status of Swinburne's reputation as a poet and a critic, bequeathed to him by Victorian critics, particularly useful.[3] As the author of the scandalous *Poems and Ballads* (1866), Swinburne represented an emergent avant-gardism which the Modernists could invoke to give their own program historical legitimacy. At the same time, as the author of *Songs Before Sunrise* (1871), Swinburne joined Arnold and Tennyson in typifying that grand style of social and moral rhetoric from which the Modernists wished to distance themselves. Consequently, as I will demonstrate, 'Swinburne' functions as a double sign in several of Eliot's major critical essays. In certain passages, 'Swinburne' signifies a Victorian past which Eliot repudiates; in others, 'Swinburne' prefigures the advent of Modernism itself. All told, 'Swinburne' becomes a sign(ature) of Eliot's ambivalent relation to literary history, which he regards as both burden and brotherhood.

## Influence or intertextuality?

Since the later 1970s, influence studies concerning Victorian and Modern writers have been problematized largely from two directions: psychoanalysis and structuralism.[4] Harold Bloom's psychoanalytic model for literary relations assumes an Oedipal dynamic of rivalry between male poets who are divided generationally into strong fathers or 'precursors' and anxious sons or 'ephebes'.[5] Bloom's model for literary history opens up the field of possible textual relations by enabling the critic to make connections between texts not only on the grounds of quotation and allusion, but also according to the transformational rule of 'repression' whereby we may find a precursor's text distorted and appropriated almost beyond formal or thematic recognition in the work of a successor. Nevertheless, Bloom's model preserves a unidirectional, linear model of literary history in its insistence on what T. S. Eliot called the 'ancestors' behind each 'individual talent'.[6]

Organized along a chronological axis, but admitting a wider range of textual relations than Bloom's model, is the theory of intertextuality in poetry proposed by Michael Riffaterre. Whereas Bloom's schema for the anxiety of influence focuses on intersubjective relations between poets from a psychoanalytic perspective, Riffaterre uses the semiotic concept of the 'interpretant' to foreground the role of cultural knowledge in the interpretation of a poem.[7] Moreover, while Bloom personalizes literary history by organizing it into pairs of rival writers, Riffaterre expands the dyad characteristic of influence study (the poem and its source) into a triangle involving a minimum of three texts, each of which refers to a 'matrix' or shared paradigm of cultural knowledge.[8]

A typical intertextual triangle consists of the present text; an earlier intertext; and an interpretant text, which is either earlier than or contemporaneous with the text in question, and which mediates between this text and its intertext. By acknowledging multiple intertextual interferences in the reading and, by implication, in the writing of any text, Riffaterre's model affords greater flexibility and range for literary analysis than does Bloom's version.

However, Riffaterre's theory of intertextual triangulation lacks criteria for determining the orientation of textual relations, that is, their motivation. This can be supplied by Bloom's idea of the simultaneous resistance to and appropriation of a precursor's work by the new poet – a dialectic between past and present that need not be referred solely to Freudian psychoanalysis for its explanatory power. Together, then, Bloom's and Riffaterre's theories of textuality suggest a critical approach that might be dubbed the intertextual hermeneutic of suspicion. As I will show in the remainder of this essay, Swinburne's ambiguous place in Eliot's criticism results from a strategy of intertextual triangulation that is motivated equally by admiration and anxiety. On one hand, the 'myth of the modern' demanded that Swinburne be rejected as a representative Victorian writer.[9] The signature of 'Swinburne' came to represent to Eliot, as also to William Butler Yeats, the quintessence of what was wrong with the literature of the 1850s–1890s.[10] On the other hand, Swinburne was one of the Victorian poets and critics who showed the way to Modernism.

## He do Swinburne in different voices: T. S. Eliot

In *Victorian and Modern Poetics*, Christ discusses the 'anti-Victorianism' embedded in 'the New Critical version of poetic history' which was primarily formulated by Eliot, Yeats, and Pound.[11] In denouncing the 'rhetoric' and didacticism which they attributed to Victorian poetry, the Modernists created a polemical opposition between past and present, old and new, often simplifying and distorting the literature of the Victorians in the process. Establishing a clear boundary between Victorian and Modern was an urgent mission for young writers like Eliot and Pound, who during the 1910s–1920s, were strenuously promoting their own work as an advance over 'the scientific and moral discursiveness of *In Memoriam* . . . the political eloquence of Swinburne, the psychological curiosity of Browning, and the poetical diction of everybody'.[12] Christ concludes: 'Although Victorian poetics contains many of the elements from which the Modernists were to build their poetic revolution, the Modernists characteristically misread Victorian poetry, identifying it with the failures which would most defeat their own enterprise'.[13]

A process of what might be termed anticipatory misprision describes T. S. Eliot's relationship to Swinburne in the field of criticism. As the latest spokesman for a literary avant-garde in England, Eliot must perforce acknowledge Swinburne's prior inscription of modernity into the English poetic tradition.[14] The crucial text here is Swinburne's review essay on 'Charles Baudelaire's *Fleurs du mal*' (1862). According to Patricia Clements, this piece was the first to define the ideal of the 'modern' writer for British criticism: 'When Swinburne recognized Baudelaire . . . he changed the course of the main current of the English tradition, altering . . . the ideal order against which the individual English talent must define itself'.[15] Furthermore, as Linda Dowling has pointed out, Swinburne also foregrounds the notion of modernity in his poetry, 'whose style always betrays an anxiety about impinging influences and about its own originality'.[16] In turn, precisely because Swinburne had made 'Frenchness' into a sign of radical originality within the English tradition, Eliot was able to mark his own avant-gardism by allusions to Baudelaire in self-consciously modernist poems such as *The Waste Land* (1922).

Theoretically speaking, Swinburne serves as an interpretant text that mediates between a set of intertexts signed by 'Baudelaire' and Eliot's new text(s) as poet and critic.[17] Note that the interpretant here consists of Swinburne's essay on Baudelaire in addition to the controversy it aroused and its position within mid-Victorian culture. This interpretant functions silently within Eliot's discourse, for nowhere does he publicly recognize Swinburne as a 'source' for his interest in French Decadent literature. As Riffaterre emphasizes, quotation of, or direct allusion to, the interpretant text is not necessary in order to establish intertextuality, which is not the same as influence.[18] Intertextuality refers to the larger cultural field of texts, or what Pound called 'the domain of culture', rather than to exact verbal parallels between pairs of texts. Thus, Eliot identifies himself as an heir of the nineteenth-century avant-garde in the British tradition by the very act of hailing Baudelaire as an important precursor of Modernism, thus 'confirm[ing] the change in direction of the main current of the English tradition that Swinburne had initiated . . . .'[19]

The theory of intertextual triangulation also sheds light on Eliot's construction of his position as a critic out of conflicting strains within Victorian criticism. For the literary historian René Wellek, Swinburne was 'the first in England to apply purely imaginative [that is, aesthetic] standards to . . . literature without . . . concessions to purely moralistic, realistic, or philosophical standards'.[20] To Eliot as a reader surveying Victorian criticism, this practice puts Swinburne in direct opposition to Arnold who, in 'The Function of Criticism at the Present Time' (1864), calls upon the literary critic to don the cloak of the moral sage, 'letting his own judgement pass along . . . as a sort of companion and clue' to readers in search of the 'truth' about life.[21] By contrast, Swinburne insists on the aesthetic autonomy of poetry in the opening paragraph of his defense of Baudelaire: 'The critical students [in France], as well as here, judging by the books they praise and the advice they proffer, seem to have pretty well forgotten that a poet's business is presumably to write good verses, and by no means to redeem the age and remould society' (*Works*. 13: 417). Through rejecting the critical establishment's demand for moral lessons in verse, Swinburne formulated a proto-formalism that would be radicalized by the Aesthetes of the 1890s.[22] During the period from 1900–20, I would suggest, Eliot developed his brand of criticism from a mixture of Victorian moralism and formalism. He skipped over, as it were, the elaborate aestheticism of Oscar Wilde's generation, going back to an earlier version of formalism to be found in Swinburne's criticism and deploying it as a sort of buffer against more immediate influences such as Arthur Symons.[23]

Significantly, Eliot begins his 'Preface' to the 1928 edition of *The Sacred Wood* with a ground-clearing gesture that recalls Swinburne's manifesto-like statement on the primarily aesthetic function of poetry in the opening of his landmark essay on Baudelaire. By positioning 'Swinburne' as an interpretant text between the intertexts of Arnoldian moralism and Wildean aestheticism, Eliot manages to avoid repeating either school of criticism and to appear to be striking out on his own *qua* Modernist critic: 'the problem appearing in these essays, which gives them what coherence they have, is the problem of the integrity of poetry, with the repeated assertion that when we are considering poetry we must consider it primarily as poetry and not another thing' (viii). Of course, 'integrity' is a usefully ambiguous word: it slides around between Arnold the moralist ('truth and the highest culture') and Arnold the formalist ('the free play of the mind upon all subjects').[24] At the same time, 'integrity' evokes Swinburne's critical stance as a Francophile formalist ('Art for art's sake first of all . . .' [*Works*, 16: 137]). As we will see again in other essays by Eliot, Swinburneian 'integrity' exemplifies a criticism that reads poetry as art 'and not another thing'. Finally, Swinburne represents 'integrity' when compared to the extreme position of Wildean aestheticism ('For in art there is no such thing as universal truth'[25]). Within this intertextual field, Swinburne provides an apt interpretant between conflicting moments in the nineteenth-century tradition because he mediates between conservative uses and radical abuses of literary criticism.[26] As Eliot himself observes in one of the essays in *The Sacred Wood*, unlike Arnold, Swinburne 'was writing not . . . to instruct a docile public, but as a poet . . . upon poets whom he admired'. And unlike Wilde, Swinburne 'was writing not to establish a critical reputation' merely for the sake of notoriety.[27] Through this intertextual triangulation of nineteenth-century critics, Eliot builds a 'new' cultural space for his own critical opinions. The palimpsest structure of Eliot's criticism is what makes it seem original.

According to a Bloomian model of influence, Eliot's anxiety over his indebtedness to Swinburne for the Victorian's prior insertions of modernity and formalism into the English tradition would account for the way in which Eliot vilipends his precursor in essays that otherwise seem to praise him. For instance, the medley entitled 'Imperfect Critics' (1919) opens with Swinburne, whose 'notes upon poets whom he admired' Eliot in his turn admires, paying great 'attention and respect' to them. Eliot emphasizes that Swinburne's 'justness of judgment' on other writers in the literary tradition is based on an exacting scholarship. This is an important point, for what Eliot has in mind entails a special kind of scholarship that can be practised only by an active poet who reads everything 'with the single interest in finding literature'. In this context, 'literature' connotes the realm of the aesthetic, and Eliot wants it clearly understood that aesthetic 'integrity' does underpin Swinburne's essays. Why, then, does Eliot not rate Swinburne as a 'perfect critic'?

What begins as a positive evaluation of Swinburne's contribution to criticism is punctuated and punctured by a list of its 'infirmities', which include superficiality and a 'blur' of ideas. Consequently, Swinburne is relegated to a representative group of 'imperfect critics'. This 'swerve' in Eliot's evaluation of Swinburne is strategic, for through it Eliot ties Swinburne to Arthur Symons, another but more recent failed critic.[28] A complex set of intratextual and intertextual relations is established here. Eliot's objections to Swinburne's work in 'Imperfect Critics' refer forward to his comparison of Swinburne and Symons as two writers who fall just short of being 'The Perfect Critic' (1920). Simultaneously, Eliot's negative remarks about Swinburne refer backward within the intratextual space created by *The Sacred Wood* itself: doubts formulated in 1920 are, as it were, confirmed by doubts expressed in 1919 since the later essay is placed before the earlier one in the book.

Applying the theory of the anxiety of influence, one might conclude that Eliot's disparagement of Swinburne and Symons is designed to fend off two strong precursors who were, like the young Eliot, critics as well as poets. However, because it retains the linearity of influence studies, the Bloomian model cannot account for literary historical formations that are intra- and intertextual at once. In the present case, the concept of intertextual triangulation may help us more fully grasp how Eliot works Swinburne and Symons against each other in order to carve out a space for his own work within the inherited discourses of Victorian and *fin-de-siècle* criticism. Thus, according to Eliot, although Swinburne's pieces on poets far excel Symons' impressionistic essays 'in the direction of analysis and construction',[29] the fact that Symons was heavily influenced by Swinburne's characteristic 'infirmities' of style undermines Symons's contribution, which, by retrospective association, tells against Swinburne's *imprimatur* of 'tumultuous . . . adjectives' and 'undisciplined sentences'. On a related point of comparison, Eliot again disparages Symons through Swinburne and vice versa. Classified as 'an appreciator and not a critic' due to his 'violent and immediate' expression of likes and dislikes for the writers he discusses, Swinburne is implicitly blamed for the faults of his heir Symons, who made Swinburne's style into a 'far more profoundly affected' mannerism. In the end, 'although Mr. Symons is far superior to most of the type' of the previous century's impressionistic critic, and although Swinburne was 'more a critic than Mr. Symons' because he was able to distinguish writing criticism from writing poetry, Swinburne because of his style and Symons because of his imitation of Swinburne both fall short of Eliot's ideal of the 'perfect critic'.[30]

Establishing his own legitimacy as both poet and critic is one of the prime motors of Eliot's practice as a canon-maker. Specifically, Eliot aims to identify and empower the Modernist as the 'perfect' poet-critic. It seems quite significant, then, that Eliot develops a definition of the poet-critic out of the mutually invidious comparison between Swinburne and Symons in 'The Perfect Critic'. All of his faults of style notwithstanding, Eliot finally prefers Swinburne over Symons and justifies this decision by putting forward a cardinal principle of Modernist poetics and criticism: '. . . the artist is – each within his own limitations – oftenest to be depended upon as a critic; his criticism will be criticism, and not the satisfaction of a suppressed creative wish . . .'.[31] Conversely, the artist (that is, the poet) who is also a serious scholar can be depended upon as the most nearly 'perfect' critic. This is an important statement on the Modernist ideal of the scholarly poet-critic, whose triply vested cultural function lends him considerable power in modern society, much like the Victorian cultural sages who were also poets and critics, such as Arnold, Swinburne, and Wilde.

Part of the project of *The Sacred Wood* is to reposition Swinburne in relation to the English canon of poet-critics from the mid-1800s through the early 1900s, for this constitutes the possibility as well as the limit of Eliot's own thinking and writing as a Modernist. The essay on 'Swinburne as a Poet' (1920) should be read in tandem with Eliot's remarks on Swinburne as a critic because these two roles were merged in the Modernist ideal of the poet-critic. Now, given Eliot's definition of the 'perfect' poet-critic, it is arguable that Swinburne had already realized this ideal, just as he had already inscribed his name in the main line of the English avant-garde. For, as a consummate scholar ('He read everything . . .'), and as an 'appreciator' of other poets' achievements from the perspective of his own, Swinburne in the 1860s–1880s largely prefigures the mode of criticism the Modernists in the 1910s–1930s are striving for. He exemplifies, to borrow Eliot's words, a 'perfect' 'integrity' of scholar, critic, and poet.

According to a Bloomian model, therefore, Swinburne would represent a rival to Eliot's ambitions in all three of these roles. But exactly how is this psychological motive worked out in 'Swinburne as Poet'? In effect, Eliot uses intertextual triangulation in order to marginalize Swinburne's poetry. Mindful of the high esteem in which late Victorian and Edwardian critics such as Edmund Gosse held Swinburne, Eliot begins by taking it 'as undisputed that Swinburne did make a contribution; that he did something that had not been done before'.[32] What is the nature of this 'something' and what is its relative worth in the present context of Modernism? After naming a small selection of titles, above all from the scandalous first collection of *Poems and Ballads*, Eliot focuses on 'The Triumph of Time' as the epitome of Swinburne's 'contribution': 'That so little [thematic] material . . . should release such an amazing number of words requires . . . genius'. The sarcasm here is palpable: not even a good editor could help Swinburne ('You could not condense . . . . You could only leave out'). True, as Eliot illustrates in detail, this Victorian poet had a positive 'genius' for 'dwell[ing] . . . exclusively and consistently among words', expanding them to the extent that 'the object has ceased to exist'. The problem is that this kind of 'genius' produces primarily negative results from the viewpoint of the Modernists and their contemporary readers: 'But the language which is more important to us is that which is struggling to digest and express new objects . . . as, for instance, the prose of Mr. James Joyce or the earlier Conrad'.

In this last sentence of the essay, Eliot all but decrees Swinburne's exile from the literary canon. The force of his judgement may be seen in the long eclipse of Swinburne's reputation over the last sixty years. Eliot's method consists of negative intertextualization, which is based here on an opposition between two symbolic signatures: that of 'Swinburne' which stands for Victorian literature and the Past, and that of 'Conrad-Joyce' which stands for Modernist literature and the Present leading into the Future. The specific issue that focuses this opposition is the proper relationship between literature and 'the object'. Swinburne may have a brilliant way with words, but what is wanted in 1920 is not mere language or 'rhetoric' (Yeats), but reference to 'new objects, new groups of objects, new feelings, new aspects'.

Equally important, this opposition between the quintessential Victorian and the quintessential Modernist(s) is mediated by a third term: Eliot's own poetics. In two well-known passages in *The Sacred Wood*, Eliot emphasizes the impersonal stance of the Modernist poet in relation to any given 'set of objects'.[33] Read intratextually, in connection with his dismissal of Swinburne's word-oriented poetics in the present essay, this doctrine of an 'objective' poetics decisively aligns 'Eliot' with 'Conrad-Joyce' over and against 'Swinburne'. In this triangulation of sign(ature)s, Swinburne's poetics of 'the most general word' serves as an intertextual foil that highlights the essential difference between 'Eliot'/Modernism and 'Swinburne'/Victorianism on the one hand, and the essential alliance between 'Eliot' and 'Conrad-Joyce' as leaders of a Modernism focused on the object on the other.[34]

Could it be a mere accident of literary history that all three of Eliot's essays concerning Swinburne were written within the same two-year period as was 'Tradition and the Individual Talent' (1919)? Eliot keeps returning to Swinburne while working out his own posture as a poet-critic in *The Sacred Wood*. Bearing this in mind, I would further suggest that 'Swinburne' functions as an important interpretant for the idea of tradition central to Eliot's poetics. My argument is not that Eliot either paraphrases or alludes to specific titles by Swinburne in his famous essay; rather, 'Swinburne' represents an intertextual site on which Eliot builds his conception of how the new poet should be situated in relation to the literary past. This intertextual site consists not only of Swinburne's 'appreciations' of a wide range of writers from Aeschylus to Arnold, but of the many poems in which he melds past and nineteenth-century poets together by way of addressing the question of what Eliot terms 'tradition and the individual talent'.[35] Unlike Yeats and the poets of the 1890s who rejected Swinburne's highly intertextual pastiches and elegies as irrelevant to their 'post-philological moment', Eliot gleaned the original poetics of tradition behind Swinburne's technique of 'seamlessly incorporating . . . whole passages from the literary past' into his poems.[36]

Among Swinburne's representations of the new poet in relation to the tradition, perhaps the best known is 'Ave Atque Vale'.[37] One might say that this elegy to Baudelaire is doubly implicated in the anxiety of influence. First, Swinburne's *succès de scandale* as a poet-critic depended in no small part upon his early adoption of 'Baudelaire' as an icon of rebellion against moral and aesthetic norms in literature. By Baudelairizing, as it were, Swinburne could distinguish himself from other mid-Victorian radicals such as Dante Gabriel Rossetti who did not look to French models for their aestheticism. Moreover, the scandalous *Poems and Ballads* (1866) self-consciously recontextualizes several themes that were foregrounded in Baudelaire's *Les Fleurs du mal* of 1857.[38] In short, as his address to the 'master' in 'Ave Atque Vale' proudly confirms, Swinburne was Baudelaire's devoted disciple in critical as well as poetic practice. Secondly, though, this text inscribes a drastic 'swerve' and an Oedipal moment of love-hate between the older and the younger poet, for Swinburne composed the elegy upon hearing a rumour that Baudelaire had died, although he had in fact not. In 'Ave Atque Vale', then, is Swinburne mourning his loss or celebrating his own ascension to the throne of aestheticism?

In Bloomian terms, Swinburne's ambivalent relation to Baudelaire as a strong precursor to whom he is indebted and whose work he must surpass offers an uncanny parallel with Eliot's relation to Swinburne. Strikingly, Swinburne and Eliot draw upon the same tropological matrix – 'life-in-death' – in order to position themselves within the avant-garde line that extends from the mid-1800s to Modernism. In both 'Ave Atque Vale' and 'Tradition and the Individual Talent', the new poet takes up the task of carrying on the literary tradition, which he views as both burden and brotherhood. The burden of tradition includes the Oedipal rivalry that drives the intergenerational *agon* between poets according to Bloom. Thus, Swinburne races against Baudelaire whom he calls a 'sweet strange elder singer' whose 'more fleet/Singing' Swinburne, as a belated poet, struggles to overtake (*Poems*, 3: 53). Likewise, Eliot's stance toward the literature of the past is markedly competitive: the present poet (that is, the Modernist) must create 'a new work of art' that will decisively alter the 'ideal order' of 'all the works of art which preceded it'.[39] In other words, the Past must change in order to accommodate the Present – an important effect of criticism as well as the ambition of poetry.

The burden of tradition is also represented by the paradoxical state of life-in-death ascribed to Swinburne's 'Baudelaire' and to Eliot's 'ancestors'. In 'Ave Atque Vale', Baudelaire remains alive both literally (the elegy was premature) and figuratively (the elegy reinscribes an array of Baudelaireian intertexts). For his part, Eliot goes as far to suggest that just as life is death in the troping of literary apotheosis, so originality *is* tradition: ' . . . we shall often find that . . . the most individual parts of [the new poet's] work may be those in which the dead poets . . . assert their immortality most vigorously'. Interestingly, the use of the same metaphors in the conclusion to 'Swinburne as Poet' implies that this essay should be read as Eliot's elegy to Swinburne, who had died only in 1909. Thus, in words recalling those used to describe the 'ancestors' of the literary tradition, Eliot states that Swinburne's 'language is not . . . dead. It is very much alive' – perhaps all the more so because of that very 'peculiar' style of his, with that 'singular life of its own', which even Eliot's own strictures cannot quite lay to rest.

The other important metaphor for the literary tradition shared by Swinburne and Eliot is that of brotherhood. As James Longenbach has pointed out, the idea of a brotherhood of poets was crucial to the friendship and literary collaboration between Pound and Yeats during 1913–16, formative years for Modernism. Through Pound, Eliot probably heard about ' "the unfounded order" ' of the ' "Brothers Minor" '.[40] Nonetheless, the brotherhood envisioned by Pound with Yeats consists of contemporary poets, whereas Swinburne and Eliot dedicate themselves, in 'Ave Atque Vale' and 'Tradition and the Individual Talent', respectively, to the 'immortal' 'dead'. Their emphasis lies on a literary kinship that can transcend the boundaries of language, nationality, and historical time. Swinburne makes the conventions of the elegy into a ritual of bonding with Baudelaire: 'For thee . . . my brother, / Take at my hands this garland . . .' *Poems*, 3: 57). Equally ritualistic, Eliot advocates a mystic 'surrender' and 'self-sacrifice' of the new poet to his 'ancestors'.[41] From the psychoanalytic perspective of the theory of the anxiety of influence, the notion of the tradition as a brotherhood represents a displacement: Oedipal rivalry between son and father, new poet and precursor, is transferred into brotherly love.

By contrast, from the perspective of a theory of intertextuality, the relationship between Swinburne and Eliot as literary *frères ennemis* becomes – to borrow a term from Eliot – 'impersonal'. As I have argued, 'Swinburne' in Eliot's work represents a nodal point within a certain area of nineteenth-century culture, an intertextual site and a symbolic signature that acquires its meaning within a field of texts. In the final analysis, 'Swinburne' is more than an influence on Eliot: he is a metonym standing for the intertextuality of tradition itself.

## Notes

(Special thanks to David DeLaura who read and commented on an earlier version of this article.)

1. Although Ezra Pound's debt to Swinburne has been extensively explored, little

has been said about Eliot's.

2. See Carol Christ's *Victorian and Modern Poetics* (Chicago, 1984) and Perry Meisel's *The Myth of the Modern* (New Haven, 1987) for the connections between Victorian and Modernist poetics.
3. See my essay 'Mixed Metaphor, Mixed Gender: Swinburne and the Victorian Critics', *Victorian Newsletter*, 73 (1988), 16–19.
4. On the differences between influence and intertextuality, see my essay 'The Space of Intertextuality' in R. C. Davis and P. O'Donnell, eds., *Intertextuality and Contemporary American Fiction* (Baltimore, 1989), 239–79.
5. For instance, Bloom uses these two terms when describing 'antithetical completion': 'the *tessera* represents any later poet's attempt to persuade himself (and us) that the precursor's Word can be worn out if not redeemed as a newly fulfilled . . . Word of the ephebe'. Quoted from Harold Bloom, *The Anxiety of Influence* (1973), 67.
6. T. S. Eliot, *The Sacred Wood: Essays on Poetry and Criticism* (1920, repr. 1972), 48. Hereafter cited as Eliot.
7. According to Riffaterre, '*intertextual* interpretants' are 'mediating texts' that 'contain a model of the equivalences and transferals' between the codes used in a given poem. Quoted from Michael Riffaterre, *Semiotics of Poetry* (Indiana, 1978), 81, his emphasis. For a more detailed explanation of Riffaterre's theory, see my 'The Space of Intertextuality', 262–266. Note that the theory of the interpretant applies to all kinds of cultural texts.
8. Riffaterre, 12–13.
9. Meisel, 4.
10. Yeats's dismissive remarks about 'Swinburneian rhetoric' (see *The Autobiography of William Butler Yeats*, 1916, repr. 1965, 57, 97) have been widely noticed. However, in *Stone Cottage: Pound, Yeats and Modernism* (1988), James Longenbach quotes Yeats as exulting on the day after Swinburne's death (11 April 1909) that he himself was now ' "King of the Cats" ' (15) – a boast that implies that he viewed Swinburne as a poet to be reckoned with.
11. Christ, 1.
12. W. B. Yeats, 'Introduction', *The Oxford Book of Modern Verse* (1936), ix.
13. Christ, 149.
14. The major poet-critic of the avant-garde intervening between Swinburne and Eliot is Oscar Wilde. On Wilde's self-conscious modernity, see Regenia Gagnier, *Idylls of the Marketplace: Oscar Wilde and the Victorian Public* (Stanford, 1986).
15. Patricia Clements, *Baudelaire and the English Tradition* (Princeton, 1985), 10.
16. Linda Dowling, *Language and Decadence in the Victorian Fin de Siècle* (Princeton, 1986), 190.
17. A diagram of this intertextual situation would be something like this:

Swinburne (interpretant)

Eliot (text) 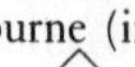 Baudelaire (intertext)

18. In a slightly later theorization, Riffaterre emphasizes: 'There is no need to prove any contact between the author and his predecessors. It suffices that the intertext exist for the reader in order to make the necessary connection between two or more texts.' See his 'Sémiotique intertextuelle: L'interprétant', *Rhétoriques, sémiotiques* (Paris, 1979), 131 (my translation).
19. Clements, 332.
20. René Wellek, *A History of Modern Criticism, 1750–1950* (New Haven, 1965), 381.

21. A. Dwight Culler (ed.), *The Poetry and Criticism of Matthew Arnold* (Boston, 1961), 257, 239.
22. With regard to Swinburne's role in transmitting the formalist strain to later nineteenth-century criticism, Dowling comments: 'To understand the situation of the inheriting Aestheticist writers of the 1890s . . . is to perceive how circumscribed they were by the two great Aestheticist writers who preceded them, namely, Pater and Swinburne' (176).
23. Much has been written about Arnold's place in Eliot's criticism. In *The Social Mission of English Criticism, 1848–1932* (1983), Chris Baldick points out the way in which Eliot tries to balance between formalism and moralism, both of which he sees in Arnold's criticism: ' . . . this central interest in the relations between creation and its cultural preconditions . . . can lead the critic to being lured out of purely literary concerns' (114).
24. Culler, 250, 245.
25. Oscar Wilde, 'The Truth of Masks: A Note on Illusion', first published as 'Shakespeare and Stage Costume', 1885, and reprinted in *Intentions*, 1891. Here cited from R. Ellmann, ed., *The Artist as Critic*, 1970, 432. See Gagnier, 41.
26. A diagram of this intertextual situation would look something like this:

    Swinburne (interpretant)
    Eliot (text) △ Wilde (intertext)
    vs. Arnold (intertext)

27. Eliot, 17.
28. 'The *clinamen* or swerve . . . is necessarily the central working concept of the theory of Poetic influence, for what divides each poet from his Poetic Father . . . is an instance of creative revisionism' (Bloom, 42).
29. Eliot, 5.
30. A diagram of this intertextual situation would look something like this:

    Swinburne (interpretant)
    Eliot (text) △ vs./=Symons (intertext)

31. Eliot, 7.
32. Upon the poet's death, Edmund Gosse observed that Swinburne's 'most active influence on living literature' was to have 'introduced . . . an attitude, an approach to literature which has affected everyone who tries to write about poetry with any distinction.' Quoted from 'The Genius and Influence of Swinburne: A Symposium', *The Bookman* 36 (London, 1909), 127.
33. Eliot, 56, 100.
34. A diagram of this intertextual situation would look something like this:

    'Swinburne'/Victorian ('diffuseness')
    'Eliot'/Modernist ('objective correlative') △ 'Conrad-Joyce'/Modernist ('objects')

35. Swinburne's poems on the poetics of tradition include 'In the Bay', memorial verses on Théophile Gautier, and 'On the Cliffs'.
36. Dowling, 178.
37. See Jerome McGann's analysis of the manifold places of 'Ave Atque Vale' within the poetic tradition (*McGann*, 292–312).
38. See Clements.
39. Eliot, 49–50.
40. Longenbach, 26.
41. Eliot, 52.

# 10 Swinburne at work: the first page of 'Anactoria'

Timothy A. J. Burnett

'He is a reed through which all things blow into music.' Tennyson's two-edged compliment (*Hyder* 113), with its imputation of a fatal facility, has dogged Swinburne's reputation. Browning went even further. 'As to Swinburne's verses . . . they are "florid impotence", to my taste, the *minimum* of thought and idea in the *maximum* of words and phraseology. Nothing said and nothing done with, left to stand alone and trust for its effect in its own worth' (*Hyder* 115). Swinburne has been regarded as a poet whose work lacked what Dante Gabriel Rossetti called 'fundamental brainwork' (*Letters* 1.xix). Examination in some detail of part of one of Swinburne's poetical manuscripts, the only records that we have of his compositional brainwork, may throw some light on whether or not this reputation is justified. The poem chosen is 'Anactoria' which was, of course, not only one of the texts which caused the outcry at the publication of *Poems and Ballads* (1866), but also contains one of Swinburne's most famous phrases: 'the mystery of the cruelty of things'. It is also, conveniently, possessed of a particularly complicated draft.

In *Notes on Poems and Reviews* (1866) Swinburne claimed that in 'Anactoria' he had tried to reproduce the spirit of Sappho's Ode 'To a Beloved Woman', a poem which he would have known since his time at Eton. Swinburne was one among the many who have considered Sappho to be the greatest lyric poet of all time. She was also, for him, a symbol of the high calling and immortality of the poet. Her verse, written in the 7th century BC, has survived only in fragmentary form in the quotations of later classical writers and commentators, and in equally fragmentary papyri. It chiefly treats of affection between women, a theme which has caused the modern world to give the name of Sappho's native island to a practice which there is no evidence that she herself pursued. Although Sappho's ode is graphically descriptive of her jealousy at seeing a woman she loved seated beside a man, and although in fragment 28 she calls love the 'giver of pain',[1] and although Swinburne incorporated several lines translated from Sappho's poems in *his* poem, it is not the spirit of Sappho that is expressed in 'Anactoria' so much as that of the Marquis de Sade whose *Justine, ou les malheurs de la vertu* Swinburne had read in 1862.[2] This is true not only of the overtly sadistic passages (lines 23–36 and 103–144), but also of the philosophical (lines 148–188), where God is portrayed as the supreme sadist, the cause and essence of 'the mystery of the cruelty of things'.

In the case of the philosophical passages study of Swinburne's draft reveals that lines 145–154 were added later, while 155–188 are not found in the manuscript at all. These are the lines closest in spirit to the philosophy of the choruses in *Atalanta in Calydon*, and their appearance out of sequence, as it were, would already have suggested that composition of the two poems proceeded coevally, even if we were not aware that a draft of lines 155–188 is to be found on folio 6b of the Fitzwilliam Museum, Cambridge, manuscript of *Atalanta*.

To quote W. R. Rutland, 'No poet ever wrote more supple rhyming couplets in iambic fives . . . The variety of caesura, the variations of enjambement and endstopping, and the skill with which the rhymes carry the sense instead of chopping it up, simply takes one's breath away'.[3] Swinburne himself, in a letter to Dante Gabriel Rossetti dated 22 December 1869 referred to '. . . my own scheme of movement and modulation in Anactoria, which I consider original in structure and combination' (*Letters*, 2:74). Perhaps by examining Swinburne's manuscript in detail we may be able to discern, however dimly, something of how this was achieved.

There are three manuscripts of 'Anactoria' known to me: the first, a draft, preserved at the Harry Ransom Humanities Research Center, at the University of Texas at Austin, is written on both sides of two folio leaves of blue wove paper (folios 1 and 2), on both sides of two folio leaves of blue laid paper (folios 4 and 5), and on one side only of two folio leaves of blue laid paper (folios 3 and 6). Folios 4 and 6 are watermarked 'Sawston/1858' and ' J & SH/ 1863' respectively. The leaves have been bound in the wrong order, and should be as follows: 1, 2, 4, 5, 3, 6. The second manuscript is the draft of lines 155–188 at the Fitzwilliam Museum mentioned above, and the third is a fair copy in the Bibliotheca Bodmeriana at Geneva. In this last manuscript the poem was originally entitled 'Philocris'.

The system of transcription employed in order to reproduce the first page of the draft may be simply explained by means of examples. Comparing line 1 of the facsimile[4] and of the transcription, it will be seen that Swinburne first wrote *lips* and then substituted *life* by writing it over *lips*; at the same time he changed *are* to *is*. When he made these changes he had got at least as far as *bitter*, so the words substituted, *life* and *is*, are italicised to show that they are substitutions within an already existing string of words. Swinburne could, theoretically at least, have come back hours or days after completing the line, and made the changes. Further along the line, however, he has written a little over half of what is probably *my*, abandoned it, and *currente calamo* substituted *thy*. In that case *thy* is not italicised. Where, as in line 4, Swinburne has deleted the first substitution and substituted a third version, as in *falters*, *quickens*, *strengthens*, the first substitution is in italics, and the second is in bold face. If there were a third, it would be in bold face italics. A fourth substitution has, happily, yet to occur.

Let us now look at the draft: Lines 1–10 may possibly have background inspiration from Sappho fragment 27 '. . . You burn me,. . .'. In Line 1 we see a change from *lips* being *bitter* (Swinburne considers *burnt*) with *my* love to the less concrete *life* being *bitter* with *thy* love. On the other hand in line 3 we see a change from the neutral *their* to the more specific, and alliterative and sibilant *soft*, and in fact Swinburne builds up a remarkable accumulation of 's's in the first five lines. In line 4 there is a change from the concept of *sight* failing to *blood* faltering – an avoidance of yet more smooth sibilant alliteration, and the substitution of a more staccato, vivid image – followed by a change of tack from *falters* through *quickens* to *strengthens* (*strengthens*, although it contains two 's's, is a harsher word than *quickens*). We also see a move from the abstract *life* to the concrete *veins*. In line 6 we see a change from the legato *that life is death* to staccato *it is not death*. In line 7 Swinburne started *I would we twain were*. He then presumably conceived an ending in two iambic feet, and therefore substituted for *were* the filler O, *thou*; he then reverted to the first version; abandoned that tack and put the agents of annihilation (the *sea* and the *fire*) in the active role, and Sappho and her beloved in the passive; after which, apart from two hesitations (*sea were* [something along the lines of *over us*] for *sea had hidden*, and juggling with *fire pyre fire* – finally preferring the smoother fricative to the more jerky plosive) the line was in its final form. Lines 8 and 9 gave Swinburne considerably more trouble. The basic concept was that fire should cleanse, purge, destroy Sappho, her beloved, and Sappho's passion together. At the same time he had to find a rhyme word for *fire*. He started with the idea of fire severing life from the lovers, abandoned that (but stored it in his memory), tried *Purged life from lips*, deleted *life from lips* (Swinburne seems to have been tempted by the image of lips while composing this section, but to have decided against it; three times he deleted *lips* or *lip*), substituted *us*, then abandoned the personal approach and substituted the general, holocaustic, concept *Consumed the earth*. It is just possible that there was an intermediate stage *Purged us, the earth* [and something else besides to be supplied], but I think not. Swinburne then dropped the general concept and returned to the personal with *Laid hold upon us like a new desire*. At that point he had a line that made sense, that rhymed and that led on to lines 9 and 10 *Severed. . .leaves*. Nevertheless, the poet with the fatal facility was not satisfied. Out went *like a new desire* and in came *as with hands*. Presumably the hands were to be 'of fire', and it was possibly at that juncture that *pyre* was substituted for *fire* in the preceding line. *As with hands* was then deleted, and a new concept introduced: *with the lip that cleaves* – the fire's lip, that is. The idea of fire suggested *ash*, but in the meantime there was a problem to be solved. Swinburne was pleased with the word *cleaves*, with its ambiguous, twin meanings of clinging on the one hand and separation on the other, but by using it he had lost his rhyme-word with *fire*. After some hesitation over how to begin it, he inserted the otherwise perhaps somewhat redundant line *Wilt thou fear that and fear not my desire*? Interestingly enough, the final word *desire* is immediately adjacent to deleted *desire* from the earlier attempt. There then follows the line that employs the rhyme-word *cleaves* (again, it is adjacent to its earlier, deleted, appearance) – a line full of paradox. It is *fire* that severs the bones, yet by a jump in time the bones are not blackened, but bleached. *Severed*, too, is an odd word to use of bones parted from flesh by fire, yet that was the concept intended, since Swinburne also tried the word *divided*. *Severed* had been lurking in his mind, and on the page, since there it is at the beginning of the aborted version of line 8. Yet *flesh that cleaves* implies a jump in time in the opposite direction, since flesh cleaves to the bones only before the fire has taken hold, *Bleach* and *cleaves* are linked by assonance, but express contrary ideas. It is a complicated line, and it cost Swinburne some pains to wrestle it out. There follows a fairly neutral line, line 10, and then two lines, 11 and 12, where the expression of pain rises to a higher pitch, but it remains a mutual pain. In line 12 the too monotonous *vein aches on vein* is changed to the more biting *and vein stings vein*.

At this point the order of composition becomes somewhat hard to follow, but appears to have gone thus: line 1–10, 67 and 68, 11–14, 64, 69–71 as far as *kisses*, 23–34 omitting 29–32, then 29–32, the second half of 71, 72, and finally 63–66. The exact order in which the lines were set down upon the page may be impossible to determine, but it is clear that 67 and 68 were written down, as a couplet, early on, if not first of all, since so many of the other lines curl around them, or are fitted in next to them. Moreover, they appear to be written with a different pen, and in a bolder hand. They relate to a passage of Sappho's own poetry, the 'Ode to Aphrodite', line 1, where the goddess is described as "poikilothron" – richly enthroned.

There are therefore at this point two opposed, but balanced, concepts in Swinburne's mind at the same time: Aphrodite on her throne offering comfort to Sappho; and the torments that Sappho wishes upon the faithless object of her desire. The latter concept leads on from, and was possible inspired by, the sentiments found in lines 11 and 12, just as lines 23–24 lead on from lines 11 and 12 physically upon the page. The desire for *mutual* destruction found in lines 7–14, however, transmutes itself into a *sadistic* desire for the lingering and painful death of the beloved. It seems clear that Swinburne was not easy about these notorious lines, and was undecided whether to include them or not, if he did include them, where. In the poem as printed line 14 is separated from line 23 by the passage beginning 'Why wilt thou follow lesser loves?', a passage possibly inspired by Sappho fragment 22. '. . .Out of all mankind, whom do you love better than you love me?. . .', but which really contributes very little to the poem, unless it be to provide a brief lull of pleading, a change of tone, between the two violent passages. In the draft it is found on folio 2, following a different sadistic passage, lines 103–112. In the fair copy lines 23–34 were originally omitted altogether, and were added later in the right hand margin of folio 1. They represent the first appearance of sadism in the poem (albeit quite an early appearance) and Swinburne seems unsure how to handle it. Whatever his difficulty in placing these lines, however, he seems not, on the whole, to have had the same difficulty in composing them. Lines 23 and 24 came easily enough. Swinburne's first attempt at lines 25 and 26 reads: *Thou art over fair; I would the grave might eat / Thy body as fruit . . .* He then abandoned the envious sentiment at the beginning of line 25, but retained the idea of the beloved's body being consumed like fruit by the earth, reinforcing it with the image of her body being eaten by some loathsome reptile. He began: *And save the worm's no mouth could find thee sweet*, but no doubt found that trite and banal. He then strengthened it to: *And no mouth but the grave-worm's* (with its echo of ballad vocabulary) *found thee sweet*, but still unsatisfied searched for a yet more 'laidly worm', trying first *viper's*, and then at last, possibly prompted by the genitive 's', arriving at the splendidly sinister and onomatopoeic *And no mouth but some serpent's found thee sweet.*

The next line, 27, which begins a new passage, and signals a raising of the emotional pitch, came easily enough, as did 28, once Swinburne had made an 180 degree turn from *Subtle* to *Intense*, and from *soft* to *superflux*. He next wrote the first version of what was eventually to be line 34, *By soft red ways*, and probably *and shuddering*, before deleting *By soft red ways* and substituting *Veiled notes and shuddering semitones of death.* At this point it must have occurred to him that *Veiled notes* etc. would make the perfect end to the whole passage. He accordingly tried to fit in a line which would rhyme with *death* before the line which he had just finished. He first wrote *Strain out with music*, then substituted *pangs like music* for *music*, followed by *all thy breath.* To strain out with music all the beloved's breath must have seemed too far fetched, or at least ambiguous, but the idea of death accompanied by music, of the beloved's screams and dying sobs being music to Sappho's ears, an idea which seems to have been introduced when *Veiled notes* were substituted for *soft red ways*, is one which Swinburne decided to retain for the end of the passage, but which, after one further attempt *With pangs like music*, he set aside for the time being. The concept that now came into his mind, perhaps suggested by another meaning of 'strain', was that of treading life out as must is trodden out of grapes. He starts with a line-ending *and tread*, followed by *Thy life out softly till the dregs were shed.* Not happy with that, he tried two line-endings both of which, unfortunately, contain words which are, for myself at least, illegible. The first reads *and [ ] it out like [ ]*, and the second *and hurt thee sore being [ ]*. Swinburne then turned to a new variation on his theme of prolonged and painful death: *Vex thee with amorous agonies, let slip / And rein thy soul up at the* – but there he could go no further. Possibly he was thinking of reining the soul up at the something's lip, for his next attempt, adhering to the equestrian metaphor, was *And curb thy soul's half-lacerated lip*. This, however, would clearly not do, since it meant abandoning the image of holding the beloved in agony on the brink of death, whilst sadistically not allowing her to die. At last everything came right, and lines 29–32 were written out with but one hesitation, the incredible line 32 – *Intolerable interludes, and infinite ill* – causing the poet, as far as can be judged from the draft, no trouble at all. After that, it only remained to balance the assonance of line 32 with the alliteration of line 33, and to substitute *Dumb tunes* for *Veiled notes*, and the passage was complete.

Surprising as it may seem after the epicene emotions and perverse passions of lines 23–34, Swinburne now returned to Aphrodite, whom he had left imperishable upon her storied seat. It is, however, clear from the draft that lines 64–66, and the second half of line 71 with line 72, were written after lines 23–34. Inspired, perhaps, by Sappho fragment 123 'I dreamt that you and I had words, Cyprus-born', Swinburne wrote first *For sleeping*, but was then struck by another concept, that of contrasting Sappho's genius with the beloved's beauty, in the deleted line *For me she loves for my song's sake, but thee*. Abandoning that, he returned to Sappho's dream. The four lines introducing the vision of Aphrodite gave him little trouble, he incorporated the two lines (67 and 68) which he had had set down for so long, and the two and a half lines which he had added earlier, completed line 71, added line 72, and was ready to continue the dream conversation between Aphrodite and Sappho on the verso of the first leaf, incorporating the idea in the abandoned *For me she loves. . .* into what was to become line 74: *but thou art sweeter, sweet, than song*.

What conclusions can be drawn after studying one of Swinburne's manuscripts in this kind of detail? For one thing, and contrary to Browning's assertion quoted at the beginning of this article, it can be seen that Swinburne's text is remarkably stable. Once he has fought his way through a draft he is faithful to the result, and with very minor adjustments the final text found in the draft is the same as the text as printed. In this he may be contrasted with Dante Gabriel Rossetti, haunted, continually seeking an ideal, whose text is very unstable, and who even uses the same poem in different contexts. Beside Rossetti, Swinburne exhibits a sublime self-confidence, and seems to declare 'Quod scripsi, scripsi'.

It can be observed that Swinburne, contrary perhaps to what is generally believed of him, does proceed from the sense to the sound. He establishes the sense first, then seeks the proper sound, as in the revisions *their* to *soft* (line 3), *quickens* to *strengthens* (line 4), or *the grave-worm's* to *some viper's* to *some serpent's* (line 26).

Two different moods and two different concepts can often be seen going forward at the same time and on the same page; on the one hand intense sadistic feelings towards the beloved, and on the other the vision of Aphrodite comforting Sappho. In the printed text these two passages are quite widely separated, and there is nothing to reveal how closely intertwined they were in the poet's mind. It is also possible to see the influence of one passage upon another, separated in the printed version, but clearly written under one impulse, as in the case of the two sadistic passages, lines 7–14 and 23–34. The fact that Swinburne had difficulty in deciding where to place the latter passage, conscious as he was of the effect that it would have upon his audience, can only be discovered by study of the manuscripts.

In his choice of vocabulary, Swinburne can move either from the precise to the vague, or from the general to the specific. He is not, as is sometimes supposed, for ever paring away at precision in order to achieve a vague and dreamy music. We are also reminded that poets do not compose logically, starting at line 1, and continuing through to the end. One idea sparks off another, inspiration for a line or lines strikes in the midst of the composition of an unconnected passage. Lines sometimes come into the brain and go down on the page pell-mell, and sometimes in an ordered, logical and apparently serene progression.

Finally it reminds us that we cannot lay hold of the nature of creative genius. We can trace influences, we can follow the course of ideas being worked out, but we cannot account for the sudden appearance, perfectly formed, with no struggle, of 'Intolerable interludes, and infinite ill'.

## Notes

1. All citations of Sappho are from the translation by D. A. Campbell in his *Greek Lyric, 1, Sappho, Alcaeus*, The Loeb Classical Library, Cambridge, Massachusetts and London, 1982.
2. In a letter to Richard Monckton Milnes, 18 August 1862, Swinburne wrote, 'I have just read "Justine ou les Malheurs de la Vertu" ' (*Letters*, 1.53). In his notes to this letter Lang points out that Swinburne actually read *La Nouvelle Justine*, the revised version of 1797.
3. W. R. Rutland, *Swinburne: A Nineteenth Century Hellene*, 1931, 289–90.
4. The first page of the manuscript is reproduced by kind permission of the Harry Ransom Humanities Research Center, The University of Texas at Austin.

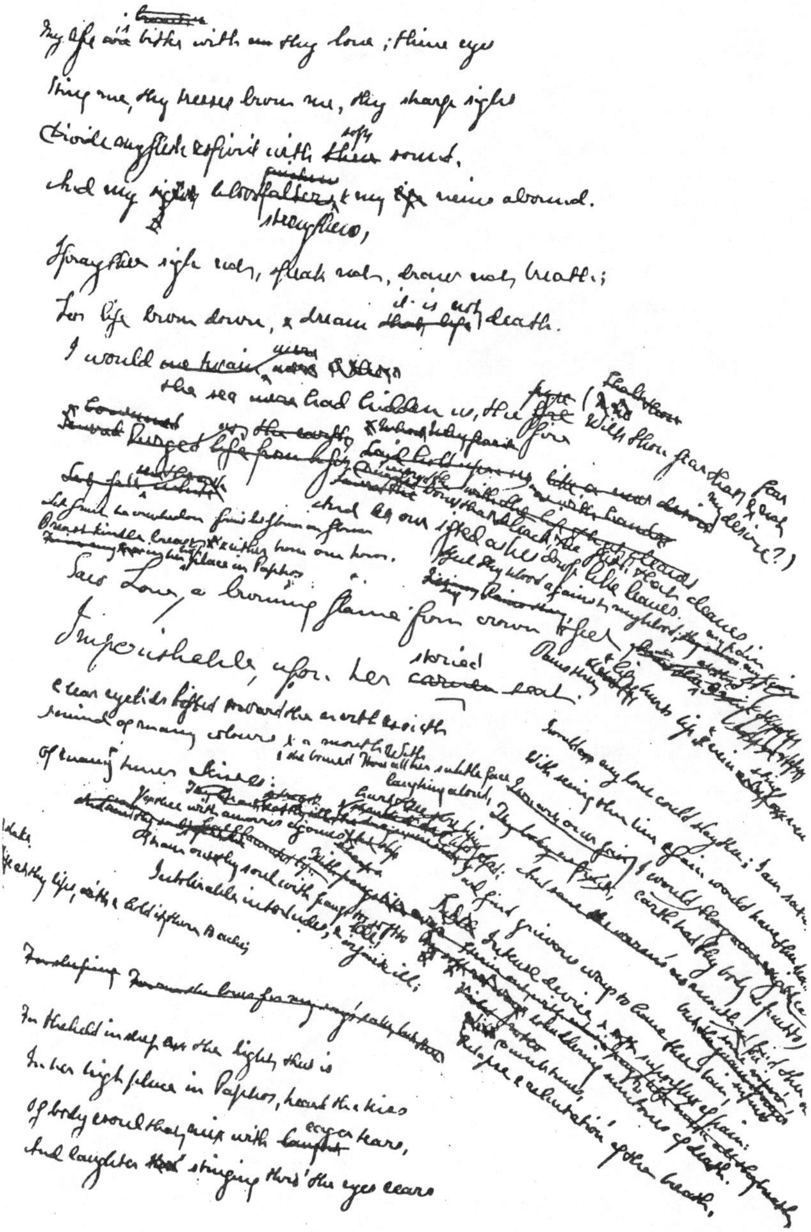

My life is bitter with thy love; thine eyes
Sting me, thy tresses burn me, thy sharp sighs
Divide my flesh & spirit with soft sound,
And my [illegible] falters, & my life veins abound.
I pray thee sigh not, speak not, draw not breath;
Let life burn down, & dream it is not death.
I would [illegible]
[illegible]
Saw Love, a burning flame from crown to feet,
Imperishable, upon her storied seat;
Clear eyelids lifted toward the north & south,
[illegible]
Of many tunes & lines;
[illegible]
In her high place in Paphos, heard the kiss
Of body & soul that mix with eager tears,
And laughter stinging through the eyes & ears

## Anactoria

*Folio 1*

1 My ‹lips› *life* ‹are› *is* bitter ‹*burnt [ ]*› with ‹m[ ]› thy love; thine eyes
2 Sting me, thy tresses burn me, thy sharp sighs
3 Divide my flesh and spirit with ‹their› *soft* sound,
4 And my ‹sight› blood ‹falters› ‹*quickens*› **strengthens**, and my ‹life› veins abound.
5 I pray thee sigh not, speak not, draw not breath;
6 Let life burn down, and dream ‹that life› it is not death.
7 I would ‹we twain ‹were› ‹, **O thou**› **were**› the sea ‹**were**› had hidden us, the ‹fire› ‹*pyre*› **fire**
‹(› ‹What› ‹Why fear it› (‹Who›
‹Shalt thou›
8 Wilt thou fear that and *fear* not my desire?)
‹Severed› ‹Purged ‹life from lips,› *us*, ‹ ‹Consumed the earth,› ‹Laid hold upon us ‹like a new desire› ‹, *as with hands[ ]*› **with the lip that cleaves**›
‹Let fall ‹*the* white› the ash›
9 ‹Severed the › ‹Divided› *Severed the* bones that bleach, the flesh
that cleaves
10 And let our sifted ashes drop like leaves.
13 Let fruit be crushed on fruit let flower on flower
11 I feel thy blood against my blood; ‹thy veins› ‹*my pain*› **my pain**
14 Breast kindle breast ‹[ ]› and either burn one hour.
64 ‹For in my› ‹Saw› in her *high* place in Paphos
‹Fill my› ‹Filling› ‹Pains thee,›
12 ‹Pains thee *all through*, and vein throbs hard on vein.› Pains thee, ‹and mouth› and lip hurts lip, ‹and› *and* vein ‹aches on› *stings* vein.
67 Saw Love, a burning flame from crown to feet
68 Imperishable, upon her ‹carven› *storied* seat.
69 Clear eyelids lifted toward the north and south
70 A mind of many colours and a mouth
71 Of many tunes and kisses: *and she bowed*
72 ‹Through› *With* all her subtle face laughing aloud,

23 I would ‹[ ]› my love could slay thee; I am satiated
24 With seeing thee live and fain would have thee dead.
25 ‹Thou art over fair;› I would ‹the grave might› *earth had thy body as fruit to* eat
26 ‹Thy body as fruit,›
And ‹save the worm's› no mouth ‹could› *but‹the grave-worm's›* **some** ‹**viper's**› **serpent's** ‹find› *found* thee sweet
27 I would find grievous ways to have thee slain,
28 ‹Subtle› Intense device, and ‹soft› superflux of pain:

‹and tread›
‹Thy life out softly ‹ till the dregs were shed› and ‹*[ ] it out like*› **hurt thee sore being** [ ]›
29 Vex thee with amorous agonies ‹, ‹let slip› *sharp*›
‹And ‹rein› *curb* thy soul'*s* ‹up at the› *half lacerated lip.*›
**and shake**
30 Life at thy lips, ‹with› and hold it there to ache;
‹With pangs ‹like music› Strain
out with ‹music› pangs like
music all thy breath›
31 Strain out thy soul with pangs too soft to kill,
32 Intolerable interludes, and infinite ill;

2

34 *‹By soft red ways› ‹Veiled notes›* ‹*With*› **Dumb tunes**, and shuddering semitones of death.

1

Relapse and reluctation of the breath,

‹For sleeping›
‹For me she loves for my song's sake, but thee›
63 For I beheld in sleep ‹her› the light that is

In her high place in Paphos, heard the kiss
Of body and soul that mix with ‹laught› eager tears
And laughter ‹through› stinging through the eyes and ears

# Appendix

## Three unpublished Poems by Algernon Charles Swinburne

As early as 1866, Swinburne's candid friend William Michael Rossetti had identified 'over-doing' as one of his most characteristic faults (*Swinburne's 'Poems and Ballads', A Criticism*, 1866, 54). Since then it has been customary to think of him as a prolix and unselective writer. It can therefore come as a shock to discover that the heroic scale of his output went hand-in-hand with a scrupulous willingness to withhold texts from publication. Even today, after the appearance of Gosse and Wise's *Posthumous Poems* in 1917 and Cecil Lang's edition of *New Writings by Swinburne* in 1964, the total quantity of Swinburne's unpublished writings remains, in Lang's own words, 'enormous' (*New Writings*, ix).

Many of these suppressed poems are indispensable for a full understanding of Swinburne's literary career. Some are also of real intrinsic merit. We here print, for the first time, two poems written in the late 1850s or early 1860s, and a distinct first draft (from the same period) of a poem published in 1866, all hitherto only accessible in manuscript.

As we argue in our Preface, the poems written by Swinburne between 1857 and 1862 (when his non-dramatic poetry for the first time appeared, professionally, in print) can be classified as juvenilia only in a rather different sense from that in which the word is customarily used. These were the years of rigorous artistic apprenticeship, in which Swinburne formed and developed his distinctive style. As early as the January of 1861 he felt that he had a volume of short poems ready for publication. His letter to Lady Trevelyan, on 19 January 1861, insisted that, on the (unrealized) condition of successful sales for *The Queen-Mother and Rosamond*, 'I shall publish my shorter poems soon: they are quite ready. . .many songs and ballads' (*Letters* 1.38). But when he chose poems from this period of composition for inclusion in *Poems and Ballads* (1866) he did so very selectively, presumably in order to leave room for the still more prolific and assured writing of the years 1862–5. By his own account, only 16 of the 62 poems in the collection were 'Early' (*Letters* 3.200).

Ten years later, in 1876, he was already expressing a wish to put more of the work of this period into print. He wrote to Andrew Chatto, on 20 July 1876, suggesting that he should publish 'at once or shortly after (if not simultaneously with) the new edition of P. and B. this companion volume of Early Poems, including The Queen-Mother and Rosamond. . .together with all the poems removed from P. and B. to this their proper and natural place, and also with additions never before published' (*Letters* 3.199). Two months later he was consulting his solicitor and literary adviser Theodore Watts (later Watts-Dunton) about this 'proposed volume of "Early Poems" (Rosamund[*sic*] etc. with the *youngest* of the Poems and Ballads)' (*Letters* 3.204). But both Chatto and Watts opposed the project, and on 15 October 1876 Swinburne wrote to Watts to concede defeat:

> You know that my own wish was to issue in one volume of the proposed new edition of my books all the poems written as an undergraduate at Oxford – viz. the two early plays and some dozen or more of the minor and less important 'Poems and Ballads' – with additions (if you should approve) from one or two remaining MSS of the same date – as Tennyson has done in his later editions. These of course will otherwise remain in MS. I certainly understood from Chatto that he thought this a good plan and likely to prove profitable to the book if duly advertised and explained – but if you are of one opinion with him that it would have the opposite effect, of course that must be the first consideration, and my *Juvenilia* must remain in dust or return to ashes (*Letters* 3.207).

Swinburne's clear wish to print these early poems therefore remained ungratified until after his death, when Gosse and Wise began (very selectively) to publish single poems in the stream of limited-edition pamphlets which they issued between 1909 and 1920. Some of these poems were then collected in Gosse and Wise's *Posthumous Poems* (1917), and the first volume of the Bonchurch Edition (1925). Some further poems were printed from manuscript by T. J. Wise in *A Swinburne Library* (1925), by Georges Lafourcade in *Swinburne's Hyperion and Other Poems* (1927) and *La Jeunesse de Swinburne* (1928), and by Cecil Lang in his article on the (very diverse) manuscripts in the Symington Collection (*Journal of the Rutgers University Library*, 18, 1954, 1–11) and his book *New Writings by Swinburne* (1964). Morse Peckham's edition of *Atalanta in Calydon* and *Poems and Ballads* in 1970 followed Swinburne's wish to separate the 'Early Poems' printed in 1866 from the rest of *Poems and Ballads* but did not add the 'remaining MSS of the same date'· which Swinburne had seen as a necessary part of such a project.

So not only have these early poems never been assembled as a group, they are still not all in print. The best list presently available of these texts is that given in *Lafourcade* 2. 174–5, which lists 54 titles from this period (sub-divided into the two categories of 'Influence Classique' and 'Influence Préraphaélite ou

"Romantique" '), roughly half of which have now been published. By kind permission of William Heinemann Ltd, and of the owners of the manuscripts, we are able to add three further titles to the list of those available in print.

Two of them are examples of the medievalist verse ('Influence Préraphaélite') which Swinburne wrote after encountering the poetry of William Morris and Dante Gabriel Rossetti in the late 1850s. Other specimens of this early, medievalist writing have been printed in the first volume of the Bonchurch *Works*, in *Lafourcade*, in T. J. Wise's *A Swinburne Library* (1925), and in James P. Carley's recent edition of Swinburne's Arthurian poems (in the Boydell Press *Arthurian Poets* series, 1990). 'The White Hind' is an early draft of the vividly Keatsian poem printed in *Poems and Ballads* (1866) as 'The Two Dreams' ('The author of "The Two Dreams",' Lafourcade comments in *Swinburne's Hyperion*, 1927, 65, 'had certainly read Chaucer; but he was no doubt familiar with *Endymion*'), and is valuable for the light which it casts on Swinburne's processes of revision. The full text of 'King Ban', established here for the first time by Timothy Burnett, corrects the widespread misunderstanding that this early poem survives only as a fragment, and helps to complete our picture of this important phase of Swinburne's work.

'By the sea-side' is an interesting early example of another aspect of Swinburne's writing: that distinctive form of nineteenth-century nature poetry which John Stuart Mill, discussing Tennyson in the *London Review* in July 1835, had called, 'the power of *creating* scenery, in keeping with some state of human feeling; so fitted to it as to be the embodied symbol of it, and to summon up the state of feeling itself, with a force not to be surpassed by anything but reality'. The state of human feeling embodied in the scenery of 'By the sea-side' is, as so often in Swinburne, closely connected with the presence of a *belle dame sans merci*, and with an invocation of that important figure in his personal mythology, Lucretia Borgia.

In the case of 'King Ban', a fragment of 120 lines was published by Gosse and Wise in their *Posthumous Poems of Algernon Charles Swinburne* (London, 1917) and reprinted by Carley in 1990. Timothy Burnett has now reconstructed the entire poem. 'The White Hind' and 'By the sea-side' are published here for the first time.

## (i) 'King Ban'

### *(a) The Text*

In their curiously named *Posthumous Poems by Algernon Charles Swinburne* (1917) the editors, Edmund Gosse and Thomas James Wise, published a poem to which they gave the title (the manuscript is untitled): 'King Ban: A Fragment'. In the Preface, Gosse describes it as follows:

> *King Ban* is a fragment from an attempt to put the early chapters of the *Morte d'Arthur* into blank verse. King Ban of Benwick and King Bors of Gaul were, it will be remembered, the two good kings who supported Arthur and fought with him against Claudas and the Eleven Bad Kings. It is interesting to note that it was from precisely this section of the Arthurian epic that Swinburne took, long afterwards, *The Tale of Balen.*
>
> (*Posthumous Poems* xxi–xxii)

That the poem was but a fragment was entirely the fault of the two editors. Later in the Preface, Gosse gives an account of how he and Wise dealt with the cache of manuscripts left at his death by Swinburne and purchased by Wise from Theodore Watts-Dunton:

> The greater part of the poems here published were hidden, unknown to Watts-Dunton, at the Pines. All round Swinburne's sitting-room there were discovered after his death unsightly rolls or parcels tied up in old newspaper, some of them looking as if they had not been opened for half a century. These parcels were found to contain proofs, bills, letters, prospectuses and every species of rubbish, together with occasional MSS. in prose and verse. On reflection, it became evident what they were. For many years Swinburne was in the habit of allowing miscellaneous material to gather on his table, until a moment came when he could bear the pressure of it no longer. He would then gather everything up, tie the whole in the current newspaper of the day, and then delicately place it on a shelf, where it never was again disturbed.
>
> (*Posthumous Poems* xxii)

If Gosse had not been so busy trying to be amusing at Swinburne's expense, he might have realized how extraordinarily valuable Swinburne's newspaper parcels could have been. The layers of newspaper, the bills, and the letters would have enabled Wise and Gosse, had they had the imagination and taken the trouble, precisely to date almost every leaf of manuscript which the poet left – a possibility unique in literary history. As it was, in Gosse's own unblushing words:

> It took a very long time to sort out the contents of these packages, and to examine and verify the poems which seemed to be unfamiliar. In this laborious and delightful work Mr. Wise was kind enough to associate me from the first, since Watts-

Dunton's interest in the matter had become entirely a financial one. At last, in the summer of 1913, we satisfied ourselves that no more early poetry of a nature fitted for publication would turn up, and we began to arrange the discovered pieces which are now at last given to the public.

(*Posthumous Poems* xxiii)

Gosse's gibe at Watts-Dunton is particularly rich since Wise's, if not his own, interest in the manuscripts was entirely a financial one. The pair must also have been easily satisfied by the results of their sorting – or worse. The manuscript of 'King Ban' later appeared in three parts, two of which Wise must have sold, for they ended up in the United States, one in the collection of Mr. John S. Mayfield, and the other in a private collection in New York. Wise's career as a forger is the best known aspect of his life of crime, but possibly the most damaging was his habit of destroying the integrity of manuscripts, and disposing of the *disjecta membra* by clandestine sales.

Having tracked down and secured copies, wherever possible, of as many of Swinburne's poetical manuscripts as I could, it became evident, in the course of trying to sort out the chronology of Swinburne's early poems, that the three fragments belonged together. The physical details are as follows: Autograph draft, written on one side only of four folio leaves of pale blue wove paper; on both sides of another folio leaf of the same paper (folio 3); and on one side only of a scrap of the same paper (folio 6). No watermark. Swinburne has numbered folios 1–3. Folios 1–4 are British Library Ashley MS. 5097. Folio 5 is in New York. Folio 6 is in the Mayfield Collection. The poem is untitled in the manuscript. Lines 48–66 were added later by Swinburne in the margins and on the verso of folio 3. The manuscript is undated, and lacks any physical evidence which might suggest a date.

The poem is printed here by kind permission of the British Library, The John S. Mayfield Collection, USA, and William Heinemann Ltd. Folio 5 is printed from a photocopy in the possession of Timothy Burnett. The MS of this folio was, at the time it was photographed, in a private collection in New York, and its present location is unknown.

Timothy Burnett

### *(b) Source and Date*

Gosse's account of Swinburne's source as 'an attempt to put the early chapters of the *Morte d'Arthur* into blank verse' is also misleading, and his error is repeated in *Lafourcade* 2.50 and J. P. Carley's *Arthurian Poets: A. C. Swinburne*, 1990, 2. Though King Ban's role as a military ally of King Arthur is described in Book 1 of Caxton's *Morte d'Arthur* (see especially Chapters 11–18), and a very brief reference is made to the fact that he is Lancelot's father in Book 4, Chapter 1, Malory does not give any account of his death – the episode with which Swinburne is here exclusively concerned. In fact Swinburne's poem is based on the account of Lancelot's childhood in *Lancelot du Lac* (one of the group of French thirteenth-century Arthurian prose romances now known as the Vulgate Cycle). He had access to a superb thirteenth-century manuscript of the *Lancelot* in the library of his uncle, the Earl of Ashburnham, where in his youth he spent a good deal of time. But when, in 1906, Sydney Cockerell happened to write to him about this manuscript, after its dispersal from the Ashburnham collection, Swinburne (for whatever reason) showed no previous knowledge of it (*Letters* 6.198), and for the purposes of composition he probably made more immediate use of the summary of its plot given in that frequent source for mid-nineteenth-century medievalist poets, John Dunlop's *The History of Fiction: Being a Critical Account of the Most Celebrated Prose Works of Fiction. From the Earliest Greek Romances to the Novels of the Present Age* (3 vols., 1814). Dunlop's summary of the 'earliest' and 'most romantic' part of Lancelot's life begins with the precise story used for Swinburne's poem:

> King Ban of Britanny was, in his old age, attacked by his enemy Claudas, a neighbouring prince, and after a long war was besieged in the strong-hold of Trible, which was the only place that now remained to him, but was considered as an impregnable fortress. Being at length reduced to extremities, he departs from this castle with his wife Helen and his infant son Lancelot, in order to beg assistance from his suzerain King Arthur; and, meanwhile, entrusts the defence of Trible to his seneschal. While prosecuting his route he ascends a hill, from the top of which he perceives his castle on fire, for it had been treacherously surrendered by the seneschal, who in romance is generally represented as a coward or traitor. At this sight the old man is struck with despair, and instantly expires.
>
> (John Dunlop, *The History of Fiction*, 1814, 1.202)

Dunlop, however, does not mention Lancelot's descent from King David, given in the Vulgate text and mentioned in line 145 of 'King Ban', which may indicate at least a memory of the actual prose *Lancelot*.

Swinburne did, of course, know Malory's *Morte d'Arthur* (the source for the 1857 paintings in the Oxford Union Debating Hall) when he wrote 'King Ban', and uses spellings closer to Malory than Dunlop for some of the personal names: Ellayne (Helen), Launcelot (Lancelot). But the *Morte d'Arthur* is not the source for the poem, any more than it is for 'Queen Yseult' (written November–December 1857), where Swinburne, a more learned medievalist than many of his Pre-Raphaelite friends, used Scott's edition of the Middle English *Sir Tristrem*, and the French and Anglo-Norman versions of Béroul and Thomas available in Michel's *Poetical Romances of Tristan* (1835). Gosse's suggestion of a significant link between 'King Ban' and *The Tale of Balen* is therefore very slightly based.

On the stylistic grounds of similarities to the 'vers blanc narratif' of William

Morris, *Lafourcade* 2. 50, 174 suggests that 'King Ban' was written in 1859. But, strictly speaking, there is no narrative blank verse in Morris's 1858 volume, *The Defence of Guenevere*, since the only blank verse poem, 'Sir Peter Harpdon's End' is dramatic. Swinburne read the poems which Morris published in the *Oxford and Cambridge Magazine* in 1856, and heard Morris read at least three more in the Autumn of 1857, when the decoration of the Oxford Union Debating Hall was under way. He read *The Defence of Guenevere* closely and enthusiastically as soon as it was published in February 1858 (*Letters* 1.15), and by September 15, 1858, was admitting to Edwin Hatch that he must 'beware of Topsification' (*Letters* 1.21). Such poems as 'Queen Yseult' (trochaic tetrameter triplets, written November to December 1857), 'Lancelot' (rhymed tetrameters and trimeters, in a dramatic dialogue), 'The Day before the Trial' (dramatic speech in rhymed iambic tetrameters and trimeters), and 'The Queen's Tragedy' (dramatic blank verse, dated 'Oxford 1859') show the influence of Morris very clearly. The narrative blank verse of 'King Ban', however, is often closer to Tennyson's narrative blank verse manner in the 1842 'Morte d'Arthur' than it is to Morris, suggesting that this is an early poem, written when Swinburne had only partially absorbed the example of Morris, and not yet escaped the influence of Tennyson ('into whose church we were all in my time born and baptised', *Letters* 1.97). James Carley (*Arthurian Poets: A. C. Swinburne* 1990, 2) and Antony H. Harrison (*Swinburne's Medievalism*, 1988, 161) suggest that 'King Ban' was written in 1857; it was probably written 1857–58.

Nicholas Shrimpton

## (i) 'King Ban'

These three held flight upon the leaning lands Folio 1
At undern, past the skirt of misty camps
Sewn thick from Benwick to the outer march –
King Ban, and, riding wrist by wrist, Ellayne,
And caught up with his coloured swathing-bands
Across her arm, a hindrance in the rein,
A bauble slipt between the bridle-ties,
The three months' trouble that was Launcelot.
For Claudas leant upon the land, and smote
This way and that way, as a pestilence
Moves with vague patience in the unclean heat
This way and that way; so the Gaulish war
Smote, moving in the marches. Then King Ban
Shut in one girdled waist of narrow stones
His gold and all his men, and set on them
A name, the name of perfect men at need,
And over them a seneschal, the man
Most inward and entailed upon his soul,
That next his will and in his pulses moved
As the close blood and purpose of his heart;
And laid the place between his hands, and rode
North to the wild rims of {distempered / the beaten} sea
That, crossed to Logres, his face might look red Folio 2
The face of Arthur, and therein light blood
Even to the eyes and to the circled hair
For shame of failure in so near a need,
Failure in service of so near a man.
Because that time King Arthur would not ride,
But lay and let his hands weaken to white
Among the stray gold of a lady's head,
His hands unwedded: neither could bring help
To Ban that helped to rend his land for him
From the steel wrist of spoilers, but the time
A sleep like yellow mould had overgrown,
A pleasure sweet and sick as marsh-flowers.
Therefore about his marches rode King Ban
With eyes that fell between his hands to count
The golden inches of the saddle-rim,
Strange with rare stones; and in his face there rose
A doubt that burnt it with red pain and fear

All over it, and plucked upon his heart,
The old weak heart that loss had eaten through,
Remembering how the seneschal went back
At coming out from Claudas in his tent;
And how they bowed together, chin by chin,
Whispered and wagged, and made lean room for words
And a sharp mutter fed the ears of them.
And he went in and set no thought thereon Folio 3
To waste; fear had not heart to fear indeed,
The king being old; since any fear in such
Is as a wound upon the fleshly sense
That drains a parcel of his time thereout.
Therefore he would not fear that as it fell
This thing should fall. For Claudas the keen thief
For some thin rounds and wretched stamps of gold
Had bought the tower and men and seneschal,
Body and breath and blood, yea, soul and shame.
They knew not this, at halt upon a hill;
Only surmise was dull upon the sense Folio 3b
And thin conjecture sickened in the speech;
So they fell silent, riding in the hills.
There on a little terrace the good king
Reined, and looked out. Far back the white lands lay,
The wind went in them like a broken man,
Lamely; the mist had set a bitter lip
To the rimmed river, and the moon burnt blank.
But outward from the castle of King Ban Folio 3
There blew a sound of trouble, and there clomb
A fire that thrust an arm across the air,
Shook a rent skirt of dragging flame, and blanched
The grey flats to such cruel white as shone
Iron against the shadow of the sky
Blurred out with its blind stars; for as the sea
Gathers to lengthen a bleached edge of foam
Whole weights of windy water, and the green
Brine flares and hisses as the heap makes up,
Till the gaunt hard wave writhes, trying to breathe,
Then turns and all the whited rims of steel
Lean over, and the hollowed round roars in
And smites the pebble forward in the weed,
And grinds the shingle in wet whirls of white
Clashed through and crossed with blank assault of foam,
Filled with hard thunder and drenched dregs of sand –

So leant and leapt the many-mouthed fire,
So curled upon the walls, dipt, crawled, smote, clung,
Caught like a beast that catches on the flesh,
Waxed hoar with sick default, shivered across,
Choked out, a snake unfed. –
Thereat King Ban Folio 4
Trembled for pain in all his blood, and death
Under the heart caught him and made his breath
Wince, as a worm does, wounded in the head;
And fear began upon his flesh, and shook
The chaste and inly sufferance of it
Almost to ruin; a small fire and keen
Eating in muscle and nerve and hinge of joint
Perilous way; so bitter was the blow
Made on his sense by treason and sharp loss.
Then he fell weeping tears with blood in them –
Like that red sweat that stained Gethsemane
With witness, when the deadly kiss had put
Shame on the mouth of Judas; and he cried,
Crying on God, and made out words and said:
'Fair lord, sweet lord, most pleasant to all men,
To me so pleasant in clean days of mine
That now are rained upon with heavy rain,
Soiled with grey grime and with the dusty years,
Because in all those tourneys and hot things
I had to do with, in all riding times
And noise of work and on smooth holidays
Sitting to see the smiting of hard spears
And spur-smiting of steeds and wrath of men
And gracious measure of the rounded game,
I held you in true honour and kept white
The hands of my allegiance as a maid's,
Being whole of faith and perfect in the will –
Therefore I pray you, O God marvellous,
See me how I am stricken among men,
And how the lip I fed with plenteousness
And cooled with wine of liberal courtesy
Turns a snake's life to poison me and clings
Here at this poor diskingdomed hand of mine, Folio 5
An old man's hand – yea thou God knowest too
No saint am I to shake it from such hold
On the blind fire that it consume therewith.
For this I thank thee, O God Merciful,

Seeing I am found { at least in my grey time
before thee and thy saints }
Worthy of want, bruised miserably, and made
In this poor thing the likeness of my Lord,
The print and likeness of thy Son my Lord,
{ Whom the hoar want impoverished utterly
Who was right poor and full of want on earth; }
Wherefore I thank thee for my grievous want.
For as mine eyes are empty, so mine hands,
And as my will hath faded, so my rule,
And none of all good men will do me good.
Yea well I praise thee for such grace of gift
On this desertless and hoar scalp of mine
Set like a crown. Only for this one thing
Have patience with me that I cry on thee
And on the perfect pity of that Christ
To show some mercy on this queen my wife,
For such a tender thing in this large world
Was not since Mary ceased thereout, nor one
So true a woman; also she is come
Of that pure seed that went to fashion him,
Being in clean line of David; for which sake
Show mercy on her that so fair a wife
And noble in all gracious offices
And delicate in making of her flesh
Be not thrown out into such loss and want
As shame hath share in; this I do well pray,
And for my fair son Launcelot that is
To her such pain and travail, that he be
Good knight and whole, and work so in thy will
That men shall praise her for the praise of him Folio 6
Cover his head that he may grow up straight,
Lest any smite him; and on her put love,
To clothe her in the naked season's edge
With thy sweet help; this do for me, my Lord.
For men will hunt them to discover them,
But thou, make peace: this is the end of all,
The sum and the completeness of the end'.
With that his knees slid and his head smote down
Flatting to earth, and sobbing in his mouth
His soul made way and went up fair to God.

## (ii) 'The White Hind'

This is an early draft of two passages of the poem printed in *Poems and Ballads* (1866) as 'The Two Dreams (from Boccaccio)'. It is found in a quarto notebook with white ruled pages formerly owned by Thomas James Wise and now Ashley MS. 1841 in the British Library, where it is entitled 'The White Hind: from Boccaccio'.

'The Two Dreams' is based on the Sixth Novella of the Fourth Day of Boccaccio's *Decameron* (the story which immediately follows Keats's source for 'Isabella; or, The Pot of Basil'), but departs from it considerably in spirit and in detail. In particular, the white hind and black greyhound of the second dream in the original are replaced by a mysterious, snake-like demon lover, or Lamia. *Lafourcade* 2.76–77 points this out as being also a difference between 'The White Hind' and 'The Two Dreams' as printed in *Poems and Ballads*, but it is difficult to be sure whether he had seen a passage (now lost) referring to a white hind in this manuscript, or whether he based his inference on the title alone. There is no evidence other than the title extant today.

Though the 'ladies' addressed in the first line of the manuscript remind one more directly of the frame-story of the *Decameron* than Swinburne's later version, 'The White Hind' is by no means a translation of Boccaccio's novella, and the text as found on folios 1r, 2r, 3r, 2v, 3v and 4r, in that order, corresponds quite closely to lines 1–101 of 'The Two Dreams'. Indeed, many lines are identical. On folio 1v is an even earlier draft corresponding to lines 27–33. In the same way, the text on folios 7r, 7v, corresponds to lines 359–367 and 382–397 of 'The Two Dreams'. The text on folio 6v contains, together with some lines discarded in 'The Two Dreams', an early draft of lines 368–371. Folios 5–6 are occupied by forty lines of a different poem, possibly part of 'The Taking of Loys Raimbault', mentioned by *Lafourcade* 2.589 as being preserved in manuscript in Wise's Ashley Library, but now otherwise no longer traceable.

According to both Wise, *Ashley Catalogue* vi, 42 and *Lafourcade* 2.76, the present manuscript should have thirteen folios. It now has only seven, of which 1–4 are a gathering of four, 5 and 6 together are a single sheet, and 7 is a single folio. The manuscript has, however, been paginated 1–13 at some time previous to its arrival in the British Library, and this may have given rise to confusion.

Another manuscript, Ashley MS. 5254, which does contain translations by Swinburne from the *Decameron*, is watermarked 1858. In a letter to Lady Trevelyan, 19 January 1861, Swinburne says, 'I have done a lot of work since I saw you, Rossetti says some of my best pieces. . .also a long one out of Boccaccio, that was begun ages ago and let drop' (*Letters* 1.38). It appears likely, therefore, that 'The White Hind' was composed in 1858, and revised into its later form, 'The Two Dreams', in 1860–61. Though it is an early draft rather than an independent poem, 'The White Hind' is valuable for the exceptionally clear picture which it gives of Swinburne's development in these years. The manner (a distinctive blend of Chaucer and Keats) remains constant. But a remarkable refining of detail transforms, for example, the unambitious directness of 'And often when the year was hardly green' ('The White Hind', 24) into the individuality and precision of line 30 of 'The Two Dreams': 'And when the windy white of March grew late'.

The poem is printed by kind permission of the British Library and William Heinemann Ltd.

Timothy Burnett
Nicholas Shrimpton

## (ii) The White Hind; from Boccaccio.

O ladies, if I say a heavy thing, Folio 1r
I pray you will forgive me; for the spring
Has bitter fits of pain to keep her sweet,
And walks somewhile with winter-bitten feet.
Moreover it is often well to let
One string, when ye make music, keep at fret
The whole song through; one petal that is dead
Confirms the roses, be they white or red:
Dead sorrow is not sorrowful to hear
As the harsh noise that comes in weeping were
And though the rain falls often, and the stain
Of autumn flecks the green with lines of pain,
I deem that God is not disquieted.
Also while men are fed with wine and bread
They shall be fed with sorrow at His hand.
  There was a rose-garden in Pisan land
Fairer than any; all the summer through
The cool thick leaves smelt sweet of rain and dew
Even when the strong light's set face stopped at once Folio 2r
All singing-music; many moons and suns
Went over it with quiet feet that showed
Like hot gold lying on a cool green road;
The garden ways were smooth to walk and clean;
And often, when the year was hardly green,
Before the trees took heart to face the sun
With their lean ravelled winter's garment on,
The place about was deep with pleasant grass.
Some roods away a lordly house there was
Cool with broad courts and latticed corridors
And tender with the hush of [? velvet] floors;
The walls were fair with many painted things;
At night one heard the fluttered noise of wings
That shook from court to court as the small birds
Settled with talk that sounded like sweet words.
Within this house a right good lord abode,
Ser Averardo, one of quiet mood,
Patient and righteous; and to child he had Folio 3r
A maid so fair that all men's eyes got glad
For sight of her, and mouths drawn fierce and straight
Forgot their ancient anger and cold hate
For new soft wonder and serene surprise.

Gold hair she had and long gold-coloured eyes
Her throat was tall and white, sad lips and sweet,
And long hands shapen like her veined feet.
Her face was white, and thereto she was tall;
In no wise lacked there any praise at all
In her most perfect and pure maidenhood;
No sin I think there was in all her blood.
And every day that kept the summer green Folio 2v
Among the leaves that shut this garden in,
She came with one she had in trust, and there
Love made himself a place to worship her
‹With tender› worship, kneeling on his knees;
For always through the low broad close of trees
One came between the flowers thick and red
From palest April till the leaves were dead.
In a poor house he dwelt some space apart;
Long time he sat and communed with his heart
If love of his might move in any wise
That maiden, or put pity in her eyes;
And after many days he said; O love Folio 3v
For love's own sake I pray you not disprove
With bitter words that gracious maidenhood;
Also I pray you for the love of God,
To give me comfort of this pain of mine;
Seeing that neither sleep nor bread nor wine
Seems pleasant to me; yea, no man that is
Seems pleasant to me; only I know this,
The ways of love are sharp for piteous feet
To travel, yet the end of them is sweet;
So shall ye do as seemeth you the best.
She said; if word of mine may give you rest Folio 4r
Take no more care of all that you have said;
And if there is no sleep will ease your head
Lo, I am fain to help you certainly;
Christ knoweth, lord, if I would have you die;
There is no pleasure when a man is dead.
– Hereat he kissed her hands and yellow head
And clipped her fair long body many times;
I have not wit to shape in written rhymes
The marvellous new pleasure they twain had.

She was pale now, and leant with earnest lips Folio 7r

In a sick tremble; as when water slips
From the beaked vessel with faint noise, so came
A ruined voice with no words right, his name
Mixed with mere breaks and babble; 'Love', she said,
And would not speak again; she held his head
Between both hands and kissed it eagerly;
Nay but your hair slips over, put it by,
That I may see you: no dream now to spoil
Our pleasant time, more than the yellow soil
On some fly's wing blurs out its colour; nay,
But lean yet closer; there's so much to say
Ere one has leave to love indeed! Thereon Folio 7v
Her breath who spoke was altered with a moan
And the face whitened.

## (iii) 'By the sea-side'

This poem exists as a manuscript of ten pages (five quarto leaves of white paper), numbered by someone other than Swinburne. There is relatively little alteration of lines or words, which suggests this may not be a first draft. At the bottom of page six, written upside down are the lines:

> Depart, and bear thy curse to him; away,
> Tempt me not lest thou perish
> On thine own head fall heavy! When it comes,
> Remember how I left thee

These seem to belong to the composition of another work. The manuscript was probably bought from T. J. Wise by J. Alex Symington, Lord Brotherton's librarian, and thus became part of the Brotherton Collection, now at Leeds University.

*Lafourcade* 2.67–68, which quotes the first twelve lines of 'By the sea-side', offers a tentative date of 1860 for the poem (though *Lafourcade* 2.590 alternatively gives 1859), and suggests that the particular landscape effect attempted here may reflect the influence of Pre-Raphaelite painters, especially Burne Jones. If the reference in lines 123–24 to studying a 'dust-grimed scroll' (containing information about Lucretia Borgia) 'yesterday' is to be taken at all literally, then it might suggest either his examination of Lucretia Borgia's letters in the Biblioteca Ambrosiana in Milan in the Spring of 1861 (*Letters* 1. 39, 91), or, more probably, his research for the composition of 'The Chronicle of Tebaldeo Tebaldei' (based on the *Diary of Johannes Burchardus*) in 1859–60. *Lafourcade* 2.589 mentions a fragment of a play on Lucretia Borgia, written in 1858, which would be another possible occasion. But as Swinburne's letter to W. M. Rossetti of 10 November 1902 explains, he had been interested in the topic ever since 'Victor Hugo introduced me to Lucrèce Borgia' at Eton, that is before 1853, and the most probable date of composition of 'By the sea-side' – a poem sometimes adolescent in emotional register but always highly sophisticated in its historical and cultural allusions – is 1859–60.

The rhythmic effect of the poem is atypical of Swinburne, but the setting and theme are familiar. As so often, we see Swinburne using a shoreline background to a difficult romantic encounter with a woman who is about to leave the speaker. She is the *femme fatale* to whom the speaker would like to sacrifice himself, and she sets him thinking of Lucretia Borgia. A number of phrases are reminiscent of 'The Triumph of Time'. Jerome McGann remarks that an interest in these motifs begins very early in Swinburne's career, as 'many of his earliest lyrics deal with the theme of a lost love and the sorrows of a memorial poet-lover. . . For Swinburne was not only absorbed by the figures of powerful and/or unattainable women at a very early age; he seems always to have been fascinated by the idea of ill-starred love' (*McGann* 216). 'By the sea-side' invites comparison with such other early texts as 'Hide and Seek' (published by John S. Mayfield in 1974), and 'Evening by the Sea' (Gosse & Wise, *Posthumous Poems* 1917, 100–101).

The poem is printed by kind permission of The Brotherton Collection, Leeds University Library, and of William Heinemann Ltd.

Rikky Rooksby
Nicholas Shrimpton

## (iii) 'By the sea-side'

It is near evening; wait a little yet. Folio 1r
See, the salt water-mark
High on the crumbling sandslope is not wet,
Tho' it must soon be dark.
But the far clouds are pierced with sunbeam-threads,
And, where their bank was close,
Loose fringes flicker into feathery shreds
Of gold and deepening rose.
The great sea, calmèd to its sunless heart
Streaks the grey shining sand
With white sharp tongues of hungry foam that dart
Straight up the level strand.
No voice in the air or water. Far behind Folio 1v
The sheer cliff cuts the sky.
In each worn crevice low the dungeoned wind
Falters a moaning cry.
Sunset is burning on the highest peak.
And where this water quivers
Wan at our feet in a rock-bedded creek,
One stray gleam slips and shivers.
Here, where the lank green oarweeds wan and sallow
Sleep in the sleepy pool
Rock-rooted, swinging in the dim grey shallow
With motion slow and cool.
Here, where the dark specks cross and flit and keep
The understream alive
Altho' the unrippled surface glares in sleep
Whence in and out they dive.
Outside, slow shadows curl across the grey Folio 2r
Of the broad evening-sea.
Over the beach, close-curtained as in day,
The house looks watchfully.
Do you not see, whene'er a sunbeam dips
Thro' dull-green water sifted,
How, where one stagnant weed-tuft hangs and drips,
The sea-fan heaves loose-drifted?
The slow salt ooze melts up thro' plashy sand
And crawls about your feet.
Come back, and by the window let us stand
Till sea and starlight meet.
Slowly the slumbrous light upgathering opes

O'er many a waveworn foreland,
Sunstricken peaks and evening-coloured slopes
Of lone and windy moorland.
And grey in the grey distance heave and scream Folio 2v
The seamew's trading lines,
Fierce breaks of sudden gold with rough red gleam
Fringe all the breezeless pines.
But softer on the trembling low-tuned sea
A rosehued light grows shoreward,
As from the starless distance timidly
A shy soft wind creeps forward.
Here where we stand, along the rippling curtain
It whispers half afraid
And heaves the sleepy folds and breathes uncertain
And mingles with the shade.
– And so to-night I have you, and to-morrow
Long miles will sweep between us.
I thought – but you look happy now – no sorrow
Till death would overlean us.
To-morrow! Well, you go then – it is said. Folio 3r
New faces there will smile,
And happy lives thro' sweet blind pleasures led
With many a chanted wile
Shall close round yours – and you shall be as they –
You that have wander'd here
When all the sea heaved eager towards the day
Alive with love and fear:
When those sharp mountain-turrets split the gold
Of the unbroken morn,
And the mute wave crept – but my words grow cold
As my heart in your scorn.
Will you remember how you used to rove
The lakeside lone and chilly
Where one Spring night in your wet hair I wove
An uptorn waterlily?
Sleeping it stirred the cold and misty wave Folio 3v
And lit the level gloom
Where, like a sleeping fairy in a cave,
O'er its blind weltering tomb
It drooped in dewy silence. Stooping over
The wet reeds of the bank
I drew it from the green and floating cover
Of water-grasses rank

And wound it in your loose dew drenched hair
  Laughing, with skillless hands.
Will you remember when the days are fair
  In the far southern lands?
On me this hour falls cold as thoughts that come Folio 4r
  Like fears across the feast,
When growing music thro' the lustrous dance
  Soars like a bird released.
You look aside – your restless fingers play
  Where the gold fringe is worn.
You smile – I would it were already day
  Or I could sleep till morn!
– Once lived a woman in whom all abhorred
  Sins found a resting place;
But no stain ever marred her smooth white forehead,
  Or changed her queenly face.
They say she lived and smiled as children do.
  And many for her sake
Died, knowing all the shame that o'er her grew
  Coiled round her like a snake.
The man, they say, whose chance eyes looked upon her Folio 4v
  Gave her his soul and died –
Ay, sinned and died for her, and called it honour,
  And kept her name with pride.
So those men used to love in the far days!
  Such might had women then.
Nay, change not – it is spoken to your praise.
  Where shall we find such men?
Is it that love is purer or more weak?
  – And still nor guilt nor woe
Stains the white brow or shadows the clear cheek
  Or soft limbs' rounded snow.
Still lives she in the heart of love, as when
  Her silent angel's face
Shook with strange pain the changing souls of men
  – Still keeps her foremost place.
Never was one like her in shape or soul Folio 5r
  – So her dead lovers say.
Her name makes bright the worn and dust-grimed scroll
  I pored on yesterday.
Of her on earth is nothing but their songs
  And one lock of her hair.
She sleeps with all her beauty, and the wrongs

She did while she was fair.
The tress they keep – sun-hued and soft as this
I touch, but cannot speak,
So sways between strange grief and stranger bliss
My spirit wild and weak.
As the last sunlight dreaming in your eyes
Darkens – as moor and sea
Darken beneath a waste of windy skies –
So darkens life in me.
What praise is written of those lovers dead? Folio 5v
They died – I love and live.
I lay my life before your onward tread –
My death were less to give.
When it shall please you, let me die – till then
I will not change nor shrink.
I will live out the life of other men
And never stay to think.
Say only – 'Faith is not in all men dead' –
And as you say it, smile
And lift up silently that royal head
And pause from joy awhile.
I live and love you, as that mute lip says
In its rich-curved pride,
No praise is mine; yet in these weak new days
Some might have loved and died.

# Index